Narratives of Doctoral Studies in Science Education

T0347293

This book explores the ways in which small scale research studies arise from issues of practice, and how they are conceptualised, theorised and implemented using a variety of methodological approaches and frameworks. The narratives written by 13 doctoral students tell real stories of projects and challenges that researchers face when making the transition from educational practitioner to researcher.

Considering case studies from the UK, Sweden and Germany, chapters seek to investigate and inform others about how doctoral students solved individual and typical problems linking practice and research. Each methodological journey highlights and illustrates the iterative and cyclic nature of research, and the normality of the process of going back and forth between data and theory, making changes of direction as research proceeds. The book includes frameworks for combining research, theory and practice, drawing from the methodological decisions and conclusions each contributor made to develop their own practice-oriented research.

Narratives of Doctoral Studies in Science Education will be key reading for researchers and academics in the fields of educational research, science education, research methods and higher education, as well as Masters and doctoral students undertaking their own research projects.

Shirley Simon is Professor of Science Education at the UCL Institute of Education, University College London, UK.

Christina Ottander is Associate Professor and Senior Lecturer in Science Education at the Department of Science and Mathematics Education, Umeå University, Sweden.

Ilka Parchmann is Professor and Head of the Chemistry Education Department at the Leibniz-Institute for Science and Mathematics Education, Germany, and Professor of Chemistry Education at the Christian-Albrechts-University of Kiel, Germany.

Routledge Research in Higher Education

Experiences of Immigrant Professors
Cross-cultural differences and challenges, and lessons for success
Edited by Charles Hutchison

Integrative Learning
International research and practice
Edited by Daniel Blackshields, James Cronin, Bettie Higgs, Shane Kilcommins, Marian McCarthy and Anthony Ryan

Developing Creativities in Higher Music Education
International perspectives and practices
Edited by Pamela Burnard

Academic Governance
Disciplines and policy
Jenny M. Lewis

Refocusing the Self in Higher Education
A phenomenological perspective
Glen L. Sherman

Activity Theory, Authentic Learning and Emerging Technologies
Towards a transformative higher education pedagogy
Edited by Vivienne Bozalek, Dick Ng'ambi, Denise Wood, Jan Herrington, Joanne Hardman and Alan Amory

Understanding HIV and STI Prevention for College Students
Edited by Leo Wilton, Robert T. Palmer and Dina C. Maramba

From Vocational to Professional Education
Educating for social welfare
Jens-Christian Smeby and Molly Sutphen

Narratives of Doctoral Studies in Science Education

Making the transition from educational practitioner to researcher

Edited by
Shirley Simon
Christina Ottander
Ilka Parchmann

Routledge
Taylor & Francis Group

LONDON AND NEW YORK

First published 2016
by Routledge

2 Park Square, Milton Park, Abingdon, Oxfordshire OX14 4RN
711 Third Avenue, New York, NY 10017

Routledge is an imprint of the Taylor & Francis Group, an informa business

First issued in paperback 2017

British Library Cataloguing in Publication Data
A catalogue record for this book is available from the British Library

Library of Congress Cataloging-in-Publication Data
Narratives of doctoral studies in science education : making the
transition from educational practitioner to researcher / edited by
Shirley Simon, Christina Ottander, and Ilka Parchmann.
pages cm
Includes bibliographical references and index.
1. Graduate students in science—Case studies. 2. Doctoral students—
Case studies. 3. Science—Study and teaching (Graduate)—Case studies.
4. Research—Methodology—Case studies. I. Simon, Shirley, 1952-
II. Ottander, Christina. III. Parchmann, Ilka.
Q181.N19 2016
507.1'1—dc23
2015009427

ISBN: 978-1-138-89028-2 (hbk)
ISBN: 978-0-8153-5767-4 (pbk)

Typeset in Baskerville
by FiSH Books Ltd, Enfield

Contents

Figures

Tables

Contributors

UCL Institute of Education, London, UK
Shirley Simon
Anne Robertson
Adrian Day
Elizabeth Wady
Tan Ying Chin

Umeå University, Umeå, Sweden
Christina Ottander
Sofie Areljung
Jenny M. Hellgren
Annika Manni
Karolina Broman
Katarina Ottander

Leibniz-Institute for Science and Mathematics Education, IPN, Kiel, Germany
Ilka Parchmann
Christine Köhler
Wilfried Wentorf
Julian Rudnik
Frederike Tirre

Preface

Being involved in educational practices means to develop, set up, support and reflect teaching and learning processes. It can also lead to observations and questions that require more time and different insights into such processes. So studying for a doctorate in education can be a next step for experienced teachers and other education practitioners who wish to explore an interesting issue in more depth, take up a position within a research team and/or achieve a further qualification. In our field of experience as supervisors we have many practitioners who become doctoral students and who have identified a range of issues for study. They work in different settings and have obtained funding from a variety of sources (including personal savings) in order to study.

What is special about doing a doctorate with such a background? All doctoral students have to change their focus to become researchers, interpret events differently and engage in a new set of literature and ideas, but for practitioners the journey can require subtle shifts in perspective that are not obvious at the outset. For science educators in particular, the theories and methodological approaches of the social sciences can be unfamiliar. Practitioners who are used to seeing and considering the whole complexity of teaching and learning in their practice, can find it difficult to focus on one aspect that they can investigate. Moreover, finding an appropriate and doable field of research and methodology might be especially difficult for someone aiming to combine the demands of practice and research.

As supervisors we are also embarking on a journey, as each individual doctoral student shapes her or his ideas from reading, working with others, developing research questions and designing their work. Questions of how to interpret literature, theory and data are constantly worked and reworked with the students as the study progresses. Decisions have to be made about whether to study for a thesis comprising stand-alone published articles or for a monograph thesis. Experiences from such journeys can differ considerably, according to the environments and traditions of doctoral studies in different places and countries. Whilst collaborating as visiting/associate professors at Umeå University, the three of us have found these journeys to be fascinating and informative, especially for two of us while also working with doctoral students in our home countries of UK and Germany. Each doctoral student's journey involves processes of engaging with research and connecting it to practice; yet each individual student story has something different to convey, as we hope to show in the narratives compiled in this book.

We initiated the reflective process in Sweden by encouraging five students to write about their journeys from practitioner to researcher (and back). We knew that reflecting in this way would be useful for writing the 'kappa' or overview of the publications thesis for four of the five doctoral students and also for the methodology section for the one student working on a monograph thesis. However, the process was so beneficial for these students that we decided to capture the essence of it in a book, to include accounts from students preparing both types of thesis in Sweden and with inputs from doctoral students studying in UK and Germany. The book provides peer to peer feedback and messages about the challenges facing practitioners becoming researchers.

After having worked on the chapters, we could clearly see the potential benefits of such reflections for our own students in Sweden, UK and Germany. We see the same potential for students in other areas and countries, even though doctoral study and the thesis are different in different environments. We hope this book can help students as well as supervisors on their journeys between practice and research.

Shirley Simon, Christina Ottander and Ilka Parchmann

1 Editorial introduction

Pathways followed by doctoral students on their research journey

Shirley Simon, Ilka Parchmann and Christina Ottander

The purpose of this introductory chapter is to set the scene for 13 narratives written by our doctoral students. We introduce the 13 doctoral student authors, the contexts in which they work in each country, and some features of their learning journeys. The students were at different phases of research at the time of writing, so we have insights from those in the early stages and those who have completed or almost completed their doctorates. Each student brings out links they have built between an issue of practice and their research; how they found a suitable theoretical framework, posed research questions, developed their methodology, drew conclusions and implications and how they managed to overcome problems. Our overall aim is to share with our audience frameworks for relating theory, research and practice in doctoral studies, and how challenges are overcome in the research journey. We aim to provide examples that expose the dilemmas faced by many research students whose task it is to create new knowledge in order to make an 'original contribution' required for examination (Trafford and Leshem 2009), often challenging for students researching issues arising from their own contexts that may or may not have been studied elsewhere. In developing research from their original concerns as practitioners our student authors have learnt how to develop research questions and methodologies that enable their own individual research to make a contribution to a wider understanding or theoretical perspective in science education.

There are tensions to encounter within education between how doctoral research is traditionally conducted (in linear stages consisting of methods training, literature review, definition of the research problem, data collection, analysis and writing up) and other approaches used in practice such as ethnography which can be 'messy' and non-linear but systematic (Troman 2002). The studies reported here can be situated in recognised fields of research in science education, which also include different approaches for educational research, some of which can carry the messiness described by Troman. The fields of research in science education are described in three major paradigms in the latest *Handbook of Research on Science Education*: 1) The post positivist paradigm in which many studies concern effectiveness of teaching – what works and why; 2) Interpretative approaches assuming that people construct their understanding based on experience, culture and context; and 3) Critical theory – dealing with power and change (Treagust *et al.* 2014). The doctoral studies presented in this book mainly refer to the first two trends, dealing with questions of effectiveness, such as developing an understanding of sustainable development, or investigating students' learning processes in different situations and contexts. Due to their role as teachers or science educators, most researchers focus on the development of students' understanding, skills or attitudes and interests. Hence, the stories told in this book do not only provide insights into research journeys but can also offer ideas for other projects combining research and practice based on authentic questions of practitioners.

The student authors

The following table provides an overview of the 13 student authors, their phase of research at the time of writing, the country in which their doctorate was, or is, being supervised and their individual research foci. As will be seen throughout the book, the narratives fall into three sections for how we have conceptualised the doctoral journeys (see Table 1.1).

Settings and background conditions

In the UK most doctoral students in science education construct a monograph thesis for their doctoral degree, which is the case for the four authors who were examined at the Institute of Education, London (now referred to as UCL IOE since the recent merger with University College London). Some students enrol for an MPhil, a preliminary status in which they work towards an upgrade examination, before becoming a PhD student. All studies are individual and most are self-funded, but sometimes students undertake their doctoral work alongside a position in a larger research project; this was the case for Anne, who was an adviser for primary school teachers. She became involved in the Cognitive Acceleration programme undertaken by King's College in partnership with an education authority in London. The outcomes of the programme involved quantitative measures and Anne decided to develop a contrasting qualitative inquiry regarding children's learning and teachers' development. Doctoral students working in such a position experience tensions and advantages, which we will discuss later.

Elizabeth and Adrian were practising teachers who funded their studies independently and who were both motivated by wanting to engage in a particular line of research. Adrian built his study on observations he had made regarding the linguistic nature of examinations, Elizabeth on observations of students doing graphical work in science. Though both starting

Table 1.1 Overview of the doctoral student authors

Student/ country of supervision	Type of thesis	Focus	Student journey	Phase
Sofie/ Sweden	Paper-based	Science and gender in preschool	Research-based design	early
Anne/ UK	Monograph	Young children's perceptions of learning	Research-based design	final
Christine/ Germany	Monograph	Abilities of students participating in science competitions	Research-based design	final
Jenny/ Sweden	Paper-based	Motivation in the science classroom	Research-based design	middle
Annika/ Sweden	Paper-based	Meaning-making in education for sustainable development	Research-based design	middle
Adrian/ UK	Monograph	The lexical and grammatical structure of science examination questions	Research-based design	completed
Wilfried/ Germany	Paper-based	Students' views about scientists and their professions	Theory-led design-based research	final
Julian/ Germany	Monograph	Students' learning progressions in the transition from school into university	Theory-led design-based research	early
Frederike/ Germany	Paper-based	Science outreach – measures to show authentic science	Theory-led design-based research	final
Karolina/ Sweden	Paper-based	Frameworks for analysing context-based chemistry	Theory-led design-based research	final
Katarina/ Sweden	Monograph	Students' meaning-making in tasks for sustainable development	Practitioner-led design-based research	middle
Elizabeth/ UK	Monograph	Different learning approaches in working with line graphs	Practitioner-led design-based research	middle
Tan Ying/ UK	Monograph	Primary science teachers' professional learning through questioning	Practitioner-led design-based research	completed

from practitioner issues, their approaches to research design were very different. Some students in the UK work towards a different doctorate in education, the EdD, which is a staged doctoral programme with taught elements and assignments that are prerequisites to developing the EdD thesis. The final award is perceived as equivalent to a PhD. There are also taught programmes for PhD students, some of which are essential, but none of these have assignments. Many international students prefer the EdD programme, one of whom is Tan Ying from Singapore, who was able to attend taught courses in a partnership programme in Singapore prior to being supervised from the UK for her final thesis. Tutors in both countries were able to advise Tan Ying as she undertook her field work study in Singapore.

All these student authors studied independently and on a part-time basis whilst remaining in their practitioner posts. Some of them met occasionally at doctoral school events designed for students to share their studies, such as poster sessions and summer schools, or at science education seminars. These opportunities to meet and discuss are voluntary and all these students worked in relative isolation.

Doctoral studies in Sweden involve the time equivalent of four years of paid full-time study, which include a number of courses (between 30–45 per cent of the marks) and a thesis. Most students complete their doctorate in five years or more, whilst carrying out teaching for payment at the university. The thesis can be a monograph or based on published papers, the latter being more common within science education research. During the last ten years the Swedish Government has invested heavily to provide teachers and preschool teachers with the opportunity to participate in training at graduate levels. The initiative aims to raise the quality of Swedish schools and to create career paths as lecturers within the teaching profession. The investment is intended to get more teachers with a doctoral degree or a licentiate degree, i.e., halfway to a PhD, into schools to develop more practitioner-centred educational research approaches and take responsibility over more systematic research-based school developments. In Sweden the PhD students can either be externally funded by research councils and be part of a larger research project, or funded by graduate schools or municipalities in which case they apply to graduate programs with their own research ideas. Different graduate schools fund three of the Swedish PhD students, i.e., the Graduate School of Educational Science (FU), The Graduate School of Gender Studies (GFS), the National Graduate School in Science, Mathematics and Technology Education Research (FontD), and National Graduate School of Education and Sustainable Development (GRESD).

Each graduate school has its own agenda. For example Sofie is co-funded by FU and GFS, which focuses on combining traditional disciplinary studies with courses and seminars that include a gender and interdisciplinary approach to developing critical reflection skills. Annika and Katarina have been teachers in secondary and upper secondary schools for a long time, hence they have brought ideas and issues from their teaching experiences into their PhD. Both Katarina and Annika started as licentiate students, but after the first period they received funding to continue to a full PhD and have belonged to two different graduate schools throughout. Karolina is also an experienced teacher, both from teaching at upper secondary school and within teacher education. She took the opportunity to do a PhD project by responding to a special call from the university. Jenny has a background with a PhD in plant physiology; she shifted focus to become a teacher and then realised that she wanted to continue in research but in science education. She started her PhD belonging to a larger project with external money, and then developed her own project idea within this frame. All graduate students are associated with graduate schools where they participate in seminars and take postgraduate courses, and they all have two supervisors and take part in seminars within the department.

In Germany different traditions in science education exist, some studies being more closely related to methods and experiments in the natural sciences, others carrying out empirical research based on social science methods. At the Leibniz-Institute for Science and Mathematics Education, IPN, where all German authors work on their doctoral projects, studies on students' learning and effects of learning environments are well established. Most research studies are embedded in larger projects and get part-time funding in that way. The student authors involved in this book work in projects funded by the German Research Foundation, the Federal Government of Education and Research, and from IPN. Doctoral students are therefore used to cooperating, and develop and integrate their own research from and within a larger picture. This often requires extra time for meetings and tasks besides their research, but also provides an environment of support and collaboration. The final product can be a monograph or paper-based thesis, while the latter is still less common than the first.

The four authors have different experiences of practice. Wilfried has a full position as a high school ('Gymnasium') teacher now, but used to work part time in a project at IPN that was set up to develop material for enrichment courses. One goal of the framework and material was to offer school students better insights into the nature of science and to encourage them to think about science studies and careers after school. While working in this project, he noticed that many students still do not have a clear picture about scientists and their everyday tasks and activities – and so that became a question of interest for him. Christine has a teaching degree from her university education and the 18 months training in school, but immediately decided to go back into research after her teacher training in practice. As she had been working with students participating in competitions like the Science Olympiads, she became curious about what makes those students different from others in terms of interest and motivation. Both Wilfried and Christine are working on their doctoral projects as members of a larger research group focusing on enrichment and supporting talents in science. This group incorporates doctoral students as well as post-doctoral workers (PostDocs), both from science education and from psychology. Frederike and Julian, the other two German authors, have never taught at school. Frederike's background of practice is in informal learning, based on her studies in science communication. Julian has a diploma in chemistry and is involved in tutoring students both from school and university. They are both working in an outreach project, aiming to develop material for students and the public, accompanying a Collaborative Research Center at Kiel University. Thus, they are not only collaborating with the science education people at IPN but also with scientists of all disciplines related to nano science. All of them participate in the doctoral program at IPN, which provides methodological courses and workshops. Christine and Julian have decided to write a monograph thesis, while the other two aim to develop a paper-based thesis.

Starting the journey: developing research from a practitioner's perspective

Our doctoral students were all involved in analysing a complex field of practice to narrow down a research interest and to develop research questions. How they addressed this was determined by their varying perspectives on practice. For Jenny, for example, an important feature was searching for ways to reach the students, and ways to communicate science in an interesting way. She took up a position within a research project in order to reflect on the interaction between the learner and the learning context with respect to motivation. In Karolina's case, while teaching, she had noticed a disparity between those students interested in chemistry and those who found it boring, which led her to initially investigate students' perspectives of chemistry. The narratives of these two students, however, show quite different journeys from their early practitioner interests: while Jenny went on to carry out studies in classrooms to develop a better understanding for future practice, Karolina developed tools for practice first and investigated their features. Wilfried's interest in investigating students' perspectives on science and scientists began during his work in enrichment programs, with a specific ambition to develop an instrument that could be used in practice arising from the unsatisfying characteristics of existing tools. Katarina's study was very practitioner-focused from the outset, but informed by reading about scientific literacy; her experience of teaching non-science students in a scientific literacy programme led her to question how much science content students actually used in their discussions, and how they worked with socio-scientific issues. Tan Ying's research was also very practitioner-focused from her need to provide professional development for primary school teachers, as was Anne's in her position as an adviser working with a major professional development project.

Engaging with literature and theory

As in every research process the students move on from thinking about their research interest into exploring theoretical frameworks and the literature on the state of research in the chosen field, often negotiating between several options of frameworks. Students would make some progress initially by recognising a useful theory that enabled them to think more deeply about their research interest. Finding a suitable connection between practice and theories has different challenges, as explained, for example, by Annika, who was a very experienced teacher with a strong focus on the teaching of environmental and sustainability issues. She was aware of the need to theorise about her research interest early on and became frustrated by her early attempts which she felt lacked theory. She was very conscious of needing to shift away from a practitioner perspective in becoming a researcher. Sofie became immersed in new disciplines as she was associated with different graduate schools; her account shows how she navigated her way through the different disciplines. Julian's journey was first guided by frameworks of context-based learning that former students in the research group had used, but was then shifted by new international developments on learning progression as these offered an additional framework for the analysis of student answers. Katarina (education for sustainable development), Elizabeth (working with graphs in mathematics and science), and Tan Ying (questioning for higher order thinking) designed their studies from a practitioner perspective, informed by background reading of issues relevant to their interest. In each case theory took a more prominent role at the point of analysis, when each student was faced with the question of what was really going on in their (large) data sets. For these students the early interest drives the study and the outcomes are very relevant to the issues first identified, but working with theory to inform analytical focus on this doctoral journey was challenging.

From initial research ideas to research questions

Making progress from the initial interest or idea through engagement with literature can be the most problematic stage – it involves thinking in a more focused way about research questions or problems, recognising when these are valuable to guide the study and having the confidence to pursue them. For students with a rich experience of practice, this involves the ability to focus only on some aspects and to narrow down a question in a specific way to be able to analyse it, well knowing that many other aspects will be connected to the complex interaction of practice. Karolina narrowed down her own broad interest in chemistry teaching to research questions about problem-solving approaches in context-based tasks due to the lack of research in this specific area. Frederike describes her back and forth movement to narrow down her research interest into researchable questions by connecting frameworks about her content of nano science, the settings of out-of-school learning and the media tools that were implemented in the project like smartphone applications. Adrian developed his research questions and design once he had developed his framework for analysing examination items for linguistic features.

Having seen how these practitioners initiated their research and began to work with the literature and enter into research design, the divergent paths have led us to conceptualise these journeys in three different ways.

Research journeys: three pathways from practice into research

Building a research project in connection to practice can follow different routes and we use here an architectural analogy to illustrate the differences in how studies are constructed. Though the ground is always laid by observations of practice, the process of developing a research 'building' shows different characteristics. Some studies implement columns of theory as a foundation first, some design a complete building including elements of theoretical structure, whereas others focus initially on practical improvements of existing buildings, only later leading to reflections and new structural elements. The role of the researcher is different in the three settings. One group of students focuses on practice, but from an outside perspective, without changing practice within the doctoral project. Their research leads to results that are meant to initiate changes later on in teaching and learning (research-based design). A second group develops new tools or approaches for practice based on theoretical assumptions and investigates them in different kinds of interventions (theory-led design-based research). A third group acts within the field, some of their projects close to action research. They collect rich data in a more open way (practitioner-led design-based research). The chapters of this book have been categorised according to these three different routes and in each chapter there is a student voice that portrays the reflective process (Johnson 2001) showing how the research is built from the tools of theory and methodology.

Research-based design

The first group of authors proceeded on a journey from practice into research that is comparable to classic research approaches: an observation of practice leads to guiding research questions, which are further grounded and explored by reviews of suitable theoretical and empirical frameworks and studies, resulting in conclusions for a change of practice (Figure 1.1). The theoretical framework is used to carry out empirical

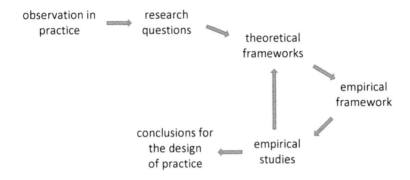

Figure 1.1 Pathway for a research-based design approach

studies and the results are used to suggest changes in practice. Some authors link the two by sub-studies and show iterative combinations of theory, research and the design of new approaches for learning practices. Sofie focuses on the challenges when exploring science and gender in preschool practice from different theoretical perspectives in the early stage of her work (Fleer 2009; Harding 1986; Hildebrand 1998). Christine describes the adaptation of theoretical frameworks, such as the RIASEC-model (Holland 1997) for the design of instruments for measuring interest. Jenny and Annika show the iterative process of going back and forth between theoretical frameworks and empirical studies prior to determining their main theoretical focus, which for Jenny was the motivation theory of Dörnyei and Ushioda (2011), and Annika the writings of Dewey (1916, 1934). Adrian and Anne each use a well-established theory to frame their research and analyse their data; for Adrian this was Systemic Functional Linguistics (Halliday and Martin 1993; Martin and Veel 1998), while Anne built on her earlier work using Kelly's construct theory (Kelly 1955).

Theory-led design-based research

The second structure (Figure 1.2) also grounds research questions in theoretical frameworks early on. But different to the first, the design of practice ·is the starting point for the empirical research, following the paradigm of design-based research (Bulte *et al.* 2006; Edelson 2002). The elements for practice these students developed range from tasks to whole lab units and diagnostic tools. These are investigated in teaching experiments, think-aloud interview studies or as pre-post-evaluations of interventions. This process usually requires several cycles of design and investigation which cannot be realised within one doctoral study. So these projects often

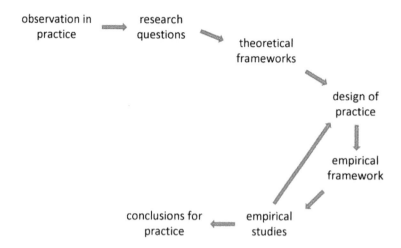

Figure 1.2 Pathway for a theory-led design-based research approach

represent phases of larger programs redeveloping practice on the basis of research. In this group, a theoretical framework, based on former research, leads to the design of a learning situation that will then be investigated and developed further in an iterative way. Karolina started from diverse findings on results of context-based learning and explains how she develops and investigates tasks in a more systematic way to better understand effects using specific analytical frameworks (Bernholt and Parchmann 2011; Zoller and Dori 2002). Frederike builds her work on the frameworks of authenticity (Braund and Reiss 2006) and the nature of science and investigates how school students develop their understanding about science. Julian analyses university entry students' learning based on diagnostic items designed according to an estimated learning progression and framed by different contexts (Neumann *et al.* 2013; Mahaffy 2006). Wilfried also designed a diagnostic instrument for use in practice, based on existing work about the nature of science and perceptions of scientists (McComas *et al.* 1998).

Practitioner-led design-based research

The design of doctoral studies in this section is based on practitioners' frameworks leading to empirical studies that are analysed using theoretical frameworks again in an iterative way (Figure 1.3). The studies involve design-based research where the design is based on practitioners' perspectives and the analysis on theoretical frameworks that provide insights into the data. Katarina designed her tasks based on her experiences of what

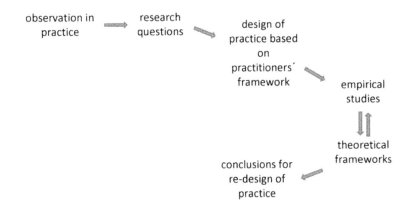

Figure 1.3 Pathway for a practitioner-led design-based research approach

would be meaningful learning experiences, Elizabeth used teacher designed tasks as the basis of her empirical work on graphs, and Tan Ying used a design based on her practitioner experience but also on earlier work with teachers. Though data collection was based on informed ideas about issues under study, essentially these authors developed more fully their analytical frameworks after data collection, Katarina drawing on the work of Potter and Wetherell (1987), Elizabeth using a range of sources such as Marton and Booth (1997), and Tan Ying finding a useful framework from Clarke and Hollingsworth (2002).

Designing research and decisions about research methods

Doctoral students need to draw on their own resources to develop research strategies, whether they are working independently from established research projects or formulating their own research alongside a wider research project. Drawing on one's own resources is not unusual for doctoral students, who often need to engage in self-tuition of research techniques for their specific needs (Troman 2002). Students were finding, adapting or developing suitable instruments to operationalise research questions and hypotheses for investigating practice, or using a framework for the design of practice to be investigated.

Refining research questions

Recognising the real working research questions that will guide the main part of the study can happen at different stages. Students who design their main study based on their earlier research and strongly developed theoretical stance find this more straightforward, for example Adrian, with his use of Systemic Functional Linguistics. Others go through several iterations between early studies, reading, understanding theory, before this next part of the design is determined. This was true for Jenny, which she documents in her chapter in her use of motivation theory, and Annika who describes how she developed her ideas with further interpretation of the writings of Dewey. For some students this shift takes them into theory-led design-based research as opposed to research-based design, in which case a theoretical framework is used to explicitly refine research questions and design an instrument that is the basis of the research, for example Karolina and Wilfried. For others the design has changed again after having added new theoretical aspects, like Julian with the idea of analysing learning progressions instead of university students' answers to context-based tasks at only one point of measurement.

Defining suitable analytical frameworks

Our authors have all accounted how they approached their analysis – analytical procedures are of course critical to the success of the study and examiners assess these in terms of validity of outcomes whatever the methodological approach. The narratives show various processes that highlight iterations between analysis and literature, theory, and even seminar discussions that all help the analytical process. To make a distinction between theoretical perspectives, as opposed to analytical frameworks, can be challenging for most students. The student narratives all exemplify this, but critical differences in how theory and analysis are constructed in the thesis can be seen across the different categories. Annika developed a deeper understanding of Dewey's theory of the cognitive and emotional aspects of learning to design the second phase of her research. Julian early on found a framework for designing his context-based tasks – Mahaffy's tetrahedron (Mahaffy 2006) – but had more difficulties in finding an analytical frame for his diagnostic items until he found papers on learning progression projects. Katarina built her practitioner-led design-based research on theoretical ideas about scientific literacy and what this means for practice; however her framework for analysing transcripts was derived from theory about interpretative repertoires and ways in which these are identified in discourse (Potter and Wetherell 1987; Edley 2001; Wiggins and Potter 2008). Likewise Tan Ying, whose practitioner-led design-based research on developing teachers' questioning was informed by Chin's work (Chin 2006, 2007), needed a theoretical model of teacher learning to analyse her teacher data and found Clarke and Hollingsworth's (2002) model useful in determining teacher growth.

Drawing appropriate conclusions and implications for practice

Students had to draw conclusions to make use of findings for the development of practice and practice-oriented research. In addition to the interpretation of data this often involves creative thinking to develop approaches for teaching and learning based on research findings and conclusions. The first cohort of students has or will draw conclusions based on their research, but they do not develop innovations for practice themselves, unless they go back into practice after finishing their doctorate. Christine, for example, has analysed the demands that science competitions set in comparison to school science, and she has also analysed how participants and non-participants of such competitions solve different tasks. The comparison of both can help to develop supporting tools and better information material for student competitions in the future. Having experienced both research and practice can help the doctoral students later on to transfer research findings into the community of practice and demands from practice back into research. The second and third group have already included changes of practice within their research journey, like Karolina's design of tasks and stepped supporting tools, or Wilfried's spider web instrument; for them the next step would certainly be to draw conclusions for further research and development, following a cyclic approach.

Challenges and opportunities of the learning journey

All doctoral students face challenges during their journeys. However, due to the transition from a practitioner to a researcher, some of these challenges might be especially difficult; and other experiences can be opportunities that students without a rich experience of practice might not have.

New disciplines, new language

For many students the engagement with theory would involve them in new disciplines, outside of the familiar science specialism they had grown up with, for example, psychology. Sofie became quickly immersed in new disciplines – gender studies and pre-school education; her account shows how reading and thinking in what she terms 'theoretical interfaces' throws light on the challenges of coming to grips with interdisciplinarity and a new language. Julian's situation was demanding, because for him as a chemist the whole area of science education theories and terminology was new.

Working alongside a larger project

Working alongside a larger project can be beneficial, as ideas and sources of collaboration can be found within the project. However, all doctoral students need to determine a project of their own, which can create tensions if their views on what this should be are different from those of project leaders. To address this need from the outset Sofie and Anne began to determine the focus for their own study early on whilst working in a larger project. Christine had to find her specific aspects in a larger project for which she was engaged to set up the whole study. She describes this not only as time consuming and difficult, due to having to overcome several organisational barriers, but also as enriching her own perspectives. Frederike describes needing a research environment with chemists, material scientists, etc. on the one hand and educational researchers on the other as challenging and supporting at the same time.

Tensions from initial studies

As a study progresses and thinking develops, recognising what was of value in earlier parts of the study can be problematic if it was deemed too superficial or insufficient, as both Jenny and Annika found until their theoretical frameworks developed and they could see the link between what was done initially and how they would proceed. Sofie's account shows the value of keeping a log of ideas from the outset as it can help to maintain confidence in the importance of early work. Holding on to what might be of value in the early stages is a dilemma faced by many students as it is tempting to ditch the early work in the light of new theoretical insights. This may be particularly the case for students' aiming to produce paper-based theses, where they are encouraged to write their first article based on initial studies that may be exploratory and lack the rigour needed for publication. Yet working with these can enable a clear focus to emerge more readily. It can also help to determine the limitations of early work, and the need to find better analytical procedures, which was the case with Katarina. Early work can help students to think more clearly about where the focus is but this can take a long time and can be a great struggle.

Dealing with uncertainty and gaining support

Students often go through periods of uncertainty when they are unsure of how to proceed, or lack confidence in their decisions. The range of possibilities and the abstract nature of theory can be overwhelming. Many accounts show how students felt during this period, and that there is much to be gained from giving a seminar, which can provide focus, feedback, and ideas for further reading with more purpose. Supervisory advice is critical in periods of uncertainty, and students need to feel supported during this time. Purposeful reading as opposed to wider more exploratory reading is critical.

In conclusion, we believe that the different stories explored in this book can help other students in their transition phases between research and practice to face challenges, to address them more explicitly – for example during supervision meetings – and to get ideas of how to overcome problems that not only they have but that are rather common for research based on practice.

References

Bernholt, S. and Parchmann, I. (2011). 'Assessing the Complexity of Students' Knowledge in Chemistry', *Chemistry Education Research and Practice* 12(2): 167–73.

Braund, M. and Reiss, M. (2006). 'Towards a More Authentic Science Curriculum: The Contribution of Out of school Learning', *International Journal of Science Education* 28(12): 1373–88.

Bulte, A.M.W., Westbroek, H.B., de Jong, O. and Pilot, A. (2006). 'A Research Approach to Designing Chemistry Education using Authentic Practices as Contexts', *International Journal of Science Education* 28(9): 1063–86.

Chin, C. (2006). 'Using Self-questioning to Promote Pupils' Process Skills Thinking', *School Science Review* 87(321): 113–19.

Chin, C. (2007). 'Teacher Questioning in Science Classrooms: Approaches that Stimulate Productive Thinking', *Journal of Research in Science Teaching* 44(6): 815–43.

Clarke, D. and Hollingsworth, H. (2002). 'Elaborating a Model of Teacher Professional Growth', *Teaching and Teacher Education* 18(8): 947–67.

Dewey, J. (1916). *Democracy and Education. An Introduction to the Philosophy of Education* (1966 edn.). New York: The Free Press.

Dewey, J. (1934). *Art as Experience.* New York: Perigee Books.

Dörnyei, Z. and Ushioda, E. (2011). *Teaching and Researching Motivation.* London: Pearson Education Ltd.

Edelson, D.C. (2002) 'Design Research: What we Learn when we Engage in Design', *The Journal of the Learning Sciences* 11(1): 105–21.

Edley, N. (2001). 'Analysing Masculinity: Interpretative Repertoires, Ideological Dilemmas and Subject Positions'. In: Wetherell, M. *et al.* (eds), *Discourse as Data: A Guide for Analysis.* London: Sage, pp. 189–228.

Fleer, M. (2009). 'Supporting Scientific Conceptual Consciousness or Learning in "a roundabout way" in Play-based Contexts', *International Journal of Science Education* 31(8): 1069–89.

Halliday, M.A.K. and Martin, J.R. (1993). *Writing Science; Literacy and Discursive Power.* London: Falmer Press.

Harding, S. (1986). *The Science Question in Feminism.* Ithaca, NY: Cornell University Press.

Hildebrand, G.M. (1998). 'Disrupting Hegemonic Writing Practices in School Science: Contesting the Right Way to Write', *Journal of Research in Science Teaching* 35(4): 345–62.

Holland, J.L. (1997). *Making Vocational Choices. A Theory of Vocational Personalities and Work Environments*, 3rd edn. Odessa: Psychological Assessment Resources.

Johnson, H. (2001). 'The PhD Student as an Adult Learner: Using Reflective Practice to Find and Speak in her own Voice', *Reflective Practice* 2(1): 53–63.

Kelly, G.A. (1955). *A Theory of Personality, The Psychology of Personal Constructs.* New York: Norton Library.

McComas, W., Clough, M. and Alamzroa, H. (1998). 'The Role and Character of the Nature of Science in Science Education', In: McComas, W. (ed.), *The Nature of Science in Science Education Rationales and Strategies.* Dordrecht: Kluwer Academic Publisher, pp. 3–38.

Mahaffy, P. (2006). 'Moving Chemistry Education into 3D – A Tetrahedral Metaphor for Understanding Chemistry', *Journal of Chemical Education* 83(1): 49–55.

Martin, J.R. and Veel, R. (1998). *Reading Science; Critical and Functional Perspectives on Discourses of Science.* London: Routledge.

Marton, F. and Booth, S. (1997). *Learning and Awareness.* Mahwah, NJ: Lawrence Erlbaum Associates.

Neumann, K., Boone, W., Viering, T. and Fischer, H.E. (2013). 'Towards a Learning Progression of Energy', *Journal of Research in Science Teaching* 50(2): 162–88.

Potter, J. and Wetherell, M. (1987). *Discourse and Social Psychology: Beyond Attitudes and Behavior.* London, Thousand Oaks, CA and New Dehli: Sage Publications.

Trafford, V. and Leshem, S. (2009). 'Doctorateness as a Threshold Concept', *Innovations in Education and Teaching International* 46(3): 305–16.

Treagust, D.F., Won, M. and Duit, R. (2014). 'Paradigms in Science Education Research', In: Lederman N.G. and Abell, S.K. (eds), *Handbook of Research on Science Education*, II: 697–726. New York: Taylor & Francis.

Troman, G. (2002). 'Method in the Messiness: Experiencing the Ethnographic PhD Process', *Doing a Doctorate in Educational Ethnography* 7: 99–118.

Wiggins, S. and Potter, J. (2008). 'Discursive Psychology'. In: Willig, C. and Stainton-Rogers, W. (eds), *The SAGE Handbook of Qualatative Research in Psychology.* London: SAGE Publications Ltd, pp. 73–90.

Zoller, U. and Dori, Y.J. (2002). 'Algorithmic, LOCS and HOCS (Chemistry) Exam Questions: Performance and Attitudes of College Students', *International Journal of Science Education* 24(2): 185–203.

Part I
Research-based design

2 Relocalisations and renegotiations

Framing a project about science in preschool

Sofie Areljung

The story told in this chapter concerns my first year of doctoral studies. In 2012 I applied for, and received, a doctoral student position where the research project was already set as being about science in preschool (children aged 1 to 5 years). The position is funded both by the Umeå School of Education and by the Umeå Centre for Gender Studies. With this funding comes compulsory participation in two postgraduate schools, and an obligation to place my thesis within the fields of educational science and gender studies. I have felt comfortable with connecting my research to educational science, since my background is in science and mathematics teaching, with experience from working with teachers and children from primary and secondary schools. However, both gender studies and preschool were relatively new areas for me. For that reason my research interest was at first mainly in science education, while my interest in gender studies and preschool developed as I engaged in readings and postgraduate school activities.

When I applied for the position I chose to associate my research study with a larger project, with five senior researchers involved. This project, from here on referred to as 'the larger project', had been going on for a semester when I arrived and its main objective was to examine how cultural factors affect the shaping of pedagogical activities with science content in preschools. I took part in project meetings and participated in the data collection, but was expected to outline an independent project design that included perspectives from gender studies.

In this chapter I will reflect on how my experience as a school science teacher comes into play when researching science practices in preschool. Initially my research interest was wide, revolving around what science for children as young as 1 to 5 years old could be. Further, I thought of examining how the science taking place in preschool was related to teachers' perceptions about preschool and science. In the following paragraphs I aim to expose how these research interests have developed and how literature, empirical work, as well as my participation in the larger research project and the two postgraduate schools, have been woven into each other in the framing of my doctoral project.

The research context and the practitioner perspective

In Sweden, 84 per cent of all children between 1 and 5 years, and nearly 95 per cent of children between 3 and 5 years, are enrolled in preschool (Statistics Sweden 2014). Sweden is part of the social pedagogy tradition that combines care, upbringing, play and a holistic view on learning and that focuses on the children's confidence in their own learning (OECD 2006). However, several studies have shown that when trying to implement activities with specific subject learning goals in preschool, social learning goals are often emphasised while subject learning goals come second (e.g., Thulin 2011). In 2010 the Swedish preschool curriculum was revised to clarify both specific learning goals and the preschool teachers' special responsibility for shaping a practice that ensured *both* learning and nurturing (Swedish National Agency of Education 2011). One reason for shedding light on science in preschool stems from this revision, as it involves an expansion from the former content regarding biological/environmental issues, to also include chemistry and physics content. Furthermore, the curriculum specifies that the preschool teacher should support children's ability to explore, record, speak about and ask questions about natural science. A general aspect that can be recognised in the 2010 revision is that the preschool curriculum is in transition. Both Lenz Taguchi (2000) and Alvestad (2011) see tendencies of school systems expanding to younger ages, and thereby introducing the school traditions to preschool. I recognise a similar tendency, that is, of school science simmering down to younger ages, in some of the formulations in the revised curriculum, such as children developing their understanding of 'chemical processes' and 'physical phenomena' (Swedish National Agency for Education 2011: 10). The new stress on scientific subject knowledge could be seen as a contrast to the preschool culture of integrating subjects in everyday practice (Thulin 2011).

While preschool practices are often guided by the children's interest, one widespread feature in preschool discourses is the resistance towards the perceived teacher-centred practices of regular school (Dahlberg and Lenz Taguchi 1994). There are reasons to believe that the reinforced knowledge focus in preschool will highlight the tensions between preschool and regular school practice. One example of this is found in a recent Swedish longitudinal study on preschool student teachers' attitudes towards science teaching (Sundberg and Ottander 2013). Sundberg and Ottander show that even though the student teachers felt confident in science many of them resisted teaching science in preschool since they wanted 'to protect the children from school culture' (2013: 80). As the students wanted their future preschool practice to be about inspiring and supporting children, this did not match their perceptions of school teaching, which were connected to compulsory activities and authoritative transmission of information.

My teaching background as a science and mathematics teacher has contributed to the nature of my engagement in researching science education in the preschool context. Having such a background means I am inescapably part of the reported tensions between preschool and school. I felt early on in my doctoral studies that researching preschool practice 'as a school science teacher' meant that I needed to renegotiate my way of interpreting and communicating about science education. I can identify two explicit reasons for this – the first comes from a methodological discussion that took place in the larger project. The discussion in the project group revolved around what standards we should use to recognise and describe science activities in preschool. We found that traditional criteria for identifying science activities, for example that they should include the elements *planning, predicting, observing, investigating,* and *interpreting results,* did not do justice to the activities we had observed in the preschool settings. The second reason was that my engagement in key texts of gender studies had highlighted that the researcher's position and way of seeing affected the research (Haraway 1988). My initial idea, before starting my doctoral studies, that the researcher was quite peripheral and somewhat untraceable was thereby challenged. When I dealt with data material of the larger project I became aware of how my practitioner perspective might influence my research. I recognised a tension between my own perceptions of science education and the stories and practices of preschool teachers, for example when it came to their approaches to children's own theories about phenomena in science. From my initial stance, I was very surprised to hear preschool teachers saying that the children's own explanations of a phenomenon were the most important, and that ready-made answers should be avoided. *What do they mean?* I remember thinking (and still to some extent do). *Could the children say just about anything and then the preschool teachers are fine with leaving it at that?* Since then my understanding of this issue has been deepened by readings and conversations with researchers and preschool staff. These experiences help me to see that the focus on the children's own explanations is in line with a long Swedish tradition of child-centred practices, meaning that activities should start from children's needs and interests (Swedish National Agency of Education 2004).

Further, my empirical work has shed light on how the preschool conditions differ to those of school when it comes to organising learning in space and time – in preschool the science activities normally occur in places other than classrooms, and a science theme can last as long as two years. So even though there might not be any answers given in conjunction with the children's own intuitive explanations, further discussions might take place in another time and place.

From what I have experienced so far the school-preschool tension opens up a fruitful spectrum for analysis, and at the same time it has led me to continuously highlight and renegotiate my views on the research material.

Looking back in retrospect I can see how my practitioner perspective, which lacks preschool experience, has influenced my methodological choices. Instead of only me judging and describing what science in preschool is, I base my interpretations on the preschool teachers' talk, their pictures, their videos, and their work-team discussions about science in preschool.

Readings and thinking in theoretical interfaces

As mentioned above, I am part of two postgraduate schools, one for educational science and one for gender studies. While having a background in education, gender theories were relatively new to me. The gender theories that I relate to in my research are those I have been acquainted with through postgraduate school activities. These theories go beyond research on gender differences and rather aim at challenging power relations and dominating views in society. These theories are not limited to gender only, as they include perspectives on ethnicity, class, age, and other social positions – and intersection of these positions – involved in subordination processes in society. My overall purpose of employing perspectives from gender theories in my research is to highlight and challenge taken-for-granted perceptions about both science and preschool. Such perceptions may affect what a person finds to be desirable and also possible practices, for instance that science might be perceived as appropriate only for older students. By challenging the taken-for-granted I hope to contribute to making science more accessible to all people, regardless of gender and age.

Because of the conditions included in the position I applied for I have had to relate my work to several fields of research: preschool, science, gender studies and educational science. In order to navigate these fields I have searched for texts that cover interfaces between some of them. These interdisciplinary readings can be illustrated using a Venn diagram (see Figure 2.1), which has turned out to be helpful, for example, when overviewing what types of previous research I include in research publications. One example of my interdisciplinary readings are the texts concerning both gender studies and science, where I encountered the works of feminist scholars who have scrutinised the value-free nature of science knowledge and the Western traditions of organising knowledge through dichotomies, that is through mutually exclusive concepts (e.g., Keller 1996). Schiebinger (1989) highlights how perceptions of gender are related to perceptions of science in dichotomies such as fact/value and reason/feeling. According to Schiebinger the first concepts in these dichotomies are associated with science, and aligned with notions of masculinity, while the second concepts are associated with non-science, and are aligned with notions of femininity. Thereby the dichotomies operate in separating science from other disciplines, and also in separating women from science.

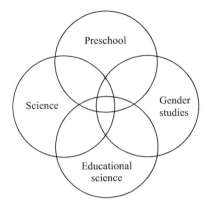

Interface	Examples of readings	Scholars
Gender studies–Science	Feminist critique of science	Harding (1986)
Preschool–Science–Educational science	Teachers' epistemological beliefs	Fleer (2009)
Gender studies–Science–Educational science	Challenging dominating science discourses	Hildebrand (1998)
Gender studies–Science–Educational science–Preschool	Challenging 'one-sided' research focus on concept knowledge	Andersson and Gullberg (2014)

Figure 2.1 The fields of research involved in the doctoral project

Referring to these types of dichotomies, Harding (1986: 24) poses a question that has lingered with me: 'can we imagine what a scientific mode of knowledge-seeking would look like that was not concerned to distinguish between objectivity and subjectivity, reason and the emotions?' In the data analysis I am currently working on with colleagues, we are using the concept pairs objective-subjective and logical-intuitive in the categorisation of the interview data, in order to examine teachers' conceptualisations of valid science in preschool. However in our use the dichotomy concepts are seen as ends of a continuum, as suggested by Parker (1997), and thereby not mutually exclusive.

Adding educational science to the interface of gender studies and science, I read a study conducted by Hildebrand (1998), who draws on feminist critique on knowledge production in science. She studied classrooms where the teachers encouraged the students to use imaginative and poetic language in their science assignments, aiming to challenge dominating science discourses. When I first encountered the feminist critique of science I was engaged in the methodological issues regarding how to recognise science practice in preschool, and these perspectives offered a way to deal with that. I see now that these readings, and certainly the idea of challenging dichotomies, have been intertwined with my aim of contributing to the discussion of what science in preschool practice can be.

The challenging of traditional science cultures is also present in the interface of preschool, science and education. Several researchers in early childhood science education contest the extensive research concerning preschool/primary teachers' (insufficient) content knowledge, by uncovering other important factors that influence how science is done in preschool. When it comes to children learning science, Fleer (2009) argues that preschool teachers' beliefs about learning make more difference than their confidence in teaching science. Further, the importance of the local preschool cultures has been stressed in the above-mentioned study conducted by Sundberg and Ottander (2013). They saw that after a whole year of teacher training with natural science orientation, resulting in students teachers' improved attitudes and self-confidence regarding the subject, the science teaching was restricted by the preschool cultures that the student teachers were situated in.

Moving to the interface of gender studies, educational science, science, and preschool, I find the discussion regarding science in early childhood education being perhaps even more intense. Andersson and Gullberg (2014) regret that researchers often point out preschool teachers' insufficient content knowledge, and in their own study they show how the researchers' shifting foci – from 'concept knowledge' to 'inclusion in a community of practice' – provides a richer account of the science activities in preschool. In a response to Andersson's and Gullberg's paper, Siry (2014) emphasises the need for science to be reconceptualised, and also reflects on the potential of this change: 'can we find spaces and support to rethink primary school science? I believe that we can, but to do so, we have to push against historically constructed, social representations that are deep seated with many teachers, researchers, and policy makers' (2014: 303). In the work of these scholars I recognised an expansion of the possibilities of how science could be framed in preschool, and the desire to, as Alvestad (2011) emphasises, acknowledge preschool teachers' pedagogical competences when handling learning goals, such as building on children's questions and experiences. This was closely connected to my own concerns regarding how to approach science practice in preschool as a researcher and not a school science teacher, and has impacted the framing of my study.

The challenge of interdisciplinarity

Since I am engaging in several fields, and taking part in two multi-disciplinary postgraduate schools, the concept of interdisciplinarity is immediately on the agenda. During a seminar in the postgraduate school for gender studies, some colleagues and I discussed Allen and Kitch's (1998) article, where the authors point out that an 'interdiscipline' yields new findings by identifying gaps in the interface between fields and by the adaptation of both disciplines to one another. This idea appeals to me as it opens up the possibility for creativity in the sense of combining knowledge in new ways. I aim for my doctoral project to be an example of disciplines adapting to each other. However, sometimes the sensation has been far away from that and I have often felt like I am outside and in-between the fields that I am supposed to be in.

I have kept a research diary throughout my doctoral studies in order to reflect on the ideas I have encountered through data collection in preschools as well as in texts and discussions. The following diary note relates to a seminar discussion in the postgraduate course *From Sex Role to Gender*, in which we handled key texts in gender theories. During the seminar I brought up a formulation in the course literature, namely Wittig's (1997: 267) statement that 'there is no nature in society', since I had wondered from what kind of ontological stance such a statement could arise.

> 11 March 2013. I feel that it is hard to make myself understandable to others. I sense that my questions about what it is to be a human being, and how society and nature belong together, are reduced to my having a different point of departure as a natural scientist, and that I thereby react on formulations that others would not react on. I can't remember ever feeling the kind of knowledge-related inferiority as I have now experienced in gender theory settings. I am not used to this sensation of feeling outside of the area that I am supposed to be in. It is strange because when I read and think about gender theory texts I don't feel foreign. But sometimes when the same issues are handled in a group discussion I feel that I am made an outsider – by myself or by others.
>
> [Personal research diary]

My location between fields has come to its head in situations involving written or oral presentations. Presenting texts in the postgraduate school settings, as well as in my home department of science and mathematics education, has shown that I can get different, and often opposing, responses depending on whose company I am in. I realise that it is reasonable that the listeners or readers are not located in the same interface as I am, and thereby see things from other positions. Though it is still sometimes frustrating, I have become more comfortable with my solitary position and with time I have learnt that the positions of other scholars need not be as polarised as I might first perceive them. Rather I have come to see it as an asset, as it brings about a gradual development of understanding different ontological and epistemological stances.

Further, my interdisciplinary point of departure has made me more aware than ever of how words carry notions with them, and what might be convenient in one field might be problematic in another. One such example is the use of feminist critique of science, and the highlighting of dichotomies that influence our perceptions of, for example, science. To contest views of science as objective and logical, and – as several feminist scholars have done before me – open up science to include aspects of subjectivity and intuition, might be supported in a setting with gender scholars. The same approach might be provoking in a setting with scholars in science education, where the idea of inviting subjective aspects into science practice can be received as a threat to a highly valued aspect of science – its objectivity.

Bringing the physical environment into my doctoral project

After four months of postgraduate studies I conducted a pilot study in order to get a glimpse of the conditions of preschool practice, and particularly an indication of what science in preschool practice can be. An additional aim with my pilot study was to practice observation, interviewing and transcription, and to see what kind of information that type of data could give. I entered the pilot study with an idea to explore the relationship between the teachers' perceived professional responsibilities and their perceptions of what science in preschool should be. At that point I was influenced by the emphasis on analysing discourses that I had perceived during several postgraduate school activities. I was interested in the concept of subject positions as presented by Davies and Harré (1990), meaning that one can only understand oneself through the categories that are available within the discourse one is in. According to Davies and Harré this implies that a limited number of subject positions are made available in each discourse. This idea appealed to me since I was interested in teachers' identity construction and the possibilities and tensions involved in being both a preschool teacher and a science teacher. Even though I am still interested in this, my research focus has shifted from teachers' identities (subject positions) to teachers' perceptions of what is appropriate science in preschool.

In my second semester of postgraduate studies, in the spring of 2013, I felt I had reached a dead end with the approach I then worked with, which focused on teachers' perceptions of science and preschool. This approach was quite similar to that of the larger research project, which was why I strived for a more independent framing of my PhD project: what perspective was I actually contributing with? I knew I was supposed to contribute with a gender perspective, but at that point I did not know enough about gender theories do so. To sum up my thoughts of that period in the spring of 2013, I was searching for some additional aspect to weave into my project, one that would make my profile clear in relation to the larger project, and one that would help me to outline how to make use of gender theories in my research. In the subsequent process of searching for such an aspect, I recalled the pilot interviews I had conducted and the teachers' talk about rearranging the preschool rooms. Further I recalled readings about sex-segregated workplaces and preschool environments as a metaphor for 'the home', and together with other influences 'the physical environment' emerged as a possible way forward. I returned to my pilot material, browsing for 'room', 'space', and 'physical environment' in the interview transcripts, and found much engagement regarding these themes in the informants' stories about preschool and science. One issue was the responsibility of keeping the preschool spaces neat and tidy, which hindered some of the informants from conducting 'messy' activities such as water play for young children. Further, the informants expressed that they would like to rearrange the preschool spaces in order to offer more opportunities to the children, as in the following quote:

> We spoke a lot about that during teacher training, about the environment, that it is the third pedagogue. And that is what I think about too – what do we offer these children? What do they see when they come in or what do they feel like doing, what do they feel like exploring? Yes, so I find these questions very exciting, and I wish it had been … I wish developing those parts had been a much larger part of my job than it is.
>
> [Teacher 2]

In the interviews I also found perceptions of science being easier to work with in certain places and certain weathers, preferably outdoors – because there is less need to clean up afterwards – but not in wintertime – because it is too cold and many things are frozen to the ground and covered in snow.

As I searched for previous research that related to the physical environment and that was relevant to science in preschool, I relocated myself in fields of research and new interfaces emerged (see Figure 2.1). When I started to read in the interface of gender studies and physical environment, I learned about the conception that spaces and people constantly constitute each other (Massey 1994) and that there is a connection between constructions of spaces and constructions of gender (McDowell 1999). Thereby the physical environment offered a way to deal with the gender perspective. Further readings in this interface guided me to theories about the things in the spaces, where scholars of posthumanism challenge anthropocentrism, claiming that non-human materialities are also important actors when it comes to directing people's possibilities (Hultman and Taguchi 2010). In the interface of physical environment and preschool I read a comparative study of English and Swedish preschool that highlighted Swedish preschool practices as limited by perceptions of 'tidy' material and 'dirty' material, where the latter was avoided since it was wet, loud, and easily spread (Nordin-Hultman 2004). This was closely related to what one of the teachers had mentioned in the pilot study:

We often speak, in the team, about not having water play for the younger children. We have such a bad conscience about that. We don't give them anything. We don't have any drainage, it will be trying to dry it all up, and we don't have time, and it will be so messy, and ... do you see? We know that they would love this, but we don't do it for the reason that it would be...

[Teacher 1]

Since the physical environment seemed to be an important issue for teachers when it came to teaching science, and since gender perspectives and spaces seemed to be closely connected, I decided to make the material perspectives central in the second study in my thesis. This study is based on data material from my collaboration project with preschool educators. Together we aim to develop physical environments that facilitate preschool teachers' and children's inquiry-based work with science. In this study I wish to learn more about how physical material matters to science education in early childhood. Further, the renegotiation theme of my thesis work continues, as I will examine how perceptions of 'science for preschool' are negotiated in our shared process of designing environments for science in preschool.

Looking forward by looking in retrospect

Writing this chapter has made me look back at my first year of postgraduate studies and synthesise the thoughts and experiences of that period into a fairly consistent story. However, the process has not been as linear as it might seem. Re-reading my research diary, I find traces of some ideas emerging much earlier in time than I can remember. This is the case of the science/non-science dichotomies. After about a year of operating in the back of my head, the dichotomies returned to the surface and are currently central to my work of analysing preschool teachers' talk about their science activities. Re-reading the diary also reveals how other things, that at some point seemed very important, have discretely faded away and ended up in oblivion.

The work of a doctoral student is not always tangible. Coming from a teacher background of 'doing', in forms of, for example, teaching, lesson planning, and marking tests, it can be difficult to take in that nowadays a whole day of thinking and reading could actually mean a whole day's work. Since doctoral work can be particularly intangible, I believe that it is sometimes hard to see one's own progression. In my case the old diary notes give comfort by assuring me that things *have* happened and that my postgraduate study pays off, since I am obviously able to see things now in a way that I did not before.

I hope the story told in this chapter helps to outline what the first year of postgraduate studies can be like and how it can be to try to locate oneself and one's work in interdisciplinary settings. I hope that it has served examples of the things that can affect the trajectory of a doctoral project, for example postgraduate school activities, readings and empirical work. I also hope that it has provided strategies for dealing with the confusing period of relating to several fields of research, that is: reading in interfaces and keeping a research diary. Even if distressing, I have found the many relocalisations and renegotiations necessary to establishing a platform of my own, one that suits and constitutes my project and research interests. I am beginning to like it here, in my place in-between.

References

Allen, J.A. and Kitch, S. L. (1998). 'Disciplined by Disciplines? The Need for an *Interdisciplinary* Research Mission in Women's Studies', *Feminist Studies* 24(2): 275–99.

Alvestad, M. (2011). 'You Can Learn Something Every Day! Children Talk about Learning in Kindergarten – Traces of Learning Cultures', *International Journal of Early Childhood* 43(3): 291–304.

Andersson, K. and Gullberg, A. (2014). 'What is Science in Preschool and what do Teachers have to Know to Empower Children?', *Cultural Studies of Science Education* 9(2): 275–96.

Dahlberg, G. and Lenz Taguchi, H. (1994). *Förskola och skola: om två skilda traditioner och om visionen om en mötesplats.* Stockholm: HLS Förlag.

Davies, B. and Harré, R. (1990). 'Positioning: The Discursive Production of Selves', *Journal for the Theory of Social Behaviour* 20(1): 44–63.

Fleer, M. (2009). 'Supporting Scientific Conceptual Consciousness or Learning in "a Roundabout Way" in Play-based Contexts', *International Journal of Science Education* 31(8): 1069–89.

Haraway, D. (1988). 'Situated Knowledges: The Science Question in Feminism and the Privilege of Partial Perspective', *Feminist Studies* 14(3): 575–99.

Harding, S. (1986). *The Science Question in Feminism.* Ithaca, NY: Cornell University Press.

Hildebrand, G.M. (1998). 'Disrupting Hegemonic Writing Practices in School Science: Contesting the Right Way to Write', *Journal of Research in Science Teaching* 35(4): 345–62.

Hultman, K. and Lenz Taguchi, H. (2010). 'Challenging Anthropocentric Analysis of Visual Data: A Relational Materialist Methodological Approach to Educational Research', *International Journal of Qualitative Studies in Education* 23(5): 525–42.

Keller, E.F. (1996). 'Feminism and Science'. In: Keller, E.F. and Longino, H.E. (eds), *Feminism and Science.* Oxford: Oxford University Press, pp. 28–40.

Lenz Taguchi, H. (2000). 'Emancipation och motstånd'. PhD thesis, Stockholm University.

McDowell, L. (1999). *Gender, Identity and Place: Understanding Feminist Geographies.* Cambridge: Polity Press.

Massey, D. 1994. *Space, Place and Gender.* Oxford: Polity Press.

Nordin-Hultman, E. (2004). 'Pedagogiska miljöer och barns subjektskapande'. PhD thesis, Stockholm University.

OECD. (2006). 'Starting Strong II. Early Childhood Education and Care'. Paris:

OECD publishing. www.oecd.org/newsroom/37425999.pdf (accessed 20 December 2014).

Parker, L.H. (1997). 'A Model for Gender-inclusive School Science: Lessons from Feminist Scholarship'. In: Marshall, C. (ed.), *Feminist Critical Policy Analysis I: A Perspective from Primary and Secondary Schooling.* London: Falmer Press, pp. 185–200.

Schiebinger, L. (1989). *The Mind has No Sex?* Cambridge, MA: Harvard University Press.

Siry, C. (2014). 'Towards Multidimensional Approaches to Early Childhood Science Education', *Cultural Studies of Science Education* 9(2): 297–304.

Statistics Sweden (2014). *Women and Men in Sweden: Facts and Figures.* http://jamda.ub.gu.se/bitstream/1/833/1/scb_eng_2014.pdf.

Sundberg, B. and Ottander, C. (2013). 'The Conflict within the Role: A Longitudinal Study of Preschool Student Teachers' Developing Competence in and Attitudes towards Science Teaching in Relation to Developing a Professional Role', *Journal of Early Childhood Teacher Education* 34(1): 80–94.

Swedish National Agency for Education. (2011). 'Curriculum for the Preschool Lpfö 98, revised 2010'. Stockholm: Fritzes. www.skolverket.se/publikationer? id=2704 (accessed 11 November 2014).

Swedish National Agency for Education. (2004). 'Förskola i brytningstid – en nationell utvärdering av förskolan'. Stockholm: Fritzes. www.skolverket.se/ publikationer?id=1272 (accessed 11 November 2014).

Thulin, S. (2011). 'Lärares tal och barns nyfikenhet: kommunikation om naturvetenskapliga innehåll i förskolan'. PhD thesis, University of Gothenburg.

Wittig, M. (1997). 'One is Not Born a Woman'. In: Nicholson, L. (ed.), *The Second Wave: A Reader in Feminist Theory.* London: Routledge, pp. 265–71.

3 Teachers learning from young children during a cognitive acceleration programme

Anne Robertson

My interest in learning about teaching from children was ignited by my own experience of schooling and then sparked into action as a young primary school teacher. My first post in the 1970s was in a school where all other members of staff had been teaching for at least 15 years, so there was plenty of experience from which to draw. However, I quickly noticed that the teachers told me about what I needed to do and how I needed to be and yet they did not mention the children. I wanted to put children first, so for over 30 years I have maintained my interest in listening to children about their experiences of learning and of what helps and hinders their learning journey.

After having taught in primary school classrooms for over 20 years, I took a post as an advisory teacher. This role entailed supporting a group of schools in a local area to develop pedagogies to meet the needs of all children. I was responsible for enabling teachers to reflect on and develop their pedagogy so that they made maximum impact on attainment. After several years, I took up a new post, again as an advisory teacher, but with a different purpose. I joined a new team of researchers set up to investigate how to develop Year 1 (5–6 years old) children's thinking through a Cognitive Acceleration (CA) Programme (Adey *et al.* 2001). The CA team was established as a joint venture between a university and a Local Education Authority (LEA). At that time, LEAs were responsible for ensuring that all the schools in their area met statutory requirements and provided the best possible education to all children. I was the member of the team who worked for the LEA as the Advisory Teacher for Teaching and Learning while all other team members worked for the university. The advisory role was created to ensure clear communication between all the schools and the university staff as well as helping to produce the programme of 27 lessons and devising and running a Professional Development (PD) programme for the participant teachers. Part of my role in the team was to support the teachers to teach the programme and also to increase teachers' understanding and implementation of the underlying theory through the PD. I was also expected to participate in an aspect of research and this was made clear to the schools from the beginning. Being a member of the CA team provided me with opportunities to work with teachers and develop a research method whereby the teachers could learn from the children about their learning experience so as to use a more effective pedagogy.

It was within this context that I started the PhD study although I subsequently left the team to work in Initial Teacher Education based at the university. My data collection was well underway by that time, and I had good relationships with the participant teachers so there was no difficulty in collecting the remaining data.

Context of cognitive acceleration (CA)

CA programmes are intervention programmes aimed at raising attainment of all pupils (Adey and Shayer 1994). They have been taught in secondary schools since the late 1980s but only began to be established in primary schools in 1999. CA is designed specifically to develop thinking through the use of collaborative group work where children work together to solve challenges as they talk and discuss various possible solutions. The children are also encouraged to use metacognitive strategies to help their development in taking control of their own learning processes.

All CA programmes are based on the theories of Piaget and Vygotsky. The main objective and emphasis of each CA lesson is for the children to develop thinking rather than focusing on developing content knowledge. Piaget (1952) suggested that one radical cognitive shift occurs in children between the ages of 4 and 7 years. According to Piaget, during this period, most children move from one way of thinking, pre-operational, to a qualitatively different way, concrete thinking (Piaget and Inhelder 1974). Vygotsky (1986) maintained that, in order to understand the mental functioning of an individual, it was necessary to consider the cultural and social processes experienced by the individual. His model of mental functioning is based on the belief that learning is a two-way operation: interpersonal processes and culture provide a framework for learning; the child constructs meaning and understanding from this structure. Mental function is, therefore, firstly action with the world and secondly reflection upon it, using the language and other symbols of the culture to make sense of it. Engaging with both Piaget and Vygotsky was very important for me to understand how their theories could be translated into meaningful contexts and implemented in Year 1 classes. In engaging with the vast literature, I tussled with becoming sure of the most relevant points of each theorist and then tried to ensure that these were communicated to teachers and included in the lessons provided.

CA lessons encourage children to verbalise their reasoning using the theoretical models of talk provided by Mercer *et al.* (1999). Talk takes place within the CA structure and revolves around aspects known as the pillars of CA: social construction, concrete preparation, cognitive challenge, bridging and metacognition all form part of a lesson. The lessons open with a period of concrete preparation when the context is introduced and the vocabulary needed is agreed. This is an important time of familiarisation with the equipment and the context for what is to follow. The context is usually linked to an aspect of the curriculum or to something familiar in daily life. When this link is made explicit, bridging is taking place. For example, when ordering sticks, one child was heard to comment, 'Oh, it's like the church piano', while another said, 'no, it's same as stairs'. Cognitive challenges are posed during the activity. These cognitive challenges are provided in the programme and the teacher can use the suggestions as appropriate to each group. The criterion here for teacher choice is to challenge each child in their thinking by providing opportunities for cognitive struggle at times within the lesson. With the teacher's facilitation, children discuss, ask questions of each other, challenge each other's assumptions, clarify ideas and gradually come to an agreed solution. This is social construction in action. Metacognition, encouraging children to become self-reflective, to monitor and evaluate their thinking and learning processes, occurs at points throughout each lesson. As the children work together to solve the problem, the teacher is alert to occasions for questioning children not only about the task but also about their thought processes.

Pre and post tests used by the larger project aimed to measure children's cognitive development through the year and were given to CA and non-CA children so that a comparison could be made. Evidence from the tests indicated that the CA children made a significant gain in cognitive development as compared to the non-participant children (Adey *et al.* 2002). These were very positive results showing that many children were making the transition from pre-operational to concrete thinking successfully, or developing within concrete thinking, thus being able to access the curriculum more effectively. However, the test results showed that while a significant number of children made a substantial gain, some made little or no gain and others appeared to regress. Furthermore, the tests gave no insight into what these discrepancies indicated. Nor did results give any indication as to how to change the pedagogy so that it could have a greater impact on more children. I was very interested in finding out more about what affected the children while working in CA lessons so as to develop the pedagogy used during the programme and inform teachers during the PD sessions. This interest also met the requirement of the LEA.

The PD programme consisted of nine days out of class as well as modelling in class lessons and coaching the teachers teaching the lessons. During the days out of class the teachers were given input on the theory and pedagogy of CA theory, observed the lessons being modelled, discussed lessons that they had taught and engaged in discussion of the theory and practice of the programme. The points of most difficulty were, firstly, encouraging the teachers to allow the children to engage in discussion between themselves. The teachers were asked to facilitate children's discussion but not lead it and this was difficult for some of them. The second most difficult point was establishing metacognition as a normal part of each lesson. Recognising what metacognition sounded like in a 5 year old and then developing thinking at that level took time and detailed attention.

Engaging with theory and research questions

Since I had worked on the team from its beginning to develop the programme I knew the CA lessons very well. I also had a key role in designing and developing the PD for teachers and had been able to develop a positive and supportive relationship with each of them, however, the children using the programme had had fewer opportunities to talk to us about how they experienced the lessons. In most classes the experience of participating in collaborative group work while trying to solve a challenge was new and different as the rest of the curriculum was generally not taught in this way. I thought that finding a way to engage the children and listen to them regarding their experiences of learning in the CA context could offer insights which could inform the CA pedagogy. I hoped that the children could indicate what differences the CA experience made to their learning and in turn, by listening to children, teachers could choose what to prioritise in their teaching to provide a better learning experience

Each experience a child has contributes to the building of their construct system and their interior narrative about him/herself and the world. This construct system, in turn, impacts upon learning outcomes with the learning experience itself being a central, key factor affecting further development. As a classroom practitioner, I had always tried to engage children in their understanding of the learning process and what being an effective learner entails. It was my belief that this reflexive experience required further exploration in order to understand more fully the factors of the CA programme that were impacting on children's understanding of what helped their learning. Finding a method to allow young children to articulate how they experienced CA as helpful/unhelpful to learning was very important to this study. In an earlier study I had used Personal Construct Theory (PCT), as defined by Kelly (1955), as a theoretical base and had interviewed children, collecting their personal constructs about their learning experience. I had found this to be an informative method providing the children with opportunities to explore how they experienced learning in the context of their classroom. In turn, the children's constructs informed teachers who were able to use the insights to adjust their teaching methods accordingly.

Kelly believed that scientists aim to make predictions about the natural world, develop theories and test them in experiments so as to formulate hypotheses. They then test their hypotheses and observe results. He asserts that human beings generally follow a similar cyclical procedure in the development of their system of constructs. Their constructs become their theories about the world in which they live, the essential difference being that scientists observe behaviours and then conduct their experiments on them by varying certain conditions. The human person-as-scientist, however, uses the behaviour itself to become the experiment. For Kelly, then, all human behaviour is seen as testing constructs which are being built and refined in a continuous process of movement. When teachers understand children from this perspective, it helps them to encourage the children to consider alternative views and to adjust their thinking. Kelly sees the human person as one whole; he circumscribes the whole human experience as one, living, moving inter-connected process. He believed that there is, inherent in the human person, the ability to take control of life and do something with it. It was this aspect of the theoretical perspective that I wanted the teachers to engage with and adopt.

The theory underpinning CA also views children as construing knowledge in scientific ways: predicting, looking for pattern and change, hypothesising with reason. From the basis of these complementary theories I began to develop the research. My questions were finalised as:

- How do Year 1 children understand what helps them to learn during the CA Programme?
- What differences emerge between CA and non-CA children's constructs?
- What differences emerge in CA pedagogy when teachers understand and take account of children's personal constructs during the CA Programme?

Research strategy

The main aim of my research was to support all children in making maximum intellectual progress while using the CA programme. In order to achieve this aim I considered that I needed to find out from the children how they experienced learning within the programme. This information then needed to be fed back to teachers who would have to think about how to use the information appropriately to maximise the learning opportunity afforded by the programme. This rationale provided the three main aspects to the research: child interviews in each of two years, CA lesson observations in each of two years and a short intervention with the participant teachers in between the two years. The teachers needed to be the same teachers in each of the two years. The children needed to be in Year 1 participating in CA so a new cohort of children was required for the second year of the study. I adopted a nested case study research strategy (Yin 2003) so that data could be analysed and presented at school, class and individual child levels in each of the two years. In the first year of the study, I examined differences in constructs between CA and non-CA participants as a way of exploring the context of the learning environment that CA creates. The second year of the study allowed for exploring differences in the children's participation during CA lessons and in their personal constructs following an intervention to heighten teachers' awareness of children's constructs.

To develop the research design, I worked on combining information gathered through observing CA lessons with information provided by the children in interviews about their CA experience. I wanted to explore what differences CA made to children's learning so in the first year I observed two non-participating classes and interviewed 12 children from those classes. I had to decide on the frequency of interviewing children, so following discussion with the CA team, we decided that three times per year was sufficient. The team was concerned that I would have more data than I could cope with and I was worried that if I interviewed the children too frequently they may lose interest.

As the first year progressed, the teachers were keen to hear what the children said in their interviews so I was able to harness this motivation and planned the short intervention with the teachers between the two years. Because I wanted the teachers to learn from the children, I had to find a way to communicate the information from the children to the teachers in a constructive way. Working with the four teachers during the first year of the study, maintaining their interest and motivation to learn was crucial to the success of the intervention and the research process.

Developing data collection protocols

As the advisory teacher on the CA team, I was able to teach the lessons in any classroom as the teachers were willing for this to happen. However, when in the role of researcher observing lessons, I had to ensure that I did not cross boundaries and stay in role. I had worked in a variety of roles in the past so maintaining boundaries was not difficult. The important consideration was how the research was introduced to the particular teachers and then establishing exactly the purpose of each visit to school. This ensured that when I was visiting in the role of advisory teacher I fulfilled that role with the teachers and certain children and when I was visiting to advance the research I observed specific groups and interviewed particular children. I sent out a termly schedule in advance to each teacher with proposed dates and purposes of visits. The teachers found this very helpful and were able to work with me in each role without difficulty.

Lesson observations

I found developing a lesson observation schedule to be a complex task. I needed to be able to see and hear the children and the teacher in the group being observed. Recording equipment was unsatisfactory as it distracted the children and got in the way of the lesson equipment. As a consequence I wrote everything that was said. I took the stance, as far as possible, of an observant presence, speaking only when necessary to minimise distraction. The spotlight was to be held firmly on the children and the teacher interacting with one another and with the activity.

Child interviews

PCT is useful in that the underpinning theory can be implemented in a range of ways, some of which have been designed with young children in mind. When I talked about PCT to the CA team, no-one had read or used Kelly's theory in their work. At first, I thought this was a disadvantage and considered that perhaps I should not use it. However, I was convinced of its value and flexibility so I persevered with it. I re-read much of Kelly's work and also literature from others who had been inspired by him and used his ideas (Salmon 1995; Fransella 1995). It was particularly useful to engage with psychologists and teachers who had based their work with young children on PCT. I explored various interview techniques and schedules based on PCT and trialled them with children. The challenge was to give the children the opportunity to speak while not leading them or putting words in their mouths. These children were 5 years of age and many were in the first few months of learning English. I found it difficult at first to find a method of interviewing them where they felt comfortable enough to try to explore their learning experiences. I eventually found that staying with one simple question was the best approach: 'I wonder if you can tell me what helps you to learn?' Because constructs are bi-polar I needed to also find a way to access the opposite pole of the construct. For this I used the group situation and asked each child following the production of a construct: 'I wonder if you all do that in the same way?' As the children elaborated I was able to access the opposite pole of each construct as well as get some explanations for how each construct helped the child to learn. For example, if a child said, 'it helps me to listen', *listen* became the construct and the opposite pole on this occasion, 'he does *not* listen really well – only a little bit sometimes'. I investigated what constructs children held with regard to learning before the teaching began and then examined the changes in the constructs on three occasions as the CA programme was taught.

The interview began with the child naming the members of their group. This was easy and non-threatening. I wrote the names on small cards and the child arranged them on the table in the seating position of the group that day. There was no pressure to produce a certain number of constructs during interviews. No judgement was passed at any time and no comments were made that could imply any kind of criticism.

Interviews explored the words children used to ensure clarity of meaning. For example, Nemy said: 'doing hard things makes you learn', while Susan said: 'easy things but they can be boring'. Allowing further time for elaboration elicited that Susan wanted some challenges (hard things) during the day to enable her to feel that she was learning something new and to keep boredom at bay. This established that the two constructs that were initially produced held the same main idea but could easily have been misrepresented. It was important to take time and effort to become as clear as possible about what the children meant when they produced their constructs.

Teacher intervention

The intervention took the form of four one hour meetings with the four teachers in July–August. We examined lesson transcripts, listened to what the children had to say through their constructs and explored how CA pedagogy was being implemented. During the fourth meeting, the teachers analysed the children's constructs against their own lesson transcripts to see where challenges were successful, which children responded to metacognitive strategies, where behaviour implementation was distracting from the thinking. Towards the end of the last meeting, the four teachers voluntarily set themselves some targets which they shared with each other. These targets were based on themes that emerged through the constructs and could be perceived in the lesson transcripts. The themes emerged from the texts of transcripts and constructs and became the focus of our discussions without prior agreement. For example, make the lessons more challenging, engage more fully in metacognition, encourage more exploratory talk and do not let the social context distract from the children's thinking. The fact that these themes developed naturally was a key factor in their being developed by the teachers and used as targets to improve the CA pedagogy.

These data collection protocols produced a vast amount of data. I made the final decisions about material to be included and excluded in the study during the writing process. This was important in order to ensure that what was included was all relevant to the key questions, main findings, conclusions and learning points.

Analytical process

Analysis of data provided a huge challenge and took many hours of thought and trying various approaches before I arrived at the final method. The analysis of observed lessons needed a clear and coherent approach. So much material was overwhelming so to extract the most relevant data from all the transcripts was important while ensuring that decisions were transparent and non-biased.

I explored ways of analysing the lesson observations by reading and re-reading the transcripts. I then analysed the lessons from the perspective of CA pedagogy. In the first instance, I highlighted the schema being used and then I identified the pillars of concrete preparation, cognitive challenge, metacognition and bridging in each lesson. I considered it to be important to recognise the pillars within each lesson as they determine the intention of any teacher action, for example, asking a question about the task, asking a question to encourage metacognition. I began the analysis of oral contributions by identifying each occasion when a child, teacher or group of children spoke. This was a word, a phrase or a sentence. Each of these occasions was classified as an 'event' on the transcripts. Each event in all the observed lessons was then examined and described by answering the question: What is this event? The types of event that were identified from this initial examination were questions, instructions, statements, descriptions and explanations. Following this, I grouped each intervention according to the intent of the contribution in line with CA pedagogy. I then developed a coding scheme that was also used by two colleagues in order to establish reliability prior to applying the codes to all the lesson observations (111 lessons observed).

Because personal constructs and their opposite pole were clearly identified, this made analysis of interviews less complicated than the analysis of lessons. I was also able to identify constructs that meant the same even when different words were used. For example, doing a challenge, doing hard work, doing a tricky puzzle are all represented by the construct 'being challenged'. I recorded the date, child, class and school, which made it easy to see changes through the year by each child in each class and school. I considered the frequency with which each construct was mentioned to be important, and tracking the frequency enabled me to identify emerging themes. For example, listening to others' ideas became a common construct mentioned by most children. These emerging themes indicated the broad aspects being experienced by the children during CA lessons.

During the intervention meetings after sharing the children's constructs, the teachers identified emerging themes. Since the main aim of the intervention was to support teachers' development it seemed appropriate for me to structure the writing around the themes emerging from the children, identified and chosen by the teachers to determine targets to work on in the following year. The themes identified were challenging children, developing metacognition, using exploratory talk and social issues.

Analysis of CA lessons across the two years indicated that in the second year the teachers not only became more competent in using CA pedagogy but also took seriously what the children communicated through the personal constructs. This is evidenced particularly by the changes in metacognitive opportunities within the lessons. Also, lesson transcripts show that teachers used shorter concrete preparation times and prioritised creating challenges for each child. All of the teachers were more accurate in their use of language especially when using instructions regarding the schemata. The social context and group dynamics aspect of the collaborative group work worked more successfully in that every child was encouraged to contribute and no child was allowed to dominate. This created a helpful, supportive environment where peer scaffolding was evident on a regular basis.

Results and reflection

Providing a summary of the study has allowed the reader to glimpse the main aspects of the underlying theory, the main methodological aspects and a brief summary of the results. However, this may appear as if the journey was straightforward. In fact, there were many false turnings and detours in direction during this long journey and these created delays, frustrations and a sense of being lost and overwhelmed at times. In analysing these sensations several challenges emerged from which to learn.

One of the main factors I identify as a difficulty was initially having expectations that were too broad and lacking in focus. Because of my lack of clarity I kept changing the questions being investigated. Having an openness to an emerging direction was useful; however, remaining unrooted on one specific road left me prey to the prevailing winds, storms and scorching sun. Looking for shelter and relief, I sauntered off the road and became distracted by all that I found there. These delays affected my motivation and the resultant slow progress lowered motivation and self-esteem even further.

At the start of the journey, I was unclear as to exactly what I aimed to achieve from the research and this resulted in a lack of clarity over what route to follow. The result of this lack of focus was that I collected data about several other aspects of children's learning that bear little relation to the final study. For a long time, I went down a 'gender' road and eventually left it behind. I veered into a 'self-concept' road where I was investigating how much a child's self-concept interacted with the personal learning journey. This too came to a dead end when I finally accepted that I had too much data and this avenue was not vital to the study. I mention these two main aspects because they cost me a lot in time and energy. Both of these routes had value, both had well established literature and both could have been informative but, to this study, they were not crucial and had to be left behind.

Another important factor was not prioritising information appropriately. The journey was well advanced before I prioritised the value of the teacher intervention, which took place between the two academic years. Once I analysed the main aspects of learning that the teachers identified during the intervention, I had the focus for the analysis of children interviews and classroom observations. Until then I was ploughing through a muddy field of too much data with no coherent way to organise it.

Despite the above aspects, there were also many positive aspects of the journey. The good relationship with the four teachers was crucial to the completion of the study. I was faithful to the observation and interview schedule and the four teachers remained committed to their schedules and availability. This meant that I was able to have a full data set in each class for each of the two years. The teachers were all willing to give up their time to attend the four intervention meetings. They were open to learn and to receive feedback then set themselves targets which they went on to use during the second year. Another positive aspect of the journey was the time taken in trialling data collection methods. This time was invaluable in that once the two years began clear protocols were in place and worked well without the need for any change.

On reflection, the journey was not pleasant and the temptation to give up was often present. I questioned what was it that held me on the journey? It required more than my normal determination and resilience to trudge on through the mire to get to the end. What was it that pierced the darkness and shone through? I can only describe it as moments of delight. These came from the children who were focussed and intent on the task. They were very keen to help teachers to understand what helps children to learn. They wanted school to be a fun place where they could learn with all the helpful things in place. I owed it to them to tell the story. The thought of all that they shared with their enthusiasm and excitement, their trust and their hope kept me going when the going was tough. It was the children who kept me on the journey and made it all worthwhile. This taught me that it is crucial to find the real meaning in a task because it is this that will see me through the journey to the end.

References

Adey, P. and Shayer, M. (1994). *Really Raising Standards: Cognitive Intervention and Academic Achievement.* London: Routledge.

Adey, P., Robertson, A. and Venville, G. (2001). *Let's Think: A Programme for the Development of Thinking in 5–6 Year Olds.* London: NFER-Nelson.

Adey, P., Robertson, A. and Venville, G. (2002). 'Effects of a Cognitive Acceleration on Year 1 Pupils', *British Journal of Educational Psychology* 72(1): 1–25.

Fransella, F. (1995). *George Kelly.* London: Sage Publications.

Kelly, G.A. (1955). *A Theory of Personality, The Psychology of Personal Constructs.* New York: Norton Library

Mercer, N., Wegerif, R. and Dawes, L. (1999). 'Children's Talk and the Development of Reasoning in the Classroom', *British Educational Research Journal* 25(1): 95–111

Piaget, J. (1952). *The Origins of Intelligence in Children.* New York: International Universities Press.

Piaget, J., and Inhelder, B. (1974). *The Child's Construction of Quantities.* London: Routledge and Kegan Paul.

Salmon, P. (1995). *Psychology in the Classroom.* London: Cassell.

Vygotsky, L.S. (1986). *Thought and Language,* A. Kozulin (ed.). Cambridge, MA: MIT Press.

Yin, R.K. (2003). *Case Study Research: Design and Methods: Applied Social Research Methods.* London: Sage.

4   Abilities of participants at students' science competitions

Christine Köhler

During my studies of Chemistry and French to obtain the teaching degree for secondary schools at Kiel University, I have been involved in scientific students' competitions such as the International Junior Science Olympiad (IJSO). I was, among other things, involved in the task development for all German qualifying rounds. For my master's thesis, I developed experiments for the German qualifying round of the International Chemistry Olympiad (IChO). Some time later, I assisted in the German final qualifying round for the IJSO. There, I had the opportunity to meet highly interested and talented students for the first time. In addition, I was involved in an interview study to assess the students' interest in science as well as their beliefs about scientists and their activities. Shortly after this, I started working at school and changed role from being involved in the organisational part of the competition to being involved as a teacher who supported students in participating in the IJSO, which was quite challenging. My own journey as a PhD student started when the project, in which the mentioned interview study was embedded, offered a PhD position which aimed to characterise students and participants at different students' science competitions. Due to my experience in the development of IJSO tasks as well as in the supervision and support of IJSO participants, developing a test for students which measures their scientific knowledge and their abilities seemed to fit perfectly to my background.

As I am now finishing my data collection with regard to the final phase of my PhD, this chapter will describe the first half of my PhD. It will focus on the development of the test and the difficulties in the different stages of the development as well as the test design and realisation in school and during competitions. I will close with an outlook on the whole project and the steps which followed until the beginning of the current data collection, based on the development and piloting of the test.

Being a teacher – becoming a researcher

During my work as a teacher, I offered an extracurricular activity to prepare students for their participation in the IJSO. I quickly realised that this was quite a challenging task: I addressed the extracurricular activity to students from fifth to eighth grades, but over the time I noticed that the competition was possibly too difficult for fifth and sixth graders. From my own experience with IJSO participants, I knew that the constant participation in a competition was useful – so I asked myself how I could motivate young students to participate in the IJSO even though their background knowledge and their scientific abilities may not, due to their age, be sufficient. Furthermore, I was unsure about the participation of a whole class. If everybody participates, will that be too much for the weak students? If I just ask high-performing students, will I miss students that may be talented but at the same time underachievers? In summary – how could I find possible participants for the IJSO? It would have been great as a teacher to have had some characteristics of participants or even talents in science which would have made the choice of participants easier.

Even though the students I supported in their participation did not reach the next round, I asked myself how I would have supported them if they had reached the next qualifying round. So, how could I support participants as talented young students in science? Not just within the context of a scientific competition or in class, but maybe even in out-of-school activities. Thus, I reached the decision to leave school for some time and to start a PhD at the IPN Kiel in a larger project, called the 'Individual Concept about Natural Sciences' (ICoN).

My PhD project: investigating the ICoN

Working in a larger project: the ICoN framework

The 'Individual Concept about Natural Sciences' (ICoN), in which my PhD project is embedded, is a larger project which started in 2010. Two other PhD students have been involved in the project alongside me, as well as a PostDoc psychologist, a leader of a Science Olympiad and a chemical education researcher, my supervisor. As the existing ideas, frameworks and studies influenced my research, I will briefly describe the state of research which existed when I started my PhD.

The starting point of the 'Individual Concept about Natural Sciences' (ICoN) was the fact that for knowledge-based economies, many people are needed to enter science and technology careers. However, the high demand can often not be satisfied. Furthermore, students' attitudes towards science in school are generally negative, which aggravates the shortage of scientists even more (Osborne and Dillon 2008: 14). Consequently, fostering talented students in science and encouraging them to enter a scientific career should be one of the main goals of science education. Unfortunately, there is hardly any systematic approach to promote young talents in science. Hence, the long-term aim of ICoN was to develop such an approach, based on a characterisation of young talented students in science.

Many existing concepts of talented individuals define them with respect to their intelligence or their specific performance (e.g. Renzulli 2005; Rost 2009). In this project, concepts which include intrapersonal and environmental factors, e.g. beliefs, interests, as well as self-concept and self-efficacy are additionally considered (e.g. Ackerman and Heggestad 1997; Gagné 2005; Heller *et al.* 2005). Furthermore, natural sciences are regarded as a specific domain. This is a contrast to the mentioned concepts which are usually considered, for example, the general interest, but not particularly the interest in natural sciences.

Based on the afore-mentioned concepts of talents, ICoN was developed as a holistic approach to characterise talented individuals in science and identify profiles among them. The ICoN includes students' views about scientists and their abilities, their interest in science, their scientific knowledge and abilities as well as their self-concept and self-efficacy. It is based on Holland's RIASEC model (Holland 1997), which was originally conceptualised as a theory of careers and vocational choices. The RIASEC model takes six dimensions of interest as a basis: realistic (R), investigative (I), artistic (A), social (S), enterprising (E), and conventional (C). These dimensions can also be associated with certain occupations.

The first step in the project was the development of belief- and interest-instruments. For the belief-instrument, the RIASEC model was adapted by assuming that the broad field of scientists' tasks and personal characters can be represented by all RIASEC dimensions. This formed the basis for developing a new construct, 'Nature of Scientists' (NoSt), which focuses on students' views about characteristics and occupational activities of scientists (see the chapter by Wilfried Wentorf in this book). By adapting the RIASEC dimensions to subdomains of interest in science, an interest-instrument which offers a promising approach for a differentiated analysis of interests in science was developed (Dierks *et al.* 2014).

My first step in the context of ICoN was to get in contact with the work which was already done within ICoN. I intended to analyse the existing state of research and to identify the desiderata of this project. Which facets could be important for my work, how had they been analysed, which aspects had yet to be analysed, which theoretical and methodological frameworks seem to be suitable?

Defining my role in ICoN

During my first weeks as a PhD student, I read the literature around ICoN and tried to familiarise with the field of interest. As I was asked to define my own research interests, these first weeks were very important for me. I read a lot of literature concerning highly gifted or talented students as well as literature about students' competitions and their participants. While I was reading, many findings made me think of my experiences with IJSO participants and students in school, and I was able to gain a deeper understanding of how talented students might act or think.

As a whole project team has been involved in ICoN, all decisions had to be agreed within this project team, including my upcoming work as a PhD student. Having a project team around was really helpful in many ways: at any time, I could ask somebody for help, talk with someone about the literature I read, or just talk about difficulties which other PhD students in the project also had. When it came to the point where I had to decide which research interest I would follow during my PhD, we agreed in our project team that my part of ICoN would be the design of a test which measures the scientific knowledge and abilities of students. This decision was reached for several reasons: ICoN aims to characterise talented students in science with regard to four different aspects as a basis to develop a systematic approach to promote them. Potential talents, in particular participants in different scientific students' competitions (where talented students might be found) and non-participating students should participate in the study. As two PhD students were already working on two ICoN aspects and the third aspect was an important part of all the other aspects, there was only one aspect left – the scientific knowledge and abilities. It is worth mentioning that this aspect was the one I was most interested in! Additionally, my experience in the development of tasks for the IJSO and the IChO as well as my experience with IJSO participants and my work in school seemed to fit perfectly to this aspect of ICoN, which lead to the decision to work on it.

Getting started with the PhD – structuring the work to be done

After my research interest was established, I had to find a starting point for the development of the test. A first fundamental question was: what do I understand by scientific knowledge and abilities? To define this construct, I read several studies in which 'a kind of' scientific knowledge was measured (e.g. Bernholt and Parchmann 2011; Neubrand *et al.* 2004; Walpuski *et al.* 2011). As a result of this literature review and due to the fact that the relation to school was very important for me, I decided to define scientific knowledge and abilities following the German National Education Standards (NES). The NES differentiate four components to mark the students' abilities: content knowledge, scientific inquiry, communication and assessment (e.g. Kultusministerkonferenz 2005). From my point of view, these four parts seemed to describe scientific knowledge and abilities in a very extensive way.

The next step concerned the choice of my sample: the project team determined that different competitions should be a part of the study as it was assumed that different competitions might require different profiles of talents. Therefore, we agreed within the project team to choose a task-oriented competition (IJSO) and a project-oriented competition (Jugend forscht, see below). Additionally, non-participating students would take part in the study. Consequently, two aspects mainly led to my research questions: the choice of the sample and the work my colleagues within the project team had done before. Their work consisted mainly in the development of questionnaires and the comparison of groups differing on various grounds, like gender or participating and non-participating students. As I intended to resume their questions and to enhance their findings with the ICoN aspect of scientific knowledge and abilities, the following questions arose:

- What scientific knowledge and abilities can be found among participants in contrast to non-participating students?
- Which factors influence scientific knowledge and abilities as well as a (successful) participation in a competition?
- Do participants at different students' competitions differ in their scientific knowledge and abilities?

Having set the main framework for my work, the next challenge needed to be overcome: the test measuring scientific knowledge and abilities had to contain tasks from all science subjects. But how could I develop a test with tasks from biology, chemistry, and physics for content knowledge, scientific inquiry, communication and assessment? And how could this test be practicable for teachers as well as students and suitable both for participants in competitions and regular students, possibly of different ages? After having read some general literature about the development of tests, I came to the conclusion that before I could start to develop the test, I first had to consider what exactly I intended to find. As I hoped to find, among others things, variations between different students' competitions, I asked myself what possible differences between the competitions and their participants might exist. Therefore, I began to analyse the characteristics of each competition and their participants.

Identifying different abilities of participants at different students' competitions

Why the IJSO and Jugend forscht?

The IJSO is a task-oriented competition for students up to a maximum age of 15. In the qualifying rounds, the goal is to find the best six students who will represent Germany in the international competition. The German qualifier consists of three different rounds. Students have to complete take-home exams in the first round, theoretical exams in the second round, and practical and theoretical exams in the last round. Participants can not choose a specific subject or topic, all exams cover tasks from biology, chemistry and physics. As IJSO participants were already involved in previous studies of the ICoN project, the project team decided to continue the studies in the last qualifying round in this competition.

As a complement of the IJSO, the project team chose *Jugend forscht* by assuming that this competition requires different skills of participants as the IJSO. *Jugend forscht* is a project-oriented competition which is comparable to a science fair: students work on a scientific project they chose by themselves out of seven different science-related fields, document their work in a written homework and present it in front of a jury during a competition day which is held on different levels. By choosing this popular competition, our project team hoped to gain a sample size which is comparable to the amount of students in the last qualifying round of the IJSO.

Preliminaries for the test development: identifying characteristics of the IJSO

At first sight, the fact that IJSO participants have to complete theoretical and practical exams made it easier for me to derive tasks for my test. But I still had the problem that it would have been too much to develop a test which contained tasks from biology, chemistry, and physics in the four different components of the NES: content knowledge, scientific inquiry, communication and assessment. So I had the idea to analyse IJSO tasks to find out which components of the NES might be most strongly represented in the qualifying exams. As a consequence, it would be possible to focus at first on the most represented components (which would hopefully be also represented in *Jugend forscht* in other dimensions). Later, it would still be possible to complete the test with the remaining components, communication and assessment.

I read many papers about task development as well as about students' competitions and found a scheme which was originally supposed to analyse tasks of the International Physics Olympiad (IPhO) (Petersen 2010). But I realised that I could not use exactly this scheme as the IJSO tasks differed in some ways. Thus, I adapted the scheme after I again read literature concerning the characteristics in which I was most interested (e.g. Fischer and Draxler 2007; Neumann *et al.* 2007; Kauertz 2008). The adapted scheme can be seen in Figure 4.1.

More than 1,000 tasks out of every German qualifying round from 2008 to 2013 were analysed and the results show that most tasks covered content knowledge and scientific inquiry.

Preliminaries for the test development: identifying characteristics of Jugend forscht

Identifying characteristics of *Jugend forscht* was far more difficult as a jury decides which projects are the best. My first step was to visit different regional competitions to gain an impression of how the assessment of the participants occurs. Although the jury members had a kind of national manual to assess the students' performance, the manual was hardly used. It

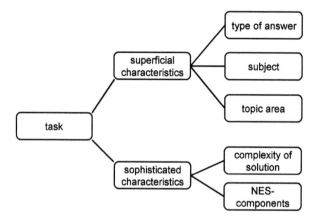

Figure 4.1 Scheme for the analysis of IJSO tasks

was rather a recommendation, not a strictly used guideline. Thus, it was not possible to identify which part of the competition was the most important: the written homework, the presentation or the jury discussion. As a consequence, to analyse just one of these parts would not have been meaningful. Moreover, pedagogical aspects were also considered, and that made it even more difficult to compare both competitions.

Consequently, I tried to draw conclusions only out of my observations and out of some conversations I had with jury members and competition officials. In addition, I read some students' written homework and tried to find the basic elements students have to fulfil to be successful in the competition. As students develop their own research questions, often conduct their own developed experiments and analyse their own data for the competition, I came to the conclusion that skills in following scientific inquiry are very important for the competition.

In comparison to the IJSO, I assumed on the one hand that the students' content knowledge would not be as extensive as the content knowledge of IJSO participants. In contrast to the IJSO, *Jugend forscht* participants are allowed to choose their subject; it is not required to have an extensive content knowledge in all disciplines. On the other hand, I assumed that participants at *Jugend forscht* were much stronger in scientific inquiry as that was, from my point of view, the most strongly represented component in the competition.

How do I organise a study all over Germany in different competitions and schools?

Besides the content of the test, the organisation of the study itself was also challenging. The qualifying round of the IJSO was a one-week meeting with enough time to question the students, but *Jugend forscht* had a tight timetable and strong regional differences concerning the duration of the competition (between 1.5 and 3 days). After talking to a competition official, a time limit of 60 minutes for the test was settled as more time would not have been practicable.

Regarding the content of the test, I had to consider that every state in Germany has its own school system. That means that students at the same age may not have the same (scientific) knowledge, due to the fact that science is mostly taught in individual subjects which may not even start in the same grade. This heterogeneity had also to be considered in the development of the test.

Developing a test to characterise different abilities of participants

Test design and task development

After the preliminary work was done, I had to start with the test development. I had to keep in mind that my aim was to develop a test which characterises the scientific knowledge and abilities of participants at different students' competitions and non-participants. Moreover, the results of my preliminary work had to be considered: IJSO tasks could mostly be classified as belonging to content knowledge and scientific inquiry. In contrast to the IJSO, *Jugend forscht* required mainly skills in the field of scientific inquiry and communication. The maximum time for the test would be 60 minutes. Therefore, it would hardly be possible in a paper and pencil test to focus on all NES components, so I decided to focus at first on the NES components of content knowledge and scientific inquiry. One last point which had to be considered: as students from all over Germany aged 12 to 16 would participate in the study, their scientific background knowledge would vary enormously.

Moreover, I intended to use existing tasks from different areas to cover a field as wide as possible: school-related tasks, competition-related tasks, creative tasks and tasks which do not correspond to typical school themes. But during the development, I found that existing tasks did not seem suitable for my purpose: they were, from my point of view, too easy, too difficult, too long, in a wrong item-format, or set in the wrong context. Consequently, almost every task was either adapted or newly developed. This was also quite challenging, as the question arose of how I could develop these tasks. Could I use existing schemes for a systematic task development? Could I adapt existing models, like the RIASEC model which my colleagues already used? I tried to weigh up the different models of task development against the adaption of, for example, the RIASEC model. The literature I read in the context of scientific knowledge and abilities in general (see above) showed me that existing schemes of task development were too complex for my purpose. But I realised also that the development of a new or adapted system of task development would take me too long. Furthermore, this would have been contrary to my aim, as I did not intend to find a new system of task development which results in as many tasks as possible, but to develop a whole test in the context of ICoN. So I tried to focus on a few points which I, based on my preliminary work, considered to be the most important for my test: the item format, the subject and themes as well as the complexity of tasks.

Concerning the item-format, I aimed to choose six multiple-choice questions and 24 open-ended questions. The multiple-choice questions were chosen because the IJSO uses this format among others (usually, this item-format is not very common in German schools). In contrast to that, I chose a relatively high amount of open-ended questions because I hoped to gain as much information as possible with a relatively low number of questions in total.

To avoid students' possible dislike for a certain subject, the tasks in the test were not classified under subject (as in the IJSO), but under themes. For the content knowledge, our project team chose energy as an interdisciplinary theme that theoretically every student among the target group had already covered in school. In contrast, our project team wanted to choose another interdisciplinary theme that is usually not treated in school, as the IJSO often contains themes that are not typical in school or at least have not been studied yet in the grades the participants are in. This theme was also supposed to be particularly interesting for the students so they would try to solve the task even if it was, at first sight, unknown or unsolvable. So I chose forensic criminology as a second theme for content knowledge. For scientific inquiry, I tried to find several interdisciplinary themes like water or cooking.

Another difficulty was the complexity of the tasks. I decided not to use the same levels of complexity I used in the analysis of the IJSO tasks because I intended to use (modified) existing tasks which were not developed following this scheme. So the tasks were ranked among three stages of difficulty (easy, relatively difficult, and difficult). This ranking was also rated by four teachers, but they hardly agreed on any ranking, due to the fact that they were from different schools and states. Consequently, besides my own ranking of difficulty, I left it up to the piloting of the test to verify the difficulties of the tasks.

Which tasks are best for the test? The selection process

After six weeks, at the end of the task developing process, I had 58 tasks from which 30 (if possible, evenly distributed to the NES components, the subjects and the difficulty) had to be selected. Therefore, I used another categorisation of the tasks following several existing schemes (e.g. Prenzel *et al.* 2002; Pickard 2007). The tasks were selected on the basis of the following characteristics:

- *Formal task characteristics:* length of the text, item format
- *Required cognitive skills:* using information which is given in the text, accessing one's knowledge, combining something, calculating something
- *Required kind of knowledge to solve the task:* factual knowledge, conceptual knowledge, procedural knowledge
- *Content of the task*
- *Difficulty* (easy, relatively difficult, and difficult).

Piloting

In several steps of piloting, I tested the difficulty of the test, the length and if the tasks were interesting to students. Furthermore, I developed a system for the test correction (see below) and revised the test. In a final step, students worked on the final version of the test. Based on their results, we agreed within the project team not to reduce or simplify the test, although the results showed that the test was, for regular students, probably too long and too difficult.

Test correction

Parallel to the development of the tasks, I formulated standard solutions for the tasks which were then completed with students' answers. For the open-ended questions, it turned out that a correction by different categories would be more suitable than to differentiate only between right and wrong. On the basis of the students' answers in the piloting steps, I developed a three-stage category system for the correction of the test. The significant Spearman's rank correlation coefficient ($\rho = 0.79$, $p < 0.000$) showed a high value for the agreement among the persons who corrected the test.

Realisation in school and during competitions – and barriers that appeared

The main idea of the study was to question students from the qualifying round of the IJSO (approximately 45 students), regular students from five schools of IJSO participants (one class from each school), *Jugend forscht* participants at the regional state level (at best the same amount of IJSO participants) as well as regular students from five schools of *Jugend forscht* participants (one class from each school as well).

As I was involved in the qualifying round of the IJSO 2013, the study could easily be integrated in the competition. Students completed the questionnaire at home before the competition, the tests were held during the one-week competition after the work for the competition itself was done.

Then, we chose different states and tried to contact teachers who had supported IJSO participants. The reactions, however, were very moderate, only three teachers agreed to participate with their classes in our study. Retrospectively, I assume that the low willingness to participate in the study could be explained by the fact that the organisational time for our study was relatively high for the teachers. Finally, I gained two classes of eighth graders, three classes of ninth graders, and two classes of tenth graders from three different states. Nevertheless, the sample remained quite heterogeneous as the different classes could not be evenly distributed to the states. Furthermore, the types of schools were also different.

Another problem that occurred during testing was the students' motivation. It turned out that the test was far too long and too difficult for regular students, they could not concentrate for such a long time. Moreover, students knew that they, personally, would not benefit from doing the test. As a result, some students did not take the test seriously although they were, of course, not forced to participate in our study (at least from my point of view; in a particular school I had the impression that the students were forced by their teacher to participate).

The study in *Jugend forscht* was, due to organisational matters, not practicable. Although a year before competition officials were quite positive towards my study and agreed to support it, it could not be organised when the competition finally took place, except in one single competition at regional state level. This confirmed again that our instruments in total were too time consuming. Competition officials were afraid that it would be too much for the participants. In addition, the time during the competitions was mostly too restricted to have enough time for the study.

As a result, I ended the information gathering after the single *Jugend forscht* competition and decided to revise the instruments and to work with the data I already had gained. In total, I had 194 complete records (as students did not work on the questionnaire and the tests at the same time, some records were incomplete).

Outlook – barriers are normal and have to be solved!

During the testing, I noticed that students worked in a more concentrated manner on tasks which were new to them than on tasks which they knew from their daily school life. In my case, they especially liked the figural tasks in the test of cognitive abilities. Furthermore, I realised that the test-time was too long for students. After 45 minutes at the most, they could no longer concentrate on the test. I explained this by the fact that written class tests usually last 45 minutes up to grade 10. Moreover, I started to read some literature around creativity as students also liked the creative tasks in my test. I found a book concerning personnel psychology (Schuler and Görlich 2007) which indicated that intelligence, creativity and content knowledge are important for successful employees. I concluded that this might be transferred to students as well. Additionally, I had already found very interesting differences between participants in scientific competitions and regular students, especially in tasks which were more open to creative ideas.

As a result of the experiences I made during the first part of my study, I limited the test time in total to 60 minutes and divided the test into three equal parts: a part for cognitive abilities, a part for scientific knowledge (including content knowledge and scientific inquiry as before), and a part for scientific creativity. The challenge is now to shorten my test and to pilot the scientific creativity test of Hu and Adey (2002) which I intend to use, due to the limited test time, in a shortened and, above all, translated German version.

With shortened instruments, I hope to gain and motivate more participants for the second part of my study. In addition, I intend to question regular students as well as students from schools that every year have many participants in *Jugend forscht*. Hopefully, this will be another opportunity to access *Jugend forscht* participants outside the competition itself.

Concerning the analysis of the IJSO tasks, the scheme is constantly improved and will be applied in other science Olympiads. Hopefully, the scheme will be communicable to other competitions besides the IJSO, which might then form the basis for a comparison of tasks of different science Olympiads. Results of a comparison might help teachers to prepare their students for participation in a competition.

Although some barriers appeared and I had to make some changes, I did not have to change my aims in general. I can still follow the development of a test which characterises the scientific knowledge and abilities of participants at different students' competitions and non-participants.

Conclusions for the design of practice

When the development of the instruments is finished, for the first time our project team will have an instrument which represents a holistic approach to characterise talented students specifically in the domain of science. On the basis of the gathered information, we might find profiles of talented students. These profiles could then form the basis for supportive measures which could be geared to the needs of specific students. In addition, our instruments might also be useful for teachers who try to find talented students in their class or participants for a competition. At the same time, possible profiles can not only be useful to identify talented students or possible participants in supportive measures, but they can also help to understand why some students may not be as interested in science as others – maybe due to a non-realistic view about science or a science class which does not focus on the interest of the students.

Furthermore, the data may give a hint at possible indicators of successful participants in scientific students' competitions such as repeated participation in competitions, performance in school, performance in general or other possible factors (Urhahne *et al.* 2012). These indicators might help to systematically promote students in their participation in a competition and, in general, in science.

Concerning the analysis of IJSO tasks, the results might help teachers in school to integrate the competition in their classes and to help them to prepare their students for the competition, which would have been helpful for me in school when I participated with my students.

The different issues I have worked on until now are all small steps with regard to the overall aim of the ICoN project: the development of a systematic approach to promote talented students in science on the basis of their characterisation. What can I say about the questions which arose while I worked in school, which motivated me to start a PhD? The question of how I could find possible participants for the IJSO, or how I could support participants as talented young students in science, are not questions I can answer in a satisfactory way after my short time as a PhD student: it is a long journey, consisting of several steps, to answer them. I know that my work will contribute to this journey, which is quite a motivating fact in my daily work. I am confident that I am taking a step in the right direction.

Acknowledgement

Funded by the German Research Foundation, the Federal Government of Education and Research.

References

Ackerman, P.L. and Heggestad, E.D. (1997). 'Intelligence, Personality, and Interests: Evidence for Overlapping Traits', *Psychological Bulletin* 121(2): 219–45.

Bernholt, S. and Parchmann, I. (2011). 'Assessing the Complexity of Students' Knowledge in Chemistry', *Chemistry Education Research and Practice* 12(2): 167–73.

Dierks, P.O., Höffler, T.N. and Parchmann, I. (2014). 'Profiling Interest of Students in Science: Learning in School and Beyond', *Research in Science & Technological Education* 32(2): 1–18.

Fischer, H.E. and Draxler, D. (2007). 'Konstruktion und Bewertung von Physikaufgaben'. In: Kircher, E., Girwidz, R. and Häußler, P. (eds), *Physikdidaktik. Theorie und Praxis*. Berlin: Springer, pp. 639–55.

Gagné, F. (2005). 'From Gifts to Talents. The DMGT as a Developmental Model'. In: Sternberg, R.J. and Davidson, J.E. (eds), *Conceptions of Giftedness*. Cambridge: Cambridge University Press, pp. 98–119.

Heller, K.A., Perleth, C. and Tock, K.L. (2005). 'The Munich Model of Giftedness Designed to Identify and Promote Gifted Students', In: Sternberg, R.J. and Davidson, J.E. (eds), *Conceptions of Giftedness*. Cambridge: Cambridge University Press, pp. 147–70.

Holland, J.L. (1997). *Making Vocational Choices. A Theory of Vocational Personalities and Work Environments*, 3rd edn. Odessa: Psychological Assessment Resources.

Hu, W. and Adey, P. (2002). 'A Scientific Creativity Test for Secondary School Students', *International Journal of Science Education* 24(4): 389–403.

Kauertz, A. (2008). *Schwierigkeitserzeugende Merkmale physikalischer Leistungstestaufgaben*. Berlin: Logos.

Kultusministerkonferenz (2005). *Bildungsstandards im Fach Chemie für den Mittleren Schulabschluss. Beschluss vom 16.12.2004*. München: Luchterhand.

Neubrand, M., Biehler, R., Blum, W., Cohors-Fresenborg, E., Flade, L., Knoche, N., Lind, D., Löding, W., Möller, G., Wynands, A. and Neubrand, J. (2004). 'Der Prozess der Itementwicklung bei der nationalen Ergänzungsuntersuchung von PISA 2000. Vom theoretischen Rahmen zu den konkreten Aufgaben'. In: Neubrand, M. (ed.), *Mathematische Kompetenzen von Schülerinnen und Schülern in Deutschland. Vertiefende Analysen im Rahmen von PISA 2000*. Wiesbaden: Verlag für Sozialwissenschaften, pp. 31–49.

Neumann, K., Kauertz, A., Lau, A., Notarp, H. and Fischer, H.E. (2007). 'Die Modellierung physikalischer Kompetenz und ihrer Entwicklung', *Zeitschrift für Didaktik der Naturwissenschaften* [Online] 13. http://archiv.ipn.uni-kiel.de/zfdn/jg13.html#Art005 (accessed 22 January 2015).

Osborne, D. and Dillon, J. (2008). *Science Education in Europe: Critical Reflections*. London: Nuffield Foundation.

Petersen, S. (2010). 'Oberflächen-und Tiefenmerkmale von Aufgaben in der Internationalen PhysikOlympiade', *PhyDid B – Didaktik der Physik – Beiträge zur DPG-Frühjahrstagung*. [Online]. www.phydid.de/index.php/phydid-b/article/view/195 (accessed 22 January 2015).

Pickard, M.J. (2007). 'The New Bloom's Taxonomy. An Overview for Family and Consumer Sciences', *Journal of Family and Consumer Sciences Education* 25(1): 45–55.

Prenzel, M., Häußler, P., Rost, J. and Senkbeil, M. (2002). 'Der PISA-Naturwissenschaftstest: Lassen sich die Aufgabenschwierigkeiten vorhersagen?', *Unterrichtswissenschaft* 30(1): 120–35.

Renzulli, J.S. (2005). 'The Three Ring Conception of Giftedness. A Developmental Model for Creative Productivity'. In: Sternberg, R.J. and Davidson, J.E. (eds), *Conceptions of Giftedness*. Cambridge: Cambridge University Press, pp. 246–79.

Rost, D.H. (ed.) (2009). *Hochbegabte und hochleistende Jugendliche. Befunde aus dem Marburger Hochbegabtenprojekt*. 2nd edn. Münster: Waxmann.

Schuler, H. and Görlich, Y. (2007). *Kreativität*. Göttingen: Hogrefe.

Urhahne, D., Ho, L.H., Parchmann, I. and Nick, S. (2012). 'Attempting to Predict Success in the Qualifying Round of the International Chemistry Olympiad', *High Ability Studies* 23(2): 167–82.

Walpuski, M., Ropohl, M. and Sumfleth, E. (2011). 'Students' Knowledge about Chemical Reactions – Development and Analysis of Standard-based Test Items', *Chemistry Education Research and Practice* 12(2): 174–83.

5 Studying motivation in the science classroom

Jenny M. Hellgren

Perhaps unusually I already had a PhD in plant physiology before I trained to become a secondary school science teacher. My background in research and in subject knowledge influenced my view of becoming a science teacher, working as a science teacher, and later also influenced my view of researching science education. The wish to become a teacher emerged from experience of teaching plant physiology and cell biology at the Swedish University of Agricultural Sciences and from the teaching I did in my spare time. During my teacher training, I wanted to learn how to communicate what I see as the essence of science, and to reach and engage a broader group of students who want to question, discuss, explore and argue around science. During this time and the years that followed when I worked as a teacher, I did what I think most teachers do. I searched for ways to reach the students; catch their interest in science and try to get them motivated to learn by challenging their thoughts and encouraging critical thinking. With the aim of helping students connect the science content to their reality and to see the importance of learning science in a larger context, I thought about ways to communicate science. With this focus, I became frustrated from not having the time to reflect upon my practice from a researcher's perspective. When the opportunity arose, I applied for a position as a doctoral student in science education. The position was part of a research project about students' motivation to learn science and mathematics that focussed on interactions between the student and the learning context.

Though I am now two thirds through the PhD and working towards my mock PhD viva, this chapter discusses the first part of my PhD, how it focused on the theoretical framework and research questions of the project, and included a large student motivation questionnaire study. It also describes the beginning of the second, more independent part of my PhD where the plan was to look more closely at student motivation in the science classroom with a mixed methods methodology. Here I had problems adapting the theoretical framework and I felt the need to look for complementary theoretical approaches to motivation. The central part of the chapter narrates my process of searching for a complementary theoretical approach to motivation, identifies the problems and questions I had to deal with, and explains how my PhD project and research fits better with an extended view of motivation that I came across during my doctoral journey. This is an account of a research training journey that has been driven by a desire to contribute new knowledge to our understanding of how the interaction between the learner and the learning context is related to motivation.

Joining a research project

The project's initial approach was to study students' motivation and affective experiences in science and mathematics with a large-scale questionnaire. The theoretical framework was mainly based on variables extracted from, or related to, self-determination theory (Deci and Ryan 1985; Ryan and Deci 2000), expectancy-value theory (Eccles and Wigfield 2002; Wigfield and Eccles 2000) and achievement goal theory (Senko *et al.* 2011), complemented by theories about emotions and beliefs. During this part of the work, the book *Motivation in Education: Theory, Research and Applications* (Schunk *et al.* 2008) was very helpful. It took me some time to realise that in addition to science and education, I was entering a third discipline – psychology – that was a completely new discipline to me as it had neither been part of my training in plant physiology nor my teaching training.

The first question addressed was 'what factors are important for student motivation?' which is a relevant question for researchers, practitioners and stakeholders. Factors important for student motivation in the classroom were also of interest from my perspective as a practitioner. Results of the large-scale questionnaire study included a prediction of students' positive emotional experiences in the classroom (Winberg *et al.* 2014). The study showed, among other things, that teacher support, clear goals, perceived learning and autonomy and intrinsic/identified motivation are important factors for predicting students' positive emotional experiences in the classroom. The study provides a valuable basis for my current work both practically and theoretically. Practically it was helpful to find the factors in the classroom important for students' positive emotional experiences; these experiences are an important part of motivation. Factors that were shown to be less important could be given less focus in my further studies. Theoretically, the study gave me a solid understanding of a lot of motivation research that has been carried out, and made me think about possible limitations of this approach when aiming to understand motivation in the everyday life of the classroom.

After the initial part of my PhD, which was undertaken collaboratively within the research project, the plan of my continued PhD research was guided by the results of the initial study and my interests. This part included more independent work. Together with my supervisor, I planned a research design in which qualitative methods were added to support data from the self-report questionnaires. The focus was still to predict student motivation and emotional experiences in the classroom, but with the addition of wanting to find out more about how different students experience different learning situations.

One of the challenges was to create comparable learning situations that differed in the aspects shown to be important for students' motivation and affective experiences in the first study. These aspects include teacher support, clear goals and autonomy. I thought about different possibilities, yet wanted to avoid experimental conditions and training teachers to teach in ways with which they were not comfortable. However, I was lucky and got a great opportunity. I was asked if I would be willing to supervise a Master's level dissertation in science education, and by doing this I came in contact with teachers participating in a student-teacher scientist partnership with their grade-eight classes. They were doing the same activities with their students during the same time period, but had freedom to adjust the activities according to their school and classroom contexts. I asked three teachers and they all welcomed me to research motivation in their classrooms when they worked with the student-teacher scientist partnership. According to my plan, I collected data using three different methods: students a) answered questionnaires about their motivation, goals, values, beliefs and attitudes related to school science; b) were audio- and video-recorded during a lesson in which they interacted with peers in an inquiry-based activity; and c) were interviewed about their experiences of this lesson.

The selection of participating classes was made so that students with different motivation focus, in terms of intrinsic and extrinsic motivation (Ryan and Deci 2000) and mastery and performance goals (Senko *et al.* 2011) were represented in each class and the classes selected had students with various motivation foci. The data collection resulted in a) pre- and post-self-reports of students' motivation, goals, values, beliefs and attitudes related to school science for all the 388 students participating in the student-teacher scientist partnership; b) audio and video data from one lesson for 24 students in three classes; and c) interviews of the same 24 students' experiences of the lesson.

Identifying my concerns

I started to analyse data based on the initial motivation framework. The aim was to find themes in the interviews and to find variables in the observations that could add to prediction of student motivation and affective experiences in the classroom. The aim was also to find interactions between personal and situational variables that could add to predictions of student motivation and affective experiences in the classroom, something I was not sure how to approach.

At this point I had to stop and think. What I was trying to do was very theoretical and abstract to me. The theoretical framework felt particularly distant from the empirical data, both when I looked at the motivation theories and when I looked at the variables extracted from the theories. To get them aligned would require an extensive operationalisation of a very broad research-area including both science education and psychology, which felt overwhelming. I was not sure if we were accessing the non-directly measureable aspects of motivation in the best ways. That is, I was not sure if we were able to access them through the observable phenomena we were using, and I was not sure if we were actually measuring the interaction between the different aspects of motivation. Moreover, I was insecure about whether it was possible to predict motivation and emotional experiences in this way. I was also wondering about the stability of motivational and positive affective experiences over time during a lesson. My experience was that a lot can happen during a lesson and that students' alertness and engagement can vary a lot during one single lesson. I had problems pinpointing what I was looking for and what was missing in the current framework for motivation that seemed so broad. Also, the initial aim and the research questions seemed too broad to fit the limited time of a PhD, and needed to be more focused. In this process I gave two seminars where I got rewarding feedback, support and new ideas on how to move on. Most importantly, I went back to read more and to develop my own understanding of motivation.

Returning to literature to develop my own understanding of motivation

In everyday life, 'motivation' and 'motivated' are used by teachers, parents and students to describe student engagement and interest in the classroom. Saying someone is motivated in everyday language would probably involve spending time on the task, being engaged in on-topic conversations with peers and learning a lot. In the literature, Koballa and Glynn (2007) defined motivation as 'an internal state that arouses, directs and sustains students' behavior' (85). As a teacher and a researcher, both the everyday understanding and the scientific definition of motivation inform my understanding. According to the everyday understanding, motivation can be seen in the classroom, but according to the scientific definition, motivation cannot be measured or observed directly. This made it challenging in many ways to operationalise motivation in the classroom. I needed to go back and find possibilities to study motivation in a meaningful way from the data material I had already collected. I also wanted to see how other people had operationalised motivation in the classroom so I started to look for existing frameworks for motivation and empirical classroom studies of motivation in scientific literature.

The first area I explored was motivation research in science education. In science education much research examines attitudes (e.g. Osborne *et al.*

2003; Saleh and Khine 2011), but far less examines motivation. Motivation and attitude research in science education is reviewed and discussed, for example, by Koballa and Glynn (2007). They also state the relationship between attitudes and motivation: 'attitudes influence motivation, which in turn influences learning, and ultimately behavior' (85), and acknowledge this relationship as complex and interactive. I conducted literature searches for motivation in science education but found few empirical studies. The examples I did find were frequently questionnaire studies, focused on differences between boys' and girls' motivation for science, based on one motivation theory, or just a few variables.

The articles I found did not help me understand how to get the most out of my mixed-methods data. I also experienced that motivation, attitudes, interest, and other related concepts were used interchangeably and in unclear ways. I began to wonder if this was an indication that not much research had been done on motivation in science education, or if I had used the wrong search terms. In Koballa and Glynn's literature review most of the references in the motivation part focus on motivation research in general and very few are empirical studies of motivation research in science education. At this point I felt very insecure.[1]

The second area I explored, or re-visited, was the motivation theories on which the original project framework had been based (self-determination theory, expectancy-value theory, and achievement goal theory). I needed to go back and understand them from my own point of view. Self-determination theory (Deci and Ryan 1985, Ryan and Deci 2000) sees motivation as based on the three basic needs: competence, autonomy and relatedness, and that motivation can be intrinsic or extrinsic. Intrinsic motivation is where an action is performed because it is valued as interesting, enjoyable, or in another way gives satisfaction to the actor, and extrinsic motivation is where an action is performed to reach an extrinsic goal, for example high grades (Ryan and Deci 2000). Expectancy-value theory considers a student's expectations about how successful s/he will be with a task and the perceived value of the task as the two most important factors controlling effort, persistence and results (Eccles and Wigfield 2002). Achievement goal theory is a motivation theory in which an individual's goal type influences their achievements and experiences in different situations. Students with mastery goals focus on mastering a task and learning new skills, whereas students with performance goals focus on performance and skills that are assessed in comparison with others and tend to link performance with self-value.

I thought about the meaning of combining theories based on different theoretical perspectives; the behavioural perspective that focuses on, for example, incentive and reinforcement, the humanistic perspective that focuses on, for example, need fulfilment and self-determination, the cognitive perspective that focuses on, for example, expectancies and goals, and social perspectives that focus on, for example, feelings of belonging to communities (Koballa and Glynn 2007). I realised that the framework I used was trying to combine all the four perspectives and felt insecure about the meaning of this. I decided to put the theories in the background for a while and find a framework that could help me more directly in my analysis of classroom data.

The third area I explored was motivation research carried out in other educational (that is, non-science education) disciplines, especially empirical studies in classroom contexts. My focus was to find approaches suitable for studying motivation in the classroom to complement motivation questionnaires from my initial PhD research. This inspired me to read, among other articles, a review of 'self report and alternative approaches' to student motivation by Fulmer and Frijters that was published in 2009. In this review, the authors made it clear that motivation can be approached from many different ways even if self-reports by questionnaires are most common. They presented phenomenological/authentic, neuropsychological/physiological and behavioural approaches as alternatives, and discussed the advantages and limitations with each approach.

To completely change the approach to motivation was not an option to me as I was halfway into my PhD and had already collected much of the data for my research project. However, I found one research area where extensive studies of motivation had been performed in classrooms that spoke to me: second language teaching and learning. Fulmer and Frijters refered to Dörnyei (2000) and his description of motivation as being 'influenced by environmental, historical, and individual factors and involves a temporal aspect, illustrating that motivation is not a stable emotional or mental state but is subject to change over time (Dörnyei 2000) and, in the case of motivation for academics, change across learning contexts' (229). I read more from Dörnyei, and the research and ideas presented in the book *Teaching and Researching Motivation* (Dörnyei and Ushioda 2011) matched well with my way of thinking about motivation in the classroom.

Dörnyei and colleagues' process-model for studying motivation in the classroom (Dörnyei and Ottó 1998; Dörnyei 2000) differs from the views of motivation I had encountered so far in my PhD training by adding a clear time perspective and drawing on the dynamic aspects of motivation that cannot be neglected in a complex classroom environment. They describe their approach as 'a situated and process-oriented account of motivation' that 'inevitably leads us to a dynamic conception of the notion of motivation that integrates the various factors related to the learner, the learning task and the learning environment into one complex system whose ultimate outcome can be seen as the regulator of learning behaviour' (Dörnyei and Ushioda 2011: 89).

The time dimension divides the functions of and influences on motivation into three stages (see Figure 5.1). The pre-actional stage involves setting goals, forming intentions and launching action, the actional stage involves generating and carrying out subtasks and self-regulating strategies,

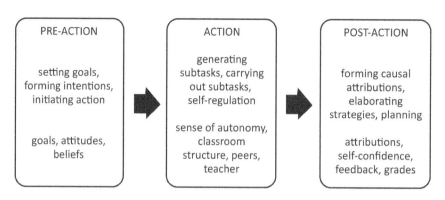

Figure 5.1 Simplified process model of motivation, derived from Dörnyei (2001)

and the post-actional stage is retrospective and evaluating. This dimension was helpful for reflecting upon my own work.

Elaborating the key issues

Reading and thinking about motivation from different perspectives helped me to develop my understanding of motivation, and this can be summarised with three key issues: what is motivation, what interactions between students and their learning environment are meaningful to study, and how can I combine results from different methods?

What is motivation?

This was the first key issue I explored. I extended my search to non-science sources, and I did a Google picture search for motivation models. In this search I found pictures where motivation and related factors were shown as an iceberg with the tip above the surface representing observable and/or conscious factors such as behaviour and skills. Below the surface were the remaining factors that are not possible to study directly yet are assumed to have an effect on or interact with motivation. In my work these factors were, for example, attitudes, beliefs and emotions (see Figure 5.2). Visualising my motivation work in this way helped me merge my everyday understanding of student motivation and the view of motivation I met when reading and doing my previous research. As teachers, we can see students' behaviour and hear them talk in the classroom. We can also see students' results in terms of short-term lesson evaluations, long-term evaluations, and fulfilment of course goals. Factors such as motivation, attitudes, beliefs and emotions that I had been studying until now, cannot be observed directly, but can be measured indirectly through questionnaires.

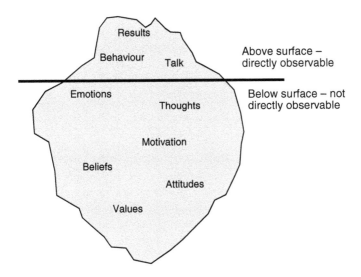

Figure 5.2 Model of motivation, showing factors that can be directly observed in the classroom and factors that are assumed to be underlying

This is adequate to get information about individual motivation at one time point but not sufficient to understand the dynamics of motivation during a science lesson.

Since my goal was to learn more about the interaction between the student, the peers, the teacher and the task, and how this related to motivation, I needed to think about the role of emotions, thoughts, motivation, beliefs, attitudes and values in the immediate classroom situation. I came to the conclusion that individual motivation, in terms of goals, beliefs, attitudes and values, are important but not of central focus, for my further doctoral studies of how students actually are motivated in the classroom.

What interactions between students and their learning environment are meaningful to study?

This was the second key issue I explored. Individual motivation had to be aligned with what happens in the classroom and how students themselves experience what happens. The first step had been to predict emotions with individual motivational aspects such as goals, beliefs and values (see Figure 5.2), and situational aspects such as perceived autonomy, teacher support, task difficulty and clarity of goals. The next step was to study interactions between individual motivational aspects and situational aspects. An alternative could be to start from the classroom observations, find sequences where motivation for the science content and the task is challenged or changed, and look for possible interactions in those sequences. In this way, I can relate motivation to the learning of science and to the scientific way of working in the classroom. This perspective opens possibilities to acknowledge and study these dynamics in the classroom based on Dörnyei's model (see Figure 5.1); this would be studying interaction focusing on the actional phase of motivation.

How can I combine results from different methods?

This was the third key issue I explored. In my previous work, the method for combining data was statistical analysis and I thought about other options that would allow more of the students' voices to be heard in the final result of the qualitative studies. Since the process-model of motivation in the classroom (Dörnyei and Ottó 1998; Dörnyei 2000) seemed helpful when exploring individual motivation and interaction, I wanted to see how my data and potential results could fit into this model.

The pre-actional stage of motivation in Dörnyei's model is where goals are set, intentions are formed and action is launched. This process is influenced by goal properties, values associated with learning, attitudes towards the subject, learner beliefs and strategies and environmental support and hindrance. In my data, the pre-actional stage of motivation is the goals, values, beliefs and attitudes students have about their school science when they enter the learning situation. The actional stage of motivation in the model is where the actual work is going on; causal attributions are formed, standards and strategies elaborated, intentions are dismissed and further planning done. Motivation is involved in, for example, generating and carrying out sub-tasks, on-going appraisal of achievement and self-regulation. None of these factors are easily measured directly in the classroom, but a few selected factors can be operationalised. This can be supported by the interviews, where students discuss pleasantness of the learning situation, sense of autonomy, perceived difficulty, and reasons for seeking, or not seeking, help from the teacher. The post-actional stage of motivation is not a focus of my study. Approaching my data in this way opens possibilities to acknowledge individual motivation (as choice motivation), yet still explore interactions between students and their peers, teachers and the scientific content in the classroom (as motivation in action), and to have a framework for discussing a combination of the different parts.

Refining the research questions from the developed perspective

The developed theoretical perspective helped me focus and narrow the research questions emerging from what happens in the classroom. This was more intuitive from my perspective as a teacher. In the second part of my PhD, individual motivation was used as a factor to select students and ensure students with different motivation foci were included in the study. Interactions are still assumed to be central to student motivation, but will be looked at in a more direct way in the classroom. Greater focus can be given to student motivation for the science content and scientific way of working. This is important to me since student motivation for science learning, for the importance of science itself, is my main didactic interest. Finally, viewing motivation as having a temporal dimension allows separating individual motivation from the interaction, and opens up the possibility for looking at motivation as choice motivation and motivation in action. This facilitates bringing meaning into motivation measured with questionnaires, and motivation as a result of classroom interaction. Leaving the holistic approach and starting in the students' experiences and actions, allows the following research questions to be posed:

1   How are students' experiences related to science- and non-science aspects of the learning situation?
2   How is students' motivation in the classroom connected to interaction with teachers, peers and scientific content?
3   Are there differences in students' experiences and/or actions related to students' motivation focus?

Question one can be answered using interviews. In the interviews, students describe how they perceive different aspects of the lesson. Analysing the interviews for affective expressions and what aspects of the learning situation the expressions refer to highlights what aspects are important to the students. Question two can be answered based on audio and video observations. The students worked with peers in an inquiry-based activity that revealed several aspects of how students interact with teachers, peers and the scientific content during a science lesson. An observation protocol for individual- and group-motivation will be developed based on the framework reported in Dörnyei (2000), Dörnyei and Ottó (1998) and Dörnyei and Ushioda (2011), and a framework for analysing motivation in the science classroom developed by Moeller Andersen and Lund Nielsen (2013). Their model focuses on the following areas of student motivation by actions and engagement: 1) content of students' talk subject matter; 2) students' actions: indicators of motivation; 3) students' actions: indicators of demotivation; 4) students' engagement. Question three can be answered in relation to both interviews and observations. After these changes, I finally felt I was back on track.

Conclusion

Doing research, in terms of asking questions, collecting and analysing data, and presenting findings, is one side of being a doctoral student. This chapter presents the other and less obvious side, the one about searching and finding possible ways forward. Starting my doctoral journey by working within a research project provided me with opportunities for collaboration. My decision to stop and think, and allow myself time to re-think, was not easy; it was a balance of loyalty and independence. It took a lot of time and energy, but was just as much of a learning experience as asking questions, collecting and analysing data, and presenting findings. I also want to point out it is not desirable to collect data first and try to find an analytical framework and research questions afterwards. However, the time for a PhD is limited and for me it was the most practical way of moving on without losing too much time. Now it is time to look forwards and try to implement my new ideas, specify the analytical framework, answer my research questions, and appraise the analytical framework. And write and defend my thesis.

Note

1   In the summer of 2013, I finally found an article describing a framework for looking at motivation by video analysis in the science classroom (Moeller Andersen and Lund Nielsen 2013). The authors clearly stated the lack of research in the area. To find this article was a confirmation that helped me believe in myself and in my abilities to search for literature. Later, in 2014, *Studies in Science Education* published the review 'Interest, Motivation and Attitude towards Science and Technology at K-12 Levels: A Systematic Review of 12 years of Educational Research' by Potvin and Hasni. This review again confirmed that little research has been done on motivation in science education and that most had focused on interest and attitudes. However, at the point in my PhD described in this chapter these two important articles had not yet been published.

References

Deci, E.L. and Ryan, R.M. (1985). *Intrinsic Motivation and Self-determination in Human Behavior.* New York: Plenum.

Dörnyei, Z. (2000). 'Motivation in Action: Towards a Process-oriented Conceptualisation of Student Motivation', *British Journal of Educational Psychology* 70(4): 519–38.

Dörnyei, Z. (2001). *Motivational Strategies in the Language Classroom.* Cambridge: Cambridge University Press.

Dörnyei, Z. and Ottó, I. (1998). 'Motivation in Action: A Process Model of L2 Motivation', *Working Papers in Applied Linguistics* 4: 43–69.

Dörnyei, Z. and Ushioda, E. (2011). *Teaching and Researching Motivation.* London: Pearson Education Ltd.

Eccles, J.S. and Wigfield, A. (2002). 'Motivational Beliefs, Values, and Goals', *Annual Review of Psychology* 53: 109–32.

Fulmer, S.M. and Frijters, J.C. (2009). 'A Review of Self-Report and Alternative Approaches in the Measurement of Student Motivation', *Educational Psychology Review* 21(3): 219–46.

Koballa, T.R. and Glynn, S.M. (2007). 'Attitudinal and Motivational Constructs in

Science Learning'. In: Abell, S. and Lederman, N. (eds), *Handbook of Research on Science Education*. Mahwah, NJ: Erlbaum Publishers, pp. 75–102.

Moeller Andersen, H. and Lund Nielsen, B. (2013). 'Video-based Analyses of Motivation and Interaction in Science Classrooms', *International Journal of Science Education* 35(6): 906–28.

Osborne, J., Simon, S. and Collins, S. (2003). 'Attitudes Towards Science: A Review of the Literature and its Implications', *International Journal of Science Education* 25(9): 1049–79.

Potvin, P. and Hasni, A. (2014). 'Interest, Motivation and Attitude towards Science and Technology at K-12 Levels: A Systematic Review of 12 years of Educational Research', *Studies in Science Education* 50(1): 85–129.

Ryan, R.M. and Deci, E.L. (2000). 'Intrinsic and Extrinsic Motivations: Classic Definitions and New Directions', *Contemporary Educational Psychology* 25(1): 54–67.

Saleh, I.M. and Khine, M.S. (2011). *Attitude Research in Science Education Classic and Contemporary Measurement*. Charlotte, NC: Information Age Publishing.

Schunk, D.H., Pintrich, P.R. and Meece, J.L. (2008). *Motivation in Education: Theory, Research and Applications*, 3rd edn. Upper Saddle River, NJ: Pearson Education, Inc.

Senko, C., Hulleman, C.S. and Harackiewicz, J.M. (2011). 'Achievement Goal Theory at the Crossroads: Old Controversies, Current Challenges, and New Directions', *Educational Psychologist* 46(1): 26–47.

Wigfield, A. and Eccles, J.S. (2000). 'Expectancy-value Theory of Achievement Motivation', *Contemporary Educational Psychology* 25(1): 68–81.

Winberg, T.M., Hellgren, J.M. and Palm, T. (2014). 'Stimulating Positive Emotional Experiences in Mathematics Learning: Influence of Situational and Personal Factors', *European Journal of Psychology of Education* 29(4): 673–91.

6 Exploring learning experiences and meaning-making in environmental and sustainability issues

Annika Manni

During my 15 years as a teacher in Swedish compulsory schools, I have acquired an interest in, and experience of, the teaching of environmental and sustainability issues. I have also considered that educational practice should meet the urgent need for environmental awareness and action. I was interested in students' learning processes regarding issues crossing different subject disciplines, and I often addressed environmental and sustainable education with an outdoor learning approach. My understanding of outdoor learning involved a holistic view of the learner, the process of learning as experiential involving all senses, and being situated and social. I had a practitioner's understanding of John Dewey's theory, which implies that learning through experience involves action between the learner and the specific context (Dewey 1916), and Howard Gardner's theory of multiple intelligences involving a widened view on intelligence (Gardner 1993). In practice, these theories guided me to use a variety of methods and attempts to activate all pupils according to their personalities.

In the schools where I have worked, the implementation of Education for Sustainable Development (ESD) was sometimes problematic since ESD was seen as a 'new' subject rather than an interdisciplinary approach. To some extent, these difficulties related to whether *learning in ESD* was similar to, or different from, learning in other areas. Recognising this, I was interested to learn more about how young students perceived sustainability problems, which formulated the focus for my PhD project. I found a student perspective important and valuable due to the character of ESD, which aimed to be participatory, democratic, and pluralistic (UNESCO 2005), but also as an educational research focus valuable for practice.

Background

The need and relevance of environmental and sustainability education is not to be questioned in our current time of climate change and human suffering. Teaching and learning in ESD are highlighted as important in national as well as international policy documents. All nations are to provide educational programmes that aim for a sustainable future regarding ecology, economy and social aspects (UN 2002). In the Decade of Education for Sustainable Development (2005–14), definitions and recommendations are formulated as guidelines for practice where education is seen as crucial if we are to reach sustainability (UNESCO 2005; 2012). In spite of these recommendations for ESD, schools are also finding themselves coping with high demand for achieving good grades in traditional subjects. In this matter, worried that ESD might be a neglected perspective, Johnston (2009) calls all teachers to step outside the 'curriculum-box' and engage in environmental issues for the sake of a sustainable future.

In the Swedish educational context, ESD is well highlighted in curricula (Skolverket 2011), and involves compulsory school traditions of outdoor environmental education (Breiting and Wickenberg 2010; Sandell *et al.* 2005). Outdoor environmental education is not only a Scandinavian approach but is also to be found in other countries (Fien 1993; Gruenewald 2008; Payne 1997). Learning outside in nature has been considered to make abstract ecological content knowledge concrete (Magntorn and Helldén 2007), to create environmental awareness and care (Palmberg and Kuru 2000), and even to foster behavioural change for the benefit of the environment (Boeve-de Pauw 2012). All these outdoor experiences are found to be relevant for the field of ESD.

Phase 1 – exploring young students' learning experiences in ESD

My research interest dealt with deepening the understanding of young students' perceptions and experiences of both the content and the learning processes of ESD as a way to develop practice. As I envisaged that one purpose of educational research is to inform practice, I considered that insights into students' perceptions and experiences could be helpful in developing the educational practice of ESD. Finding myself as a practitioner in academia, I recognised some of the dilemmas referred to in Anderson and Herr's 'The New Paradigm Wars: Is there Room for Rigorous Practitioner Knowledge in Schools and Universities' (1999). These authors address the old debate of real research versus school development within educational research and argue that these two paradigms should benefit from getting closer to, and learning from, each other. For the sake of developing educational research and most of all 'to seek more effective and equitable ways to educate children' (Anderson and Herr 1999: 20), the authors find this cooperation necessary. Recognising both the importance of educational research questions springing from issues of practice, and the challenges involved in theorising these issues for the purposes of research, I was concerned with changing but also retaining my perspective as a teacher whilst becoming a researcher.

The choice of methods was made not only on the basis of being most appropriate for the research questions, but also with a consideration of moving from the teacher role to the researcher role without bias when doing research within my own area of work experience. I had worries about influencing and acting as a teacher in student interviews, and taking outdoor educational approaches for granted. These different considerations led to the choice of a mixed-methods design with a questionnaire as a first quantitative investigation and a qualitative in-depth part as a follow up. The main purpose of that choice was to get a broad picture of students' learning experiences of ESD initially through the questions asked in the questionnaire (and in which I could more easily take the researcher's role not the teacher's). The results of that quantitative part would then be followed up qualitatively and more in-depth to refine and seek deeper understandings of the main findings from the first phase, as a common way of conducting mixed-methods research (Cohen *et al.* 2010; Creswell 2005).

Constructing the questionnaire

When constructing the comprehensive questionnaire, with both open and closed questions, few theoretical distinctions on a philosophical level were made in respect of the concept of 'learning experiences in ESD'. From a practitioner's point of view, understanding and emotion were related to the content of sustainable development together with experiences of the learning activities such as more physical, emotional, social and situated experiences, as in common understandings of learning. The questionnaire consisted of two parts: students' understandings and values in respect of aspects of sustainable development, and experiences of learning activities. The first part presented questions in the ecological, economic and social areas of sustainable development as defined in policy documents and literature. The questions asked 'What do you know about ...?' and 'How do you feel about that?', and had pictures working as conversation pieces for students' responses (Manni *et al.* 2013a).

The second part of the questionnaire focused on experiences of learning activities relating to ESD. UNESCO guidelines regarding multi-method approaches, the holistic view on teaching and learning in environmental and outdoor learning (Rickinsson *et al.* 2004), and my own experience from school practice influenced the questions asked. Closed questions with levels of agreement on a Likert scale were presented involving cognitive, emotional, physical, social and situated aspects of learning in sustainability related issues (Manni *et al.* 2013b). The statements could be as follows: 'We've worked with animals, nature, and the environment', 'I have learned to co-operate with others', and 'We do investigations in nature'.

This broad entrance was due to the exploratory character of the study investigating factors of importance for students' learning experiences in ESD. A presupposition regarding the definition of learning experiences was that this is a complex issue involving many important aspects, not just cognitive understanding. These presuppositions were strengthened by Dewey's emphasis on the holistic view of the child and the importance of situated context (Dewey 1916). Rickinsson *et al.* (2004) further describe the impact of environmental, outdoor education across cognitive, affective, social/interpersonal, physical and behavioural domains. These aspects were not further problematised from any theoretical point of view. Basically, when constructing the questionnaire, cognitive, emotional, physical, social and situated aspects of learning experiences were considered separately (Figure 6.1a).

Results and analysis of the questionnaire

A content analysis, based on a phenomenographic approach (Marton and Booth 1997), of the open questions revealed that students' relational understanding and valuing of the different aspects of SD varied within and between the areas (Manni *et al.* 2013a). Furthermore, and of most importance here, the results showed that student perceptions were not only a variation of 'cognitive understanding', but were interwoven with 'emotional expressions'. This was seen in both the questions asking for understanding and the questions asking for values.

Students' experiences of learning activities were analysed with statistical analyses when searching for relationships between the separate aspects. The factor analysis resulted in five factors out of 38 items: perceived experiences of ESD, perceived experiences of outdoor education, perceived content of ESD, values towards outdoor activities and finally values towards nature. Positive correlations were found between experiences of outdoor education and values of the same, perceived ESD content and experiences of outdoor activities, and finally values of outdoor education and values of nature. Some differences between schools, mainly regarding the perception of ESD, were also found (Manni *et al.* 2013b).

Critical reflections, analyses and theoretical insights

Reflecting on the results of both parts of the questionnaire exploring young students' learning experiences in ESD, I began to question the theoretical framework regarding the division of learning into separate domains presented by Rickinsson *et al.* (2004). The results showed both emotional expressions integrated in cognitive knowledge, and correlations between the separate aspects of emotional and cognitive experiences. These results clashed with my earlier interpretation of Gardner's theory of multiple intelligences. The results showed an intimate relationship between different learning aspects. From these results it seemed incorrect to understand other domains than the cognitive as helpers.

In Dewey's theories, learning experiences were acknowledged as a unit with different properties merged into the whole with equal value given to the different properties (Dewey 1916, 1934). More specifically, through the concept of 'aesthetic experience' Dewey describes emotion and cognition as merged in the normal processes of living (Dewey 1934). Additionally to Dewey, I also found neo-Aristotelian theories emphasising emotions as cognitive value judgements, i.e emotions are not to be seen as separate from, but instead foundations of, values of a cognitive kind (Nussbaum 2001). Furthermore, the situated outdoor experiences proved to have impact and be related to both cognitive and emotional questions, a result putting focus on the importance of the situated aspects of learning. Since the results revealed that higher levels of students' complex/relational cognitive understandings contained more firm emotional expressions as well, a conclusion was drawn that cognition and emotion interrelate in a positive way regarding perceptions of the content of ESD, even though this was not anticipated when developing the questionnaire.

Developing theory

Rethinking the framing of learning experiences into separate domains of cognitive, emotional, physical, social and situated aspects made me re-read Dewey's writings. Learning experience, in his theories, was not to be seen as *either* cognitive *or* emotional, it was *both* at the same time, i.e. *aesthetic*. I learned that my, somewhat unreflected, division of the important aspects within an experience had historical underpinnings. From the roots of modernism, 'real, rational' learning was considered to be of a cognitive kind in contrast to practical knowledge as learning belonging to craftsmen, or emotions as belonging to the female character. Emotions were further seen as irrational, and thereby in contrast to rational cognitive learning. Knowledge in a modern perspective was connected to facts and general truths, and research was conducted through positivistic approaches. This is in contrast to post-modern theories where relativism, contexts and situations play a greater role (Nussbaum 2001; Sauvé 1999). Sauvé (1999), in particular, suggests a framework other than the modern one for environmental education and learning in postmodern times; three interrelated spheres of personal and social development (the environment, the others, and the self). When learning about transdisciplinary phenomena, such as sustainable development, it can also be argued that a more holistic approach is needed when understanding learning complexities (Wylie *et al.* 1998).

From these conclusions another troublesome issue came to hand: the definition and use of the word 'learning'. I became troubled with the cognitive claims and traditional use of the word learning, since my understanding and definition had now changed and I actually included more than cognition in my definition of learning. Undertaking a lot of reading, the crucial question still remained: was learning understanding, to undergo a practical activity, to get an emotional experience or even all of this together? Reflections led to scrutinising learning experiences in terms of the process not just the product. In my readings of mainly Dewey and Biesta, I found that the word *meaning-making* instead of *learning* better defined what this PhD project was all about (Biesta 2006, 2010; Dewey 1916). Furthermore, meaning-making is seen as learning and socialisation processes interwoven (see Öhman 2008).

From my empirical results, critical reflections and theoretical interpretations, I developed a new picture of what learning experiences in environmental and sustainability issues could be (Figure 6.1b).

An unexpected effect of this critical reflexivity made me self-critical and caused a minor crisis in my work: How could I have foreseen the ontological and epistemological assumptions behind different research methods and approaches? Would my whole project be criticised for being eclectic if using different theories and methods? I suddenly felt my shortcomings as if I was a practitioner in researcher's clothes and, recognising the challenges of being an adult learner, I risked loss of self-confidence in this PhD process (Johnson 2001).

I met criticism concerning my use of statistical analyses in research groups representing sociocultural and critical theory paradigms, and the content analysis of the open questions was not seen as strong evidence when presenting the results in other research groups of positivistic, more quantitative paradigms. The article by Kincheloe and Tobin (2009), *The Much Exaggerated Death of Positivism*, caused me even more agony since

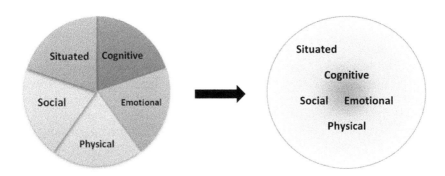

Figure 6.1a The questionnaire was developed based on personal teacher experiences and Rickinsson (2004), and included questions in relation to different domains of learning experiences in ESD

Figure 6.1b View of learning experiences as "meaning-making" in environmental and sustainability issues as a holistic activity involving different properties (derived from Dewey 1934)

positivism was here stated as the evil force in educational research and maybe was hidden in my choice of initially using a quantitative question-naire. Lund (2005), however, argues that both approaches, qualitative and quantitative, have similar aims but different tools and methods. He argues that the two approaches could learn from each other instead of arguing against. Kincheloe and Tobin (2009) argue that this is not possible since the ontological foundations are totally incomparable. This discussion became a great concern of mine as I gained more insights into research matters during this reflective part. Obviously there were other assumptions than mine, more practical ones, in the choice of methods. I felt uncom-fortable with the accusation of a positivistic view of knowledge through the choice of a questionnaire for my study. But, I could also see the point of that argument since I now agree that context and situation are both impor-tant for learning experiences. A questionnaire might not be the optimal tool for gathering data even though contextual issues were part of the ques-tions. Through somewhat painful experiences and reflections, this part must indeed be seen as the most crucial part for developing the PhD proj-ect further.

What in the end mattered was that the results of the questionnaire, in phase one, had served their purpose by giving this overview and pointed at important aspects for further more in-depth research, and according to the chosen mixed methods design this was a compulsory and necessary step (Creswell 2009). I also realised that ESD-related research was to be found in the 'between space' of more traditional research approaches aiming for either effectiveness in teaching, interpretive and sociocultural or critical theoretical approaches dealing with power and change. Traditions from different research fields and paradigms meet and sometimes disagree. Besides my initial reasons for conducting this research stepwise and with different methods, I was strengthened by more philosophical arguments for a mixed methods design; according to a pragmatic worldview, the world is what we experience through situated actions (Biesta 2010). First and foremost the research questions are formulated, and the choice of meth-ods is that which could best explore them. Theory is not to be seen as a framework that limits your analyses but rather as lenses through which you obtain new perspectives on your empirical results (Creswell 2009: 10).

Transitions from phase 1 to 2

The mixed-methods design chosen for this study was a 'Sequential Explanatory Design' where the second phase is to deepen and further explain the result of the first phase. It is typically conducted as a quantita-tive data collection in the first phase, followed by a qualitative second phase. Equal weight (equal importance) are in this study given to the two separate phases in which the first informs the second. In other words, the analyses of the first phase are to inform the design of the data collection, and specific research in the second phase (Creswell 2009). The overall structure for my PhD project is shown in Figure 6.2.

Phase 2 – a case study of meaning-making in ESD

The main arguments for a case study as phase 2 (Flyvbjerg 2011; Merriam 1988) dealt with the results and theoretical development of phase 1, namely:

- Attention to the situated context of the learning practice was important, since the results showed some school differences, and correlations between outdoor activities and perceptions of content.
- A changed understanding of learning as meaning-making includes paying attention to social aspects as well. Meaning-making also implies that learning is an activity and hence processes are preferably studied instead of perceptions, in a temporal perspective.
- From a strengthened theoretical perspective, the concept of aesthetic experience was used to study the meaning-making processes of ESD.

Phase 1. Questionnaire (6 schools, 209 students)	
RQ1. How do young students understand and value the aspects of SD? **RQ2.** How can the relationships between understanding and valuing SD be described? (Open questions with picture support. Content analysis)	**RQ1.** How do young students perceive their learning experiences in relation to ESD? **RQ2.** What, if any, relationships can be found between the different aspects of learning? **RQ3.** Can relationships be found between the different schools and the students' learning descriptions? (Closed questions. Factor analysis, correlation, and descriptive statistics)

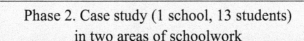

Analyses and reflections, transition from phase 1 to 2

Phase 2. Case study (1 school, 13 students) in two areas of schoolwork	
RQ. How are students' aesthetic experiences manifested, and functioning in young students' meaning-making processes? (Observations, field-notes, interviews and written responses. Content analysis of five environmental outdoor days)	**RQ1.** How are students' aesthetic experiences expressed in meaning-making processes over time? **RQ2.** What, if any, relationships are there between students' emotions and values in ESD? (Observations, field-notes, interviews and written responses. Narrative reporting of a thematic work on 'food- human- and environmental' issues)

Figure 6.2 Mixed-methods structure for this PhD project

The data collection for the case study was done through conducting observations, field notes, log book entries, interviews and gathering of written school documents. Focus was maintained on learning activities and transactions, not just students' reflections of those as in the previous questionnaire, since the process of meaning-making was now defined as the ongoing activity between experience and reflection (Dewey 1916).

Methodological concerns regarding my pre-understandings were now formulated in an even greater sense. I wanted the participating students and teachers to describe *what* ESD was to them in their school practice, without me giving any framings. I wanted to have an inductive approach and explore *how* ESD was constructed in this case and how meaning-making occurred. An ethnographic approach was adopted and initially I visited the class daily for one month, during all classes. After that, two areas of schoolwork were chosen which I followed for another two months: environmental outdoor activities, and a group work project focusing on food, humans and environmental issues.

The research plan for the case study involved analyses with an ethnographic approach, with these ideas in mind: 'Humans actively construct their own meanings of situations', 'Meaning arises out of social situations and is handled through interpretive processes', and 'Realities are multiple, constructed and holistic' (Cohen *et al.* 2010: 167). I found these methodological standpoints correlate with Dewey's view on learning where, additional to the emphasis on meaning-making processes, general phases of the processes are described. The phases of anticipation, courses of action, and fulfilment (Dewey 1934) were used as a framework for the qualitative content analysis. Secondly, an assumption was made that students' experiences within these ESD related activities were to be of an aesthetic character. The research question dealt then with how these aesthetic experiences would be expressed within the processes and how that might contribute to the continuous process of meaning-making (cf. Dewey 1934; Wickman 2006).

Discussion and conclusions

On the journey of exploring young students' learning experiences of ESD, the results of the two parts of the questionnaire gave new understandings and insights. Halfway through the PhD project this 'reflective middle' was of critical importance for the transition from phase 1 to phase 2. The experienced crisis developed into a deeper understanding of different perspectives and assumptions regarding methodology, epistemology and ontology. I would even claim it was necessary in order to continue the project with a broadened understanding and deeper focus of learning as meaning-making. Looking back at this narrative of being an interested practitioner, given the possibility of immersion in educational research, a description is given of how an abductive mixed-method approach might work in a PhD project and develop theoretical and methodological insights in educational research. This concluding part will highlight the three most crucial issues of the focus of this research process.

Developing understanding of 'learning experiences in ESD'

When constructing the questionnaire, the assumptions of important areas of learning experiences in ESD were mainly grounded in teacher experiences from practice. These areas focused on students' perceptions of the content as complex understandings and value-laden, and a variety of teaching methods, especially place-based nature encounters. The understanding of learning experiences included Dewey's theory of embodied action and Gardner's emphasis on multiple intelligences given that learning experiences could be found in a variety of separate aspects.

When analysing the empirical data from the open questions of the questionnaire, and dealing with the content of sustainability issues, the focus was on investigating variations of complex understanding concerning why phenomenographic theoretical lenses were used (Marton and Booth 1997). Those lenses provided a clear picture of how young students' perceptions of content varied within this group regarding more or less complex levels of relational understandings. Furthermore, there were parts of the empirical material that were 'blurry' using phenomenographic lenses, but which turned out to be clearer when putting on the neo-Aristotelian lenses (Nussbaum 2001). Those new lenses explained how understanding and emotions were interwoven generating even higher complex levels of student perceptions; i.e. emotions were not to be treated separately from understandings as they were put forward in the questionnaire. At this point, the understanding of learning experience was sharpened to include this 'cogni-emotional' dimension as found in the empirical results.

In the second analytical part of the questionnaire, questions had now been formulated to search for more relationships between the areas involved in learning. Using statistical tools to search for relationships in learning and theoretical lenses to understand the result brought me back to Dewey in a deeper sense. The results showed quite strong correlations between the areas of learning, especially the cognitive and the emotional areas (again). Now the lenses of Dewey (Dewey 1916) showed that instead of understanding experiences as divided in either a cognitive, social or physical way we could view experience as one whole, with different properties. The strong correlations pointed towards this understanding and made sense of the results in the first part as well. Situated and more context-related results regarding students' learning experiences were also found, thereby calling for further attention.

Choice of methods and methodology

The questionnaire gave valuable results and a general overview of students' learning experiences, but the pre-formulated questions had at the same time been shown to carry, and to some extent sustain, prior assumptions regarding theoretical perspectives on learning; especially the division of learning into separate domains. The new theoretical insights generated in turn more concern about other aspects of method than before. Furthermore, not enough could be said about the situated conditions of the participating school practices through the results from the questionnaire. Since the new understanding was of a holistic kind, a change was needed regarding methodology for the next phase. A case study was then chosen for in-depth investigation of learning in context, using a variety of empirical data. Seeing the empirical results from the first phase of the PhD project in the light of Dewey's theory of learning experience as a transactional activity of aesthetic character (Dewey 1934), made me choose a case study to empirically investigate aesthetic experiences in young students' meaning-making processes, within the context of an outdoor and environmental education school practice.

The importance of reflection in research

Finally, emphasising and recognising many aspects in Johnson's (2001) article 'The PhD Student as an Adult Learner: Using Reflective Practice to Find and Speak in her own Voice', I find important conclusions for the process of my own work. Schön (1983) develops the concepts of reflection *on* action and reflection *in* action as the difference between looking back on classroom practice and seeing it from within. Past experiences are essential to adult learners according to Knowles (1990), implicating the importance of reflection on action. As a practising teacher I was often reflecting *in* action on mostly technical or contextual matters for the best of my students. Now, as a PhD student, I have the opportunity to reflect *on* action in a more dialectical and theoretical way. This is one of the differences moving from practitioner to researcher; the character of reflection as *in* or *on*. From this point of view, I no longer consider the researcher as neutral or without importance for the results and analyses. This is not to be seen as discrediting the researcher; on the contrary, the reflective researcher is what is needed and wanted for trustworthiness and relevance in educational research.

The project of writing this self-reflective chapter has, in itself, been of great help when aligning the parts of the thesis and developing theoretical understanding. Through the abductive approach of the mixed-method methodology when moving through reflection between empirical findings and theoretical explanations it was possible to achieve change and development. There was a change from an understanding of learning experiences as separate aspects, to a holistic perspective of experiences including different properties in the process of meaning-making.

References

Anderson, G.L. and Herr, K. (1999). 'The New Paradigm Wars: Is There Room for Rigorous Practitioner Knowledge in Schools and Universities?', *Educational Researcher* 28(5): 12–40.

Biesta, G. (2006). *Beyond Learning, Democratic Education for a Human Future.* Colorado: Paradigm Publishers.

Biesta, G. (2010). 'Pragmatism and the Philosophical Foundations of Mixed Methods Research'. In: Tashakkori, A. and Teddlie, C. (eds), *Sage Handbook of Mixed Methods in Social & Behavioural Research*, 2nd edn. Thousand Oaks, CA: SAGE Publications, Inc., pp. 95–117.

Boeve-de Pauw, J. (2012). 'Valuing the Invaluable – Effects of Individual, School and Cultural Factors on the Environmental Values of Children'. PhD thesis, University of Antwerp.

Breiting, S. and Wickenberg, P. (2010). 'The Progressive Development of Environmental Education in Sweden and Denmark', *Environmental Education Research* 16(1): 9–37.

Cohen, L., Manion, L. and Morrison, K. (2010). *Research Methods in Education*, 6th edn. Abingdon, Oxon: Routledge.

Creswell, J.W. (2005). *Educational Research, Planning, Conducting, and Evaluating Quantitative and Qualitative Research*, 2nd edn. Upper Saddle River, NJ: Pearson Education.

Creswell, J.W. (2009). *Research Design, Quantitative, Qualitative, and Mixed Methods Approaches*, 3rd edn. Thousand Oaks, CA: Sage Publications.

Dewey, J. (1916). *Democracy and Education, An Introduction to the Philosophy of Education.* New York: The Free Press (1966 edn).

Dewey, J. (1934). *Art as Experience.* New York: Perigee Books.

Fien, J. (1993). *Education for the Environment – Critical Curriculum Theorising and Environmental Education.* Melbourne: Deakin University.

Flyvbjerg, B. (2011). 'Case Study'. In: Denzin, N.K. and Lincoln, Y.S. (eds), *The Sage Handbook of Qualitative Research*, 4th edn. Thousand Oaks, CA: Sage, pp. 301–16.

Gardner, H. (1993). *Multiple Intelligences: The Theory in Practice.* New York: Basic Books.

Gruenewald, D.A. (2008). 'The Best of Both Worlds: A Critical Pedagogy of Place', *Environmental Education Research* 14(3): 308–24.

Johnson, H. (2001). 'The PhD Student as an Adult Learner: Using Reflective Practice to Find and Speak in her own Voice', *Reflective Practice* 2(1): 53–63.

Johnston, J. (2009). 'Transformative Environmental Education: Stepping Outside the Curriculum Box', *Canadian Journal of Environmental Education* 14: 149–57.

Kincheloe, J. and Tobin, K. (2009. 'The Much Exaggerated Death of Positivism', *Cultural Studies of Science Education* 4(3): 513–28.

Knowles, M. (1990). *The Adult Learner: A Neglected Species*, 4th edn. Houston, TX: Gulf.

Lund, T. (2005). 'The Qualitative-Quantitative Distinction: Some Comments', *Scandinavian Journal of Educational Research* 49(2): 115–32.

Magntorn, O. and Helldén, G. (2007). 'Reading Nature from a "bottom-up" Perspective', *Journal of Biological Education (Society of Biology)* 41(2): 68–75.

Manni, A., Sporre, K. and Ottander, C. (2013a). 'Mapping What Young Students Understand and Value regarding Sustainable Development', *International Electronic Journal of Environmantal Education* 3(1): 17–35.

Manni, A., Ottander, C., Sporre, K. and Parchmann, I. (2013b). 'Perceived Learning Experiences Regarding Education for Sustainable Development – Within Swedish Outdoor Education Traditions', *NorDiNa* 9(2): 187–205.

Marton, F. and Booth, S. (1997). *Learning and Awareness*. Mahwah, NJ: Erlbaum.

Merriam, S.B. (1988). *Case Study Research in Education – A Qualitative Approach*. San Francisco, CA: Jossey-Bass Publishers.

Nussbaum, M.C. (2001). *Upheavals of Thought: The Intelligence of Emotions*. Cambridge: Cambridge University Press.

Öhman, J. (2008). 'Erfarenhet och meningsskapande', *Utbildning & Demokrati* 17(3): 25–46.

Palmberg, I.E. and Kuru, J. (2000). 'Outdoor Activities as a Basis for Environmental Responsibility', *The Journal of Environmental Education* 31(4): 32–6.

Payne, P. (1997). 'Embodiment and Environmental Education', *Environmental Education Research* 3(2), p.133–53.

Rickinsson, M., Dillon, J., Teamey, K., Morris, M., Choi, M.Y., Sanders, D. and Benefield, P. (2004). *A Review of Research on Outdoor Learning*. Slough: National Foundation for Educational Research.

Sandell, K., Öhman, J. and Östman, L. (2005). *Education for Sustainable Development: Nature, School and Democracy*. Lund: Studentlitteratur.

Sauvé, L. (1999). 'Environmental Education between Modernity and Postmodernity: Searching for an Integrating Educational Framework', *Canadian Journal of Environmental Education* 4: 9–35.

Schön, D. (1983). *The Reflective Practitioner*. New York: Basic Books.

Skolverket [The Swedish National Agency for Education] (2011). 'Curriculum for the Compulsary School, Pre-school Class and the Leisure-time Centre'. www.skolverket.se/ (acccessed 8 January 2015).

UN (2002). *World Summit on Sustainable Development – Implementation Plan*. Johannesburg

UNESCO. (2005). *UN Decade of Education for Sustainable Development 2005–2014 International Implementation Scheme. Draft*. Paris: UNESCO Education Sector.

UNESCO (2012). *Shaping the Education of Tomorrow, 2012 Report on the UN Decade of Education for Sustainable Development, Abridged*. Nolan, Cathy (ed.) Paris: UNESCO Education Sector.

Wickman, P.-O. (2006). *Aesthetic Experience in Science Education: Learning and Meaning- making as Situated Talk and Action*. London: Lawrence Erlbaum Associates.

Wylie, J., Sheehy, N., McGuinness, C. and Orchard, G. (1998). 'Childrens' Thinking about Air Pollution: A Systems Theory Analysis', *Environmental Education Research* 4(2), 117–37.

7 The lexical and grammatical structure of science examination questions

Adrian Day

A recurrent complaint among science teachers is that examination questions seem to engender the strangest responses from their pupils. All too frequently, capable and comprehending students will supply answers that lie beyond any obvious explanation. My complaints were no different to those of any other teacher and one evening, while marking a particularly incongruous set of examination scripts, it occurred to me that the peculiar answers in front of me might have arisen from the unique form of discourse that constitutes examinations. I say 'unique' because the participants of most forms of discourse perform two distinct roles. There are those who relay information and those who receive it. One might think of authors and readers for example or performers and their audiences. Yet in examinations, there are three roles; the examiner, the candidate and the marker. In many discourses, such as conversations, the role of each participant alternates as information is exchanged in a give-and-take. Yet in examinations, the role of each participant is fixed into a kind of chain and information passes along this chain in only one direction. Misunderstandings are inevitable for at no point can any request be made for clarification or rephrasing. Perhaps, given the atypical nature of the discourse, it is not so surprising that it contains extraordinary outcomes.

Learning the theory

My interest in linguistics originates from my Master's studies. I had been impressed by the work of Clive Sutton (1992) and by Jerry Wellington (1994) and both authors had greatly influenced my teaching. By following Sutton's recommendation that science teachers should bring to life the 'fossils of old thoughts', some potentially dull lessons had been transformed into lively, creative exercises in imagination. For example, instead of asking children to label materials as gases, liquids and solids, one can draw their attention to the word 'gas'. This term was coined by the alchemist Jan Baptist van Helmont, his neologism being inspired by the Greek word for chaos. One can ask them why he employed such a term. What ideas about gases was he trying to convey to other alchemists? Of course such a question has no correct answer but it does provide an opportunity to think in novel ways about the topic and to shift the focus of the lesson from a labelling, classifying exercise to a speculation about the nature of matter. Typically pupils' explanations for van Helmont's term draw on the bubbling and foaming that one sees in a flask when gases are generated. A pupil in one lesson suggested that the word 'gas' was a pejorative; its connotation of unruliness being used as an expression of van Helmont's frustration as he tried to collect and keep his gases. Interestingly, one idea that commonly occurs is that of particles moving randomly and at great speed. Given that the pupils involved in these lessons are usually no more than 11 years old, it is quite an advanced idea to volunteer without prompting or suggestion from a teacher.

By contrast, Wellington does not focus on the metaphorical attributes of a word. Instead, he draws attention to the way that a term is defined. For example, the words atrium and density both have precise scientific definitions and may be regarded as scientific terms that must, at some time, be learned by every science student. Yet they are defined in quite different ways. The first is simply a label that refers to a tangible thing, while the second is more abstract. Density refers to something that is rather more like a mathematical model since it is the quotient of mass and volume. Needless to say, it will be much harder to teach and to learn than the first kind of term. Consequently, when planning a lesson, great care must be taken to ensure that time and resources are organised in such a way as to correspond with the level of difficulty of the language that is associated with it. Now one might think that such a task would be impossible given the large number of terms that must be learned in school science. Nevertheless Wellington was able to create a simple taxonomy of these terms, consisting of three main groups; 'naming words', 'process words' and 'concept words'. These groups are hierarchical, the first group being easier to learn than the third group. Within each group there are sub-divisions and these too have a hierarchy. In all, there are nine of these sub-divisions and almost any scientific word from the lexicon of school science can be assigned to them. To be sure, these classifications may depend on the circumstance of the use of the term. The result may also be somewhat idiosyncratic since the ultimate assignment of a term may depend on the individual who classifies it. However such criticisms miss the point, for Wellington's taxonomy is a very practical heuristic. Once the words that will be introduced in a lesson have been listed and classified, it is a simple task to structure that lesson accordingly. Very often, the approach suggested by Wellington's taxonomy can be counterintuitive but it usually leads to satisfactory results.

Naturally, these early successes in language-focused science teaching led to a desire to explore further and, of these explorations, the most significant was the realisation that scientific language involved much more than technical words. Scientific language has a distinctive grammar. Sentences in scientific writing are structured so as to present processes and relationships as though they were things. These sentences are linked in particular ways because scientific writers are usually required to link observations, ideas and concepts into long, logical sequences. In addition, scientific literature includes items other than written text: graphs, diagrams, formulae, etc. Of course such items do not exist independently of the written text and authors must structure their writing in order to tie every element into a cohesive whole.

These aspects of scientific writing are outlined in two key books, these being *Writing Science* (Halliday and Martin eds 1993) and *Reading Science* (Martin and Veel eds 1998). They are both written by researchers from one linguistic discipline, Systemic Functional Linguistics (SFL). The content of both books is based on a multi-layered series of analyses called Systemic Functional Analysis (SFA). Underlying SFL is the theory of 'metafunction'. Here language is conceived of as an evolved structure that has developed to facilitate the survival of its users, each metafunction meeting a certain need. There are three metafunctions, the 'ideational' which relates to the need to communicate information about the world, the 'interpersonal' where language serves to initiate and develop the relationships between language users and the 'textual' which meets the need to organise this information in such a way as to allow communication. The needs that these metafunctions meet vary according to circumstance. Thus in scientific language the ideational metafunction is quite different to that of the vernacular. After all, scientists must communicate information about worlds that lie beyond the everyday experiences of most language users. The interpersonal metafunction can be quite distinct too. A scientist will have very different relationships to his readers and peers than would be normal in other genres of writing. So, at a fundamental level scientific text can be regarded as an exceptional form of language use.

I found that the articles based on this theory of language were quite uncomfortable to read, since there was an implied disdain for my exclusively lexical approach to scientific writing. It seemed that I had unwittingly accepted a fallacy that is common amongst science teachers, which is the belief that difficult language arises exclusively from difficult words. However, the ideas presented in these books did point to an explanation of my original problem: why do perfectly intelligent and capable pupils give such strange responses when answering examination questions?

If science has a special language then it follows that this language must be learned along with the concepts, processes and formulae that constitute school science. It also follows that when writing examination questions examiners must 'pitch' a question so that its content presents an appropriate level of challenge. However it is not so easy to do this since the use of language is very intuitive. Those who study science acquire this language without consciously doing so, and it is this unconscious fluency that allows them to communicate effectively with their peers. However, when communicating with novices this skill can become an impediment. Explanations and descriptions that seem simple, and indeed often are simple, require a considerable concentration of thought.

Now by its nature an examination is a communication between a relative expert and a beginner. This means that the author of a question has the difficult task of gauging the appropriate level of language and, moreover, they must do this without the cues and signs that are available to teachers. Questions from pupils, their requests for clarification, or their distracted behaviour are all indications that the language of the lesson is failing to meet its purpose. Yet the examination author has none of these guides and it is a matter of faith as to whether the language of the questions that they pose is suitable. Certainly, they might be able to trial questions prior to an examination but how are they to tell whether incorrect answers are due to a lack of knowledge or an inability to comprehend the question? If the language of the examination were beyond the ability of the candidates then the answers given by those candidates would inevitably appear strange. This is to say that text which appears to be common sense to the expert would be unintelligible to the pupil and text which appears to be common sense to the pupil would appear unintelligible to the expert. Almost anyone who has tried inexpertly to converse in a foreign tongue with a native speaker will have experienced a similar problem.

Of course, to follow this idea further I needed to acquire a working knowledge of Systemic Functional Analysis. Perhaps surprisingly there are no books for science teachers or science educationists that explain how to apply the theory and practices of systemic functional linguistics. However, there are SFL primers which are principally written for teachers of English for speakers of other languages. Notable among these are *An Introduction to Functional Grammar* (Halliday and Matthiessen 2004) and *The Functional Analysis of English* (Bloor and Bloor 1995). The latter was particularly useful because, at the end of each chapter, it provides a series of exercises that allow the reader to test and evaluate their understanding. As I progressed through these books, I used each new analytical method to scrutinise examination questions and their accompanying answers. As I did so it became clear that the linguistic structures of examination questions did appear to influence the responses that were given by the candidates.

I also started to believe that this enquiry might form the basis of a research degree. In fact, there was no other way in which the investigation could develop further. To arrive at an opinion is easy but it is quite another thing to substantiate that opinion and I could see that, to formulate a reliable and valid experimental design, I would require a large amount of guidance. Moreover although I was gaining in confidence in my understanding of Systemic Functional Analysis I was aware that I needed the support and critique of experienced Systemic Functional Analysts.

Yet to apply for a research degree one must write a research proposal, and a research proposal must have a research question. Now, at this point,

I had nothing of the kind; simply an assortment of ideas about the research that I wished to do. Firstly, I wanted to evaluate SFA as a tool for linguistic analysis. Secondly, I wanted to get some indication of the proportion of failed answers that result from the linguistic structures of an examination. Thirdly, I wanted to know if the findings of this analysis could usefully be applied. Could it be used as a basis for the creation of more effective questions? Of course this is a list of aspirations rather than the basis of a research project. To address these issues in any substantial way would take many years of work and would involve many researchers. What I really wanted to do was to carry out a small research project that would go some way to answering these questions. One that would, if successful, make a case for the linguistic analysis of examination questions. What I needed was a research question that would form the basis of such a project.

Finding a research question

In a search for ideas that might lead to something suitable I reread *Reading Science* (Martin and Veel 1998) and *Writing Science* (Halliday and Martin 1993), and found what I was looking for in a chapter by Halliday in *Writing Science* ('Some Grammatical Problems in Scientific English'). In this chapter he lists seven grammatical features that occur frequently in scientific texts and which can be problematical for school science pupils. It occurred to me that if these features could be found within the texts of science examination questions, and if they could be shown to adversely affect the outcomes of these examinations, then there would be a strong argument for the linguistic analysis of such questions. Furthermore I believed that it should be possible to modify selected questions so that the problematical features were removed. This being the case, I could evaluate the extent of the problems that they had caused by comparing the scores of a modified question with those of the unmodified form. If the difference in these scores were large then one could conclude that the identified grammatical procedure had had a correspondingly large effect. Thus, by gauging the significance of Halliday's problematical grammatical features I could assess the value of SFL as an analytical tool. In a way, Halliday had provided a set of predictions about the grammar of scientific texts. If these predictions did not hold true for science examinations then the validity, or at least the usefulness, of SFL would be doubtful. If, on the other hand, the features that are predicted by SFL did occur in the texts of examination questions, then the validity of SFL would be supported. The research question was formulated thus: Do Halliday's seven grammatical features affect candidates' performance?

Satisfied that I had found a promising starting point for my research degree, I submitted a proposal to the London Institute of Education and in due course attended an interview with my future supervisor. These application interviews were, at the time, described as informal discussions although it would be fair to say that the nature of this discussion was far more rigorous and thought provoking than many job interviews that I have experienced.

At one point, a question was raised concerning my choice of SFL: Why this and not some other analytical tool? It seems such an obvious question to ask and, in preparation for such a meeting, one that should have been anticipated. Now SFL does have a number of attributes that makes it appear suitable for the kind of analysis that I had in mind. In particular, there is a small though significant canon of SFL research and literature that pertains directly to the language of school science. In addition, the kind of detailed analysis that is involved in SFL is particularly suited to the short texts of examination questions. Yet these were rather superficial answers to my supervisor's question since they do not explain why SFL is better than any other form of analytical discipline. I felt uneasy when I presented these answers and she was clearly unconvinced. However, at the time she pointed out that to eliminate every other possible alternative would be far too large a task and that what was required at the outset were reasonable grounds for believing that I had chosen a suitable instrument. She also added the caveat that if, during the course of my research, it transpired that something better could have been selected then this could have serious implications for the whole undertaking.

Working with the research question

In fact, within a few months of this meeting, such a crisis nearly did occur. I was given the opportunity to present some of my early findings at a seminar at the Institute of Education and attending this seminar were researchers in cognitive psychology. These people had analysed examination papers using a cognitive theory rather than a linguistic one. Although I was aware of some of their literature (e.g. Pollitt and Ahmed 2000; Pollitt *et al.* 2000), I believed that their work dealt more with mathematics and I was not aware of the extent to which they had studied comprehension failure in science examinations (Sweiry *et al.* 2002; Crisp and Sweiry 2003). However, rather than rendering my study redundant, it became clear that the two approaches were complementary; the cognitive analysis revealing some aspects about science examination questions and the linguistic study revealing others. This was the first time that I had come across a triangulation-by-theory. In fact I had always naively believed that the rigour of a study demanded that the methodology should be confined to one paradigm. What particularly impressed me was the fact that the cognitive psychology researchers had found that diagrams and images, which are added to many scientific texts in order to aid clarity, were a significant source of confusion for examination candidates and, quite independently, my own analyses were leading me to a similar conclusion. Now if two distinct studies, with methodologies derived from completely different theories, identify one particular problem, then this must indicate some significance. Clearly an analysis of the images within the text of examination questions was desirable.

At about this time I learned that the theoretical basis of SFL is such that it is possible to analyse simple images in a way similar to that of written text. Kress and van Leeuwen (1996) explain these analyses in *Reading Images, The Grammar of Visual Design*. As I learned these analyses and applied them to examination questions, further light was shed on the problems that candidates face when answering these questions. Here then was a much better answer to my supervisor's question since SFL allows the analysis of a wider range of texts than other linguistic disciplines. In fact, systemic functional linguists may refer to any form language use as 'text', providing that it is used by real people, for the purposes of communication, in actual circumstances.

However, this new understanding brought new doubts about the research question. If images are identified as a significant source of comprehension failure, then a study that was centred on Halliday's seven grammatical features would be unable to take this issue into account; after all Halliday's features occur in written text rather than pictures or graphs. Of course it is always possible to change a research question as new information comes to light and this course of action did seem tempting. However, as my supervisor pointed out, it is very difficult to do this without losing cohesion. If the research question is changed too frequently then the experiments, observations and studies that constitute the research will address a series of disparate, evanescent questions and this would make it difficult to pull the resulting strands into a structured conclusion. In the end, I decided to keep to the original question but to use Kress and van Leeuwen's analysis in addition. All things considered, the purpose of the research question was to evaluate SFA as a means for gauging the effect of language on the performance of examination candidates. If I could find instances where image analysis gave a better insight into the structure of the question, then these findings could be included in the final chapter of the thesis. This, in turn, would allow me to discuss the way in which the analysis could be developed further.

Even so, I will never know if this was the best decision. It is always possible that a shift in focus from written text to multi-modal analysis might perhaps have resulted in a more informative study. For me, such decisions were the most challenging part of the PhD for there are no 'right' answers, and yet a bad choice at any stage can result in disappointing outcomes. No doubt an experienced researcher may develop an ability to navigate through the network of potential inquiries, but without the guidance of such an expert, the novice is likely to become lost in some unproductive back water.

Evolving methodology

A similar instance of this guidance concerned the experimental design. In the initial part of the study my supervisor and other experienced researchers expressed concern at its exclusively quantitative nature. In my early designs Halliday's grammatical features were to be judged on a comparison of the scores achieved by students who completed an original version of a question with those who had completed a modified version. However, it was suggested that interviews should also be conducted with some of these candidates in order to get a better idea of the problems that they had experienced. I was not at all persuaded by these recommendations. Examinations, I argued, are traditionally evaluated by statistical procedures and these are by their nature quantitative. Therefore, any evidence that did not follow a similar methodology would not be sufficiently convincing to justify the expenditure of my time which, as with most research degrees, was strictly limited.

However, my rationale was challenged when I was invited to explain the use of SFA at another seminar which was held at the offices of the Qualification and Curriculum Authority in London. It was, at the time, the independent regulator of state education assessments in England. They also produced a series of national examinations called the Statutory Assessment Tests. In addition, there were representatives from several examination boards. At the end of this seminar I was able to ask those attending what kind of experimental design they would accept. The unanimous preference was for a triangulated methodology that used both quantitative analysis and interview data. Thus, I was left with no alternative but to concede the argument and to plan a series of interviews.

Here, I was fortunate in that the cognitive psychologists had already established a technique for the evaluation of examination questions by interviewing pupils in pairs. This arrangement facilitated a much more open discussion than would be expected from an interview with a single pupil and also avoided the complications created by larger interview groups (Woods and Pollitt 2006). To my surprise, the value of interview data became clear even before the pilot studies had been finished. In these pilot studies, a number of pupils pointed out that their successful responses to the modified version of one question had been because in creating the modification, I had inadvertently provided cues for the correct answer. Here then was a good way of testing the validity of the experiment. However, as my technique developed, these interviews started to yield rather more fundamental findings and, by the end of the research period, it would be fair to say that I regarded this data as being just as important as that provided by any of the quantitative studies.

The relationship between quantitative and qualitative analysis can be exemplified by reference to a Hallidayan feature known as semantic discontinuity. This feature was omitted from the early study because it did not seem relevant to examination texts. However the paired interviews showed that, in fact, it was operating albeit in an unexpected way. As such it provides a good illustration of the dissonances and resolutions that occurred between the qualitative and quantitative methodologies. Yet in order to use this aspect of scientific writing as an illustration it is first necessary to explain some of the theory that lies behind it.

Semantic discontinuity

Semantic Discontinuity arises frequently in scientific explanations or in any other discourse that involves a series of linked steps such as the short passage below.

> The rise in temperature means that the particles in the gas move faster. The faster the particles move, the more they collide and the more they collide, the faster the reaction.

Here the temperature is linked to the motion of the gas particles and this motion is then linked to the number of collisions. However a discontinuity occurs because there is no explicit link from the number of collisions to the speed of the reaction and the reader is required to make the connection for themselves. A succession of such discontinuities can be seen in the following passage from a text book that was written for 11–16 year olds:

> Living things tend to adapt themselves to the conditions under which they live. Cactus plants which live in dry deserts have swollen stems for the storage of sap. Flightless penguins can swim in water. The lungfish of tropical Africa breathes through its lungs and not its gills during dry spells.
>
> [Windridge 1958: 64]

Within this passage there is nothing to explain how the storage of sap helps a plant to survive in dry deserts or how the penguin's lack of flight enables it to swim or how lungs allow the lungfish to live through dry spells. No doubt, to the reader of this chapter, these missing connections are obvious and do not need any further explanation, but one cannot assume that they are so obvious to a school science student. Such omissions do not result from the poor communication skills of the writer. Yet when carefully used, semantic discontinuities help the writer to create a more concise text. In fact when communication between experts takes place, these omissions are inevitable because both participants will assume that the other is accustomed to these ellipses. However when experts communicate with non experts, such assumptions should not be made. This might seem obvious but the trouble is that language use is so intuitive it is actually very difficult to avoid the creation of semantic discontinuities.

Now the questions in examination papers can contain explanations but these are usually very short. One would not expect texts like this to contain many semantic discontinuities because the authors of these questions are not required to link long sequences of idea and facts. Accordingly, analysis of a large number of examination questions detected very few of these Hallidayian features. When counted, there was no more than one for every 30 questions analysed. This being the case, the decision to drop semantic discontinuity from the study was unavoidable. However, this seemingly obvious decision was challenged when the paired interviews were conducted. In these interviews a large number of pupils expressed concern about the content of their answers. For some questions they did not know what information to include and what information to exclude. Very often this was their principal worry and many of the interview transcripts indicated a large degree of frustration, for they knew the answers to the questions but were unable to frame these answers in a way that would be acceptable to a marker.

Accordingly, I re-examined the texts of the questions and realised that I had forgotten an important tenet of systemic functional analysis, which is that every part of the text plays a part in the act of communication. In fact, in a work-shop on multimodal analysis at the Institute of Education, Gunther Kress had even advised us to consider the quality of the paper. What I had failed to take into account was not the written text of the question or the accompanying images but the spaces that were set aside for candidates to provide their answers. These spaces were very small and, at most, allowed no more than two or three sentences to be written. When I checked the questions against the corresponding mark schemes, in many cases, it appeared that an acceptable answer would have required the candidate to make a number of semantic discontinuities in order to produce a sufficiently concise answer. In my early analysis, I had failed to appreciate that, although the author of an examination question was not required to provide explanations, the candidate was. Now an expert scientific writer might find this kind of grammatical feature easy to employ but, as the interviews showed, this is not the case for young students.

In the light of my findings, I created modified forms of the questions in which the answer spaces were exchanged for a choice of four answers; three being incorrect and one being correct. The difference in the outcomes of the modified questions and their original versions was surprising and exceeded any expectation. In one case 45 per cent of candidates answered the original version correctly while 75 per cent answered the modified version correctly. In another comparison, 30 per cent gave a correct answer to the original version while 51 per cent answered the modified counterpart correctly. Now one might think that the modified versions may have been too easy and that the correct answer that lay within the multiple choices were a little too evident. However, the 'dummy' answers in the multiple choice questions were answers that had been frequently provided in the original examination scripts and also in the paired interviews. Hence, answers that pupils would have considered acceptable in the original version were considered to be unacceptable in the modified version.

Subsequently these results formed the basis of another set of paired interviews which in turn yielded more information about the way in which these pupils interpreted and responded to examination questions. Thus a kind of cyclical relationship developed between the two methodological elements, the qualitative information being used to inform the construction of quantitative experiments and data from these quantitative experiments being used to form the basis for further qualitative interviews. This dynamic association between two methodologies was something that I had not envisaged at the outset. Nevertheless, it proved to be a very useful technique throughout the research phase of the PhD.

Of course the open-ended nature of this kind of methodology meant that as many questions were generated as conclusions and this, in turn, lead to some very difficult editorial decisions in the writing-up phase. Certainly, my methodology was facilitating sophisticated linguistic insight into the challenges faced by examination candidates but, on the other hand, many of these insights lay so far from the original research question as to make them inappropriate for inclusion in the thesis. On reflection, it would have been perfectly feasible to have based an entire PhD thesis on the material generated by one question alone, such is the intricate nature of human language. Yet this intricacy is deceptive for as born language users we are misled into thinking that we perform a simple act when we communicate with each other. This research forced me to contend with the real complexity of language and the lessons I learned will be of enduring benefit to my teaching.

References

Bloor, T. and Bloor, M. (1995). *The Functional Analysis of English; a Hallidayan Approach*. London: Arnold.

Crisp, V. and Sweiry, E. (2003). 'Can a Picture Ruin a Thousand Words? Physical Aspects of the way Exam Questions are laid out and the Impact of Changing them'. Paper presented at the British Educational Research Association Annual Conference, University of Cambridge Local Examinations Syndicate.

Day, A. (2013). *The Structure of Scientific Examination Questions*. Dortrecht, Heidelberg, New York, London: Springer.

Halliday, M.A.K. and Martin, J.R. (eds) (1993). *Writing Science; Literacy and Discursive Power*. London: Falmer Press.

Halliday, M.A.K. and Mattheissen, M.I.M. (2004). *An Introduction to Functional Grammar*, 3rd edn. London: Arnold.

Kress, G. and van Leeuwen, T. (1996). *Reading Images; The Grammar of Visual Design*. London: Routledge.

Martin, J.R. and Veel, R. (eds) (1998). *Reading Science; Critical and Functional Perspectives on Discourses of Science*. London: Routledge.

Pollitt, A. and Ahmed, A. (2000). 'Comprehension Failures in Educational Assessment'. Paper presented at the European Conference on Education Research, Edinburgh. University of Cambridge Local Examinations Sydicate.

Pollitt, A., Marriott, C. and Ahmed A. (2000). 'Language, Contextual and Cultural Constraints on Examination Performance'. Paper presented to the International Association for Educational Assessment in Jerusalem. University of Cambridge Local Examinations Syndicate.

Sutton, C. (1992). *Words, Science and Learning.* Buckingham: OUP.

Sweiry, E., Crisp, V., Ahmed, A. and Pollitt, A. (2002). 'Tales of the Expected: The Influence of Students' Expectations on Exam Validity'. Paper presented to the Annual Conference of the British Educational Research Association, University of Exeter.

Wellington, J. (1994). *Secondary Science; Contemporary Issues and Practical Approaches.* London: Routledge.

Windridge, C. (1958). *General Science; Book 2.* Huddersfield: Schofield & Sims Ltd.

Woods, A.J. and Pollitt, A. (2006). 'The Development of the Preferred Alternative Construction Elicitation (PACE) Approach to Eliciting the Construct of Demand from Student Reviewers'. QCA Unpublished Report.

Part II

Theory-led design-based research

8 What do students think about scientists and their professions?

Wilfried Wentorf

Since my pre-service teacher training at school as a biology and chemistry teacher I have become very interested in projects fostering young talents in science. I started to build up various activities at my school next to my teaching, mostly in cooperation with several science institutes in the surrounding area, for example, an interdisciplinary science working group for upper secondary school students (grades 11–13) in cooperation with institutes at Kiel University. I also undertook scientific excursions to the Cape Verden islands in cooperation with the Helmholtz research institute GEOMAR, an institute for marine sciences. After many conversations with scientists during these projects I felt confident that strengthening authentic views about modern science is really important to support young scientists for and in the future. They should be aware of the tasks, skills and activities in modern science if they intend to study natural sciences. I observed a lack of knowledge about these aspects of science among my students. Besides I discovered the impact that my own and other out-of-school-activities in cooperation with real scientists and institutes had on students' commitment in science. Some of the students seemed to identify themselves with the scientists and authentic scientific activities more and more. They extended their contacts within the institutes on their own initiative and took part in different additional projects. After talking to the participants of these activities I estimated that most of these students had decided early on to study natural science at university after school. Based on these and other experiences and observations I became optimistic that students' views about scientists' characteristics and their concrete activities and skills could strongly influence students' commitment in science. I assumed furthermore that different interventions, especially those out-of-school activities in science institutes, have the potential to change stereotypes about scientists and their field of work.

Several questions arose from these experiences: What are these concrete activities and skills in modern science? How do they interact with students' views and their own personality? Is it possible to detect and analyse concrete students' views about scientists and their activities? Can I foster these authentic views systematically and check the impact of my assessments in a simple way? With these questions in mind I started my PhD at the Leibniz-Institute for Science and Mathematics Education (IPN) where I was offered a position in a project working with participants of science competitions. Therefore I was given part-time employment (temporary delegation) at the IPN for project activities and my empirical work, next to my part-time teaching at school. So I had the opportunity to try and reflect on some empirical and practical approaches before I studied them systematically.

Our institute is organised not only through domain-specific departments but also through interdisciplinary project teams. My supervisor associated me with a newly constituted group for characterising and fostering talents in science for my empirical work, and with an established group for designing interdisciplinary didactic concepts and materials for my project activities. Step by step my impressions and experiences from both parts merged, as you will see in the following narration.

Theoretical and empirical framework

The first months of the PhD qualification started with reading special literature and discussions in the working group, exchanging ideas with external experts and defining my own role within the working group. This process helped me to find orientation in the wide field of acknowledged constructs, theories and studies on the one hand, and in the organisational frame of bigger project structures of the working group on the other.

Step 1: Find a convenient field of research: from talent theories to nature of science

My PhD was integrated in a project called 'ICoN – Individual Concept about Natural Sciences'. This research project aimed to identify predictors and their interactions for commitment and success of young potential talents in science. I joined a group of six scientists including my supervisor during the initial phase of composing the research proposal. After initial discussions on theories and studies about talent and aptitude our group selected important predictors for commitment and success in science. My first tasks began with reading, selecting and summarising literature.

In different multidimensional models about talents and giftedness (e.g. Eccles 1983; Heller *et al.* 2001) factors like cognitive abilities, interests and self-concepts or self-efficacy are mentioned as variables to tap the full potential of talents. Additional to these personal aspects we added the views about science, scientists and their activities to the ICoN-model. The relationship between students' prototypes of different science subjects, their own identification with science and their commitment in science has been reviewed (Hannover and Kessels 2002). Although single correlations and interactions between the variables are well-known (e.g. Köller *et al.* 2006), we wanted to create an instrument to detect the influences and their inter-actions in common along analogue scales.

During debates in our working group I focused increasingly on the domain specific part of the ICoN-model: the concrete characteristics, skills and activities of scientists. These aspects matched my personal interests and my experiences with scientific school projects very well. After getting an overview about the wide field of literature incorporated in the ICoN-approach in general, I focused on the constructs Nature of Science (NoS) and Nature of Scientific Inquiry (NoSI). These constructs include philo-sophical, sociological and historical aspects about scientific methods and thinking. This wide field was a fascinating challenge for me because I like the complexity of these perspectives and I realised the tentativeness and maybe the fragility of these constructs.

This journey through the literature was very important to clarify my research question and its capacity for myself. Finally my practical experi-ences, personal research interests, content and conditions in the working-group and the chosen theoretical frame matched very well and led to the research question: What do students think about scientists and their professions?

Step 2: Analyse established constructs, the appropriateness, borders and desiderata for own research: nature of science (NoS) and nature of scientific inquiry (NoSI)

There is a wide field of theoretical approaches, empirical work and inter-ventions focusing on students' views about science itself (NoS) and knowledge about general methods in science (NoSI). The borders between these constructs are not always clear (McComas *et al.* 1998). The tentative and controversial character of the construct nature of science and science itself tends to result in synopses of acknowledged aspects. Lederman (2007), for example, characterises nature of science as tentative, empiri-cally based, subjective, involving human inference, socially and culturally embedded. Furthermore, he includes the differences between observa-tions and inference and the relation between theories and laws within the construct. This approach defines the scope of nature of science exclusively on scientific inquiry (SI), whereas other authors include methods and purposes of scientific work within the NoS-construct (Osborne *et al.* 2003).

Those scientific activities and methods, however, only refer to a closely defined inquiry process. The field of activities in science, in my opinion, is wider as can be deduced from previously postulated aspects of science and methods. Sociologists of science emphasise the impact of cooperation, socialising and the scientific community, on the one hand (Hara *et al.* 2003), and the importance of science management and marketing, on the other (Peter and Olson 1983). Among other things, these social, collabo-rative and enterprising aspects of scientists and their fields of activities are integrated into my new approach 'Nature of Scientists' (NoSt). Thus, this construct might serve as a practical interface between the Nature of Science and Scientific Inquiry constructs.

Although I was aware of many theoretical and empirical NoS-approaches at that time I decided to go a step back temporarily. After discussions with different scientists about their authentic research and their occupational every-day life I changed to a more pragmatic view. I focused on the concrete skills, characteristics and activities of scientists henceforward. So it should be possible to correlate students' images about science and scientists with their own interests, skills and characteristics later on.

Step 3: Analyse empirical framework: the lack of a pragmatic and detailed instrument about scientists and their activities

Previous studies concerning students' views about the Nature of Science mainly focused on epistemological beliefs, especially on the nature and status of scientific knowledge (Höttecke 2004; Lederman 2007). There is a limited range of tools that focus on students' conceptions about scientists and their characteristics, abilities and professional areas. Open formats such as Draw-a-Scientist tests are frequently used but often provoke stigmatising prejudices and sometimes do not reflect existing differentiated conceptions of the students (Finson 2002). Questionnaires and interviews helped to define four different types of students' images about scientists (Solomon *et al.* 1996): the weird scientist, the helpful authority, the technically adept scientist and the intellectual scientist. These types of image gave references to possible attitudes and general students' views about scientists, but there was still a lack of an instrument to detect students' views about concrete activities of scientists inside their modern field of professions. This was a challenge I wanted to approach!

Step 4: Extend the perspectives of activities for the 'nature of scientists'-instrument

To identify the wide field of job-related activity patterns corresponding to interests and characteristics, our working group has adapted Holland's (1985) RIASEC model to the field of natural sciences. RIASEC is based on six different dimensions of interest which can be associated with certain occupations: realistic, investigative, artistic, social, enterprising and conventional. Natural scientific professions were originally attributed exclusively to the investigative area. Some studies have shown that the RIASEC model can be regarded as a rather concentric continuum (e.g. Tracey and Rounds 1995). It enables occupational and interest profiles and this is also valid for the RIASEC dimensions. Based on previous reasoning, our adaptation assumes that the broad field of scientists' tasks necessarily requires activities and abilities which can be located in all

RIASEC dimensions. The RIASEC-model was a good frame especially for my work because it connected concrete occupational activities with personal aspects like interests. At that time I neither knew if it was possible to transfer this general model for occupational interests to the special field of scientists' professions nor if students' views about scientists' activities reflected the RIASEC dimensions. So now I had a suitable framework and a demand for the development of instruments – and my own empirical research journey started!

My own empirical research

It was my aim to explore students' views about scientists and their professions. This would be an empirical base to create adaptive activities to foster authentic views about the wide field of scientists' skills and activities according to a student's own personality. In the absence of adequate instruments it was necessary to develop a new instrument. So my scientific work includes three parts:

1   Development and piloting the NoSt-instruments.
2   Analysing students' views about scientists and their professions.
3   Development of practice: 'Simulating Science' – A NoSt-based intervention to foster authentic views about natural science, research and their actors.

Developing and piloting the NoSt-instruments

First of all, I compiled a synopsis of potential scientists' activities and linked this list with attributes and characteristics of the RIASEC dimensions that were postulated by Holland (1985). I validated this compendium of activities first with a small group of scientists and educational researchers and integrated it into a first version of a NoSt-questionnaire. Concerning these activities of scientists (see Table 8.1), students were asked about their views on scientific activities, their interests in them and their self-concept on a 4-point Likert scale:

1   A scientist performs the following activities on a regular basis ...
2   Would you like to perform the activity yourself in the future?
3   Please estimate your ability to exercise this activity in the future.

The questionnaire was applied in a pilot-study with 14–15-year old high-school students ($N = 305$). An explorative factor analysis mirrored the six RIASEC scales but also an additional one which includes collaborative and networking activities in science. The reliabilities were barely sufficient to identify these scales and to measure interferences. This was disappointing, of course, but also in the *Journal of Counseling Psychology* quite common as I

Table 8.1 Adaption of the RIASEC model: Characteristics and exemplary activities of scientists

RIASEC-Dimension	Attributes	Exemplary activities of scientists
Realistic	technically adept	take samples, produce substances in the lab
Investigative	analytic, task-oriented	analyse data, read specialist literature
Artistic	creative	develop instruments, create ideas for research
Social	sociable, caring	attend to students, teach students
Enterprising	leadership	manage a working group, acquire money for research projects
Conventional	conforming, precise	compile settlements, administrative tasks

learned from others. So after critically revising the questionnaire I conducted a second survey with high-school students ($N = 100$), and new results now emphasised a sufficient reliability of the NoSt-Questionnaire (Wentorf *et al.* submitted).

A qualitative study ($N = 28$) was done afterwards by a Master's candidate (Fischer 2014) to check the validity with regard to the students' understanding in addition to the theoretical and expert construct validity. The results depicted that the construct validity is suitable. The content validity of almost all items was sufficient. In some cases the content validity was limited: students did not see the whole authentic process of complex scientific activities and they compared it strongly with similar activities in school. Nevertheless their verbal descriptions matched the RIASEC categories. So I decided that the NoSt-questionnaire was suitable for my following research studies. The questionnaire is currently applied to the ICoN-project in combination with other scales, such as interest or understanding (Köhler, chapter 4, this book).

Connecting research with teaching practice

As a teacher I liked the potential of a questionnaire that would enable me to evaluate the influence of my own lessons and units or out-of-school activities about scientific inquiry and authentic cooperation projects with scientists. But of course it would be impossible to do the testing and empirical analysis of a large questionnaire in normal school every-day life. So I added a second, very simple part to the instrument for such a pragmatic use in school: The 'NoSt-Spider' was developed as an instrument to show students' views about scientists' characteristics. It includes all RIASEC dimensions by asking for the RIASEC attributes explicitly (Figure 8.1). Students can mark with a cross how important these characteristics are for a scientist from their point of view.

I used this spider in terms of pre-/post-tests for my projects at the IPN as well as evaluation of some school activities. In addition to views about scientists' characteristics it can also be used to detect self-assessments according to the RIASEC attributes of students. This should be a very easy way to find congruence between students' views and their self-concepts. Although I am aware of the limitations for generalisation of results revealed by this instrument there are firm grounds for its validity: Holland himself combined job-related activities and interests along his RIASEC scales with attributes/characteristics (Holland 1985). We used these attributes for the NoSt-spider almost literally. Just one dimension includes more than one aspect: the dimension 'artistic' relates to the items 'creative' and 'aesthetic'. Furthermore we added a scale 'cooperative', according to the NoSt-Questionnaire about activities. The content validity was proved by a discriminant approach: students should emphasise important characteristics of a scientist on the one hand and important characteristics of a manager on the other. Although professions of scientists include aspects of

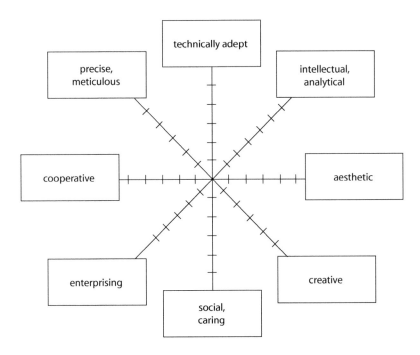

Figure 8.1 The NoSt spider

management I decided to use this example because the manager showed the strongest mismatch to scientist in former studies about the RIASEC model in the context of occupational choices (Armstrong *et al.* 2008). Students' estimations about scientists and managers differed significantly in all categories. This was confirmation of content validity of the NoSt-spider, which I decided to also use for further research studies.

Analysing views about scientists and their professions

The NoSt-instrument and first results of pilot surveys with this instrument were discussed early on at several national and international conferences. The expert feedback from these presentations was really helpful to examine results from different perspectives and especially to ensure the validity of the instrument for many ideas and points of view. The discussions were particularly important for my work because the NoSt-approach contains constructs from very different fields of research like psychology, philosophy and sociology. The development of the questionnaire raised new meaningful aspects of these discourses. After piloting and optimising the NoSt-questionnaire it was given to different groups who decided to commit to science in different ways, e.g.:

- High-school-students (partly with an optional subject in science)
- Participants of science competitions
- Bachelor degree university students in natural sciences.

The results of the first part of the questionnaire (views about scientists' activities) demonstrate especially the lack of students' knowledge about collaboration and management in science. Realistic and investigative aspects are much better known. The results based on surveys with the NoSt-spider will be shown here to exemplify outcomes of my PhD work. Students ($N = 434$) had been asked to estimate the importance of the RIASEC attributes for the professions of scientists on the one hand; on the other hand scientists ($N = 81$) had been asked for self-assessments about required characteristics in their field of work; this had been carried out during a conference. Both groups estimated the importance of the aspects 'intellectual' and 'precise' relatively highly. Strong differences were expressed with the aspects 'aesthetic', 'creative' and 'social'. Students seemed not to be aware of the importance of creativity and social aspects for success in science (Figure 8.2).

My first results based on both instruments already induced me to focus on creative and social scientific activities in my projects more than before. I examined the results about the importance of scientists' characteristics by cluster analysis to have a closer view of different types of students and their images about scientists' characteristics. The dendrogram of the cluster analysis led to four different profiles of students' views about scientists. The

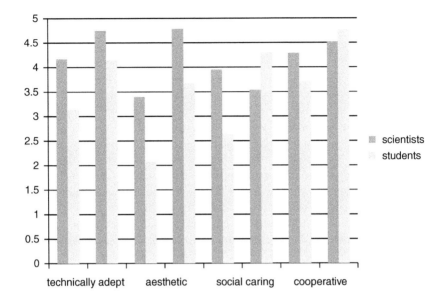

Figure 8.2 NoSt-characteristics: comparison between students and scientists

profiles include, for example, a group of students with low values in social and cooperative dimensions, whereas another profile shows high values in artistic, social and cooperative aspects. The latter group consists predominantly of girls. Findings from the interviews help characterise these types in more detail and validate the construct 'Nature of Scientists'. These findings also afford some hints for possible causes for different students' images about scientists and their characteristics. Even singular out-of-school activities or scientific projects in school or in institutes seem to influence views about the occupational field of scientists. So for innovations and interventions, it seems to be important to enable students to experience the whole field of scientists' activities along all RIASEC dimensions.

Implications for research and practice

I took the opportunity to develop a new program to foster scientific inquiry in German schools and started to concretise this approach based on my NoSt approach and my results. My supervisor arranged a cooperation project with the ministry of education and some special schools and allowed me to coordinate it. So I had the chance to transfer my empirical and practical experiences in a systematic intervention to foster differentiated authentic views about science and scientists. The ten cooperating schools in Northern Germany teach students from 8th and 9th grade for two years in a special subject called 'Simulating Science' for four lessons a week. They used the methods and materials I developed in cooperation with a group of science teachers (Blankenburg *et al.* 2013; Wentorf *et al.* 2014). The dissemination of this approach has already started based on the experiences of the first pilot schools in Schleswig-Holstein. I now teach this special subject based on my own research in school.

Next to the impact for my own way of teaching and my colleagues' teaching methods I am satisfied to see first implications and practical use of the NoSt-instrument for subsequent studies in my own institute and out of it. In the already mentioned ICoN-project it is used as one part to detect characteristics about potential talents in science competitions. Beside this the NoSt-instrument is used in European research projects to analyse students' views about scientists' professions corresponding to students' interests and self-concepts. I am looking forward to the results of these studies.

Looking back at my PhD journey I admit that sometimes I was in doubt about the compatibility between empirical research and praxis at school. Now I am sure that it is possible to find bridges between some gaps of theory and praxis, especially through the use of pragmatic instruments and designs of teaching based on an empirical background. I hope to continue to combine research and practical approaches for science teaching and find enough open-minded colleagues in science and school to give us the chance to close more gaps between research and every-day school life.

References

Armstrong, P.I., Day, S.X., McVay, J.P. and Rounds, J. (2008). 'Holland's RIASEC Model as an Integrative Framework for Individual Differences', *Journal of Counseling Psychology* 55(1): 1–18.

Blankenburg, J., Wentorf, W., Peters, H. and Parchmann, I. (2013). 'Brücken bauen zwischen Unterricht und Wettbewerben – Beispiele für die Verankerung von Wettbewerben an Schulen', *Naturwissenschaften im Unterricht Chemie* 24(4): 34–42.

Eccles, J.S. (1983). 'Expectancies, Values, and Academic Choice: Origins and Changes'. In: Spence, J. (ed.), *Achievement and Achievement Motivation*. San Francisco, CA: W.H. Freeman, pp. 87–134.

Finson, K.D. (2002. 'Drawing a Scientist. What we Do and Do Not Know after Fifty Years of Drawings', *School, Science and Mathematics* 102(7): 335–45.

Fischer, J. (2014). 'Empirische Untersuchung zur Konstrukt- und Inhaltsvalidität des Fragebogens "Eigenschaften und Tätigkeiten eines Naturwissenschaftlers" in verschiedenen Jahrgangsstufen'. unpublished Master's thesis. Christian-Albrechts-Universität zu Kiel.

Hannover, B. and Kessels, U. (2002). 'Challenge the Science-stereotype. Der Einfluss von Technik-Freizeitkursen auf das Naturwissenschaften-Stereotyp von Schülerinnen und Schülern'. In *Bildungsqualität von Schule: Schulische und außerschulische Bedingungen mathematischer, naturwissenschaftlicher und überfachlicher Kompetenzen*, pp. 341–58.

Hara, N., Solomon, P., Kim, S. and Sonnenwald, H. (2003). 'An Emerging View of

Scientific Collaboration: Scientists Perspectives on Collaboration and Factors that Impact Collaboration', *Journal of the American Society for Information Science and Technology* 54(10): 952–65.

Heller, K.A., Sternberg, R.J. and Subotnik, R.F. (2001). *International Handbook of Giftedness and Talent.* Oxford: Pergamon.

Holland, J.L. (1985). *Making Vocational Choices: A Theory of Vocational Personalities and work Environments.* Englewood Cliffs, NJ: Prentice-Hall.

Höttecke, D. (2004). 'Schülervorstellungen über die "Natur der Naturwissenschaften"'. In: Hößle, C., Höttecke, D. and Kircher, E. (eds), *Lehren und Lernen über die Natur der Naturwissenschaften – Wissenschaftspropädeutik für die Lehrerbildung und die Schulpraxis.* Baltmannsweiler: Schneider-Verlag Hohengehren, pp. 264–77.

Köller, O., Trautwein, U., Lüdtke, O. and Baumert, J. (2006). 'Zum Zusammenspiel von schulischer Leistung, Selbstkonzept und Interesse in der gymnasialen Oberstufe'. *Zeitschrift für pädagogische Psychologie* 20(1): 27–39.

Lederman, N.G. (2007). 'Nature of Science: Past, Present and Future'. In: Abell, S. and Lederman, N.G. (eds), *Handbook of Research on Science Education.* Mahwah, NJ: Erlbaum, pp. 831–79.

McComas, W., Clough, M. and Alamzroa, H. (1998). 'The Role and Character of the Nature of Science in Science Education'. In: McComas, W. (ed.), *The Nature of Science in Science Education Rationales and Strategies.* Dordrecht: Kluwer Academic Publisher, pp. 3–38.

Osborne, J., Collins, S., Ratcliffe, M., Millar, R. and Duschl, R. (2003). 'What "ideas about science" should be Taught in School Science? A Delphi Study of the Expert Community', *Journal of Research in Science Education* 40(7): 692–720.

Peter, J. and Olson, J. (1983). 'Is Science Marketing?', *Journal of Marketing* 47(4): 111–25.

Solomon, J., Scott, L. and Duveen, J. (1996). 'Large-scale Exploration of Pupils' Understanding of the Nature of Science', *Science Education* 80(5): 493–508.

Tracey, T.J.G. and Rounds, J. (1995). 'The Arbitrary Nature of Holland's RIASEC Types: A Concentric-circles Structure'. *Journal of Counseling Psychology*, 42(4): 431–9.

Wentorf, W., Höffler, T. and Parchmann, I. (submitted). 'Schülerkonzepte über das Tätigkeitsspektrum von Naturwissenschaftlerinnen und Naturwissenschaftlern – Vorstellungen, Interessen und Selbstwirksamkeitserwartungen', *Zeitschrift für Didaktik der Naturwissenschaften.*

Wentorf, W., Lüthjohann, F., Stein, G., Küster, J. and Parchmann, I. (2014). 'Planspiel Wissenschaft und Beruf – Was macht man eigentlich, wenn man Naturwissenschaftler wird?', *Naturwissenschaften im Unterricht Chemie* 25(2): 18–23.

9 How to develop an understanding for chemistry?

Investigating learning progressions for university entrants

Julian Rudnik

My first experience with chemistry was in school. Chemistry was one of the most fascinating subjects for me. Experiments like the production of sulphuric acid with a lot of glass tubes, funnels, pipes and gas-washing bottles fascinated me, and I became curious about understanding the theory behind chemical reactions. So I decided to study chemistry after school.

At Kiel University, I enjoyed getting deeper insights into the theories of chemistry and the diversity of activities in different areas of chemistry. It was inspiring for me to learn about chemistry in different fields and on different levels. As I was motivated to learn more about chemistry, I also wanted to support others to experience and understand the fascination of chemistry. During my voluntary work at the student council I offered tutorials in chemistry for students of agricultural sciences and medicine. I soon found out that the students did not refer to any concepts of chemistry in a systematic way but rather applied rote-learning strategies. During an internship at a school after my first year at university, I got similar feedback from school students, and I could also see how difficult it was for most of them to link phenomena with abstract explanations in chemistry.

After these experiences in school and university I decided that I wanted to learn more about the different abilities of students and about ways to support them better.

Taking opportunities: the offer of a position with a university entry program

My journey from being a chemist and a layperson chemistry educator to becoming a more professional educator and a researcher in chemistry education started with a project called 'Project for successful teaching and learning' (PerLe), where I applied for a position as a teacher and coordinator of prep courses and tutorials for first year students in chemistry. The project was funded by the German Federal Ministry of Education and

Research (BMBF) and aimed to support students during their transfer from school into university. So I became involved in a large endeavour, offering a professional environment for my own interests but also a lot of organisational demands, as I found out during my first year.

My duties were to set up a chemistry prep-course and additional tutorials accompanying the modules of the students' first year in chemistry, including general chemistry as well as mathematics. The prep-course aimed to give the students an orientation about first year expectations and also to clarify the differences between school and university with regard to content and learning strategies. The students completed questionnaires and tests at the beginning of the prep-course, offering a reflection tool for themselves and information for us and the other lecturers. As I – a chemist – had no experience at all in setting up measures like questionnaires and tests, I was lucky to be able to use existing instruments (Busker 2010; Klostermann 2014) from former studies at the IPN, the Institute for Science and Mathematics Education in Kiel. Through that I moved along on my journey: I was offered an opportunity to carry out a PhD in chemistry education alongside my position in the PerLe project.

Most interesting for me was to be able to analyse and support students' understanding of chemical concepts, and to build links between phenomena and conceptual explanations. Soon I experienced again that students learned by rote, not even trying to apply and deepen basic concepts. So my challenge was to raise interest using questions like 'Why does a certain molecule react in a specific way?' and to initiate a process of 'chemical thinking' (Sevian and Talanquer 2014) at the beginning of the students' university studies. However, all I did up to that point was based solely on my own experiences. So the first thing I needed to do was to learn more about learning theories, evaluation methods and approaches to initiate and develop learning progressions (a term I had not heard of at that time), based on theories and research about learning. Due to my own motivation in chemistry I also wanted to build links between basic concepts already taught in first-year chemistry courses and fields of current research in chemistry. My assumption was that students could be motivated if they were made aware of possible future directions.

So I became like a first-year student again myself, starting to learn about chemistry education from scratch!

Finding a suitable framework and design – the need for reviewing literature

For this part of my journey on becoming a science education researcher I was lucky. I became involved in the IPN chemistry education group where many different PhD students and PostDocs with different backgrounds in chemistry, chemistry education, science communication and psychology were working in different projects and project groups. Every PhD student not only has his/her supervisor, but also two PostDocs as mentors. I was working with Stefan, a former chemist and now a leader of an outreach project on nano science, and with Jan Christoph who got his PhD for research on learning progressions. Even though he left to become a teacher in South Africa early on, he gave me a very important idea for my own work – but this will be explored later on.

Initially I learned about former studies that I could directly build upon. Maike, now an assistant professor at a nearby university, and Mareike, now a school teacher, had both investigated first year students' interests, self-efficacy and chemical knowledge (Busker 2010; Klostermann 2014). Maike had also developed tasks for tutorials for different student cohorts. These tasks build bridges between basic concepts of chemistry and applications in different study contexts, such as medicine, the chemical industry or agriculture. Therefore I was able to continue with her work, adding the bridge between basic concepts and current research, which was one of my own interests; this has already led to a joint chapter in a book with her and others (Parchmann *et al.* 2015).

The theoretical background Maike had used for the design of her tasks was situated in the area of context-based learning (CBL). In the literature I found many papers describing approaches and effects of context-based learning at secondary/high school level, like 'The Salters' Approach' (Campbell *et al.* 1994; Benett and Lubben 2006), or the 'Chemie im Kontext' approach (Parchmann *et al.* 2006). For the tertiary level, Mahaffy's work has been influential for me (Mahaffy 1992). Design elements for CBL have also been described and reflected (Nentwig and Waddington 2005; Bulte *et al.* 2006). Bulte *et al.* (2006) discussed 'authentic practices as contexts' for students in chemistry education in school, and summarised that 'students are expected to give meaning to the chemical concepts they learn' (p.1063) by the context. The relation of contexts to authentic practices seemed very promising to me for the application of context-based learning at the university level, as students in first year chemistry courses come from different study programs and therefore have different perspectives of the practices which they are going to do in the future with regard to chemistry. Going through the literature on CBL has also offered insights into effects: while I was immediately stimulated by this approach, the empirical findings have been more diverse. Obviously, CBL does have positive effects especially on interest and motivation, but these effects are less clear with regard to knowledge (e.g. Bennett *et al.* 2007; King and Ritchie 2012). This raised my curiosity to learn more about the students' progression in explaining context-based phenomena based on conceptual knowledge. The work of Karolina Broman which is also described in this book (Chapter 11) has helped me to go in this direction on my own research journey.

How did I develop CBL tasks for university tutorials?

Following Maike's experiences, I also decided to connect chemical phenomena and basic concepts with contexts from different study programs (Parchmann *et al.* 2015). To do this in a systematic way, I applied Mahaffy's tetrahedron (Figure 9.1), an enlargement of the well-known 'Johnstone triangle' (Johnstone 1991). Johnstone has pointed out the necessity to combine the phenomenological level with the submicroscopic level of models and the representational level of, for example, formulae, when learning to understand chemistry. Mahaffy added the 'human element' to this triangle, reflecting that explanations can have different meanings for different people in different situations. This was exactly my assumption when working with students from different study programs. A simple example can illustrate this: the term 'neutral' with regard to pH means a pH=7 in chemistry, while it is often used as equivalent to the pH of the skin in biology or medicine.

Next to the different study programs I wanted to include current research in chemistry to the tasks for those students who do not need to repeat their basics. Due to my work with Stefan I studied the research of the Collaborative Research Center 'Function by switching' at Kiel University, which connects different areas of research within chemistry, like physical and organic chemistry, but also between chemistry and other sciences, like physics or material science. Table 9.1 gives an insight into the different levels of context-based tasks, which I developed for the tutorials.

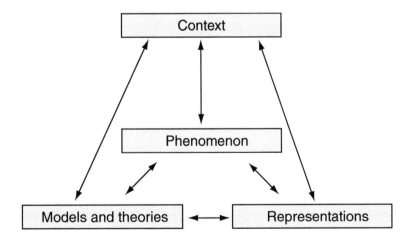

Figure 9.1 Applying the theory of Mahaffy (2006)

Table 9.1 Examples for different levels of context-based tasks

Topic	Basic questions	Context-based questions	Chemical research questions
Stoichiometry	In the lab you have to prepare a water-based solution of hydrochloric acid with a ratio of mass $\omega=10\%$. How much water and concentrated hydrochloric acid ($\omega=37\%$) do you have to mix?	As a student of chemistry and economics you might later be working in a company producing sulphuric acid. In the fabrication you cannot get 100% of the product. How much sulphuric acid ($\omega=65\%$) is formed, if 20 kg of sulphur is burnt to sulphur dioxide? You have to count on losses of 3.2%.	In an experiment you take stoichiometric amounts of chloroauric acid and sodium citrate in water for preparing colloidal gold ... You carried out the experiment twice, but in the second experiment you did not 'shock-cool' the mixture after heating it. Finally you get two different coloured colloids. Why? Try to use literature to explain this phenomenon. Consider that you used stoichiometric amounts of the substances!
Acids and bases	Which acids and bases do you know from your experience as a school student, which ones do you know from your daily-life experience? Please explore theories explaining characteristics of acids and bases and their theories. If you have already heard about a buffer, please also explain how it works.	Biological processes rely on buffer systems, e.g. to stabilise the concentration of protons in the blood or in cells ... Please describe how a buffer system works, using chemical equations. Please also explain how to calculate the concentration of protons (pH) of a buffer system.	In an on-going research project in the department of organic chemistry in Kiel there is a group working on molecular machines named Rotaxanes. They contain a loop-molecule which can move along an axis of another molecule. Both molecules have a polarity. The loop molecule moves after protonation (getting a real charge) in direction of an opposite polarity. Please give an explanation for this process based on an acid-base theory.

When working on the design of such tasks, I noticed that I did not have any system for the design of levels of difficulty, and as a consequence, for the analyses of students' answers. So I realised that I actually needed a second framework to do this, again based on theoretical assumptions about learning. This was the point where Jan Christoph gave me the idea of looking into projects on learning progression.

From a design framework to an analytical framework – enlarging perspectives

Further literature research gave me an idea about how to conceptualise the development of students' understanding. Comparable to the historical development of chemistry, empirical research has shown that students also progress along certain conceptual ideas (Parchmann *et al.* 2009; Neumann *et al.* 2013; Lee and Liu 2010; Hadenfeldt *et al.* 2013).

So if I was able to assume a theoretical progression for basic concepts in chemistry, such as understanding structure-property-relations, I should be able to categorise students' answers in a systematic and comparable way. The first level contains explanations on the phenomenological level only, like describing properties of objects. The next level incorporates properties related to substances. The third level includes models of atoms/molecules/lattices; and these models become more and more complex and abstract on the following levels. As my supervisor had done work in this field, it was not difficult for me to find articles I could use as starting points (e.g. Parchmann *et al.* 2010). So I developed hypothetical progressions for university students, adapting and prolonging existing progressions for school level (Figure 9.2).

For the design of diagnostic tools to analyse progressions in practice I kept using my adaptation of Mahaffy's tetrahedron. I chose phenomena that all students would know from their everyday experiences, like observing globules of fat in a soup, and connected them to conceptual explanations that students should have met at school, like hydrophobic and hydrophilic characters. The contexts were chosen again from different study programs, like agriculture and nutritional sciences.

My plan was to use these tools at the beginning of the students' first course in chemistry and again after their first and second semester. One problem I had to overcome when reviewing the literature on learning progressions was that the other studies had used large instruments with many items, which was not possible during my tutorials. So I had to rely on approaches of using diagnostic tools, such as those described by Treagust (1988).

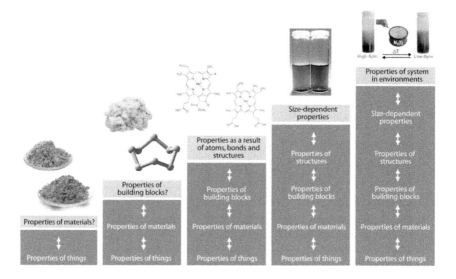

Figure 9.2 Structure-property-relations (adapted from Parchmann *et al.* 2010 and Schwarzer *et al.* 2013). The author would like to acknowledge the permissions granted to use the individual photos in this figure, from left to right: "pigment" © Schlierner; "pigment" © Schlierner; "yellow crystal" © marcel; "Cyclooctasulfur-above-3D-balls.png" public domain; "porphyrine structures" © Schwarzer; "the two glasses with the liquids" © Schwarzer; "Spin-crossover of 4-Methylphenanthroline-iron(II)bispyrazolylborate" © Naggert

My first experiences with using the tasks and analysing the students' answers

Before starting the 'real research', I tested both the acceptance of the tasks and the analysis of the diagnostic items. During the tutorials the students gave positive feedback and mentioned that they were interested in exercises testing basic knowledge to enable them to pass the examination. They also enjoyed applications of basic knowledge with regard to their field of study. Only for the examples of current chemical research did the students not see the relevance. As the students could choose the questions they wished to work on, my impression was that students with weaker prior knowledge would rather not decide to work on context-based tasks; this was also identified by Busker (2010). Those students primarily wished to get support to understand the relevant content of the lectures, the practical lab courses and guidance for future exams.

The analyses of the diagnostic tasks revealed progressions of students' levels of explanation and the knowledge they applied from the first testing at the beginning of their study to the second after approximately three months. There were more conceptual explanations given for the observed phenomena, as shown by the following example.

Task A: Please explain why rapeseed oil cannot be dissolved in water.

In the first survey (N=92) most students answered on the phenomenological level, giving explanations like 'oil and water cannot be mixed', or 'oil is insoluble in water' (closest translation). Some gave conceptual reasons, like 'water is polar and oil nonpolar' (closest translation). In the second survey (N=65) the students used more explanations based on chemical concepts (68 per cent instead of 46 per cent). Still, both surveys showed that about 50 per cent of the students did not use a model for their explanations, like comparing polar and nonpolar substances. This result is clearly not satisfying considering the fact that all students have chosen study courses in the field of science.

How to move on from here – challenges and opportunities

Currently I am analysing students' results from the first and the second test times in a systematic way for all diagnostic tasks. As the content of the tasks relates to different topics of the first and second semester lectures, I will also link results to the time of progression. The next step would then be to improve the tasks and – if necessary – the grain size of the analytical scheme.

One constraint that hinders my PhD work is the position that I have in the PerLe project. I appreciate the learning opportunity, of course, and also the funding I get, but the preparation of the courses and the exchange with other team members is very time consuming, since this is a part-time job alongside my doctoral research.

I also experienced more difficulties than expected in finding my way into the theoretical and methodological fields of science education. Being a chemist by training I had not heard of those theories and even many terms before, so I often felt like a first-year student again.

References

Bennett, J. and Lubben, F. (2006). 'Context-based Chemistry: The Salters Approach'. *International Journal of Science Education* 28(9): 999–1015.

Bennett, J., Lubben, F. and Hogarth, S. (2007). 'Bringing Science to Life: A Synthesis of the Research Evidence on the Effects of Context-Based and STS Approaches to Science Teaching'. *Science Education* 91(3): 347–70.

Bulte, A.M.W., Westbroek, H.B., de Jong, O. and Pilot, A. (2006). 'A Research Approach to Designing Chemistry Education using Authentic Practices as Contexts'. *International Journal of Science Education* 28(9): 1063–86.

Busker, M. (2010). *Entwicklung einer adressatenorientierten Übungskonzeption im Übergang Schule – Universität auf Basis empirischer Analysen von Studieneingangsvoraussetzungen im Fach Chemie.* Tönning: Der Andere Verlag.

Campbell, B., Lazonby, J., Millar, R., Nicolsen, P., Ramsden, J. and Weddington, D. (1994). 'Science: The Salters' Approach – A Case Study of the Process of Large Scale Curriculum Development'. *Science Education* 78(5): 415–47.

Hadenfeldt, J.-C., Bernholt, S., Liu, X., Neumann, K. and Parchmann, I. (2013). 'Using Ordered Multiple-Choice Items to Assess Students' Understanding of the Structure and Composition of Matter'. *Journal of Chemical Education* 90(12): 1602–8.

Johnstone, A.H. (1991). 'Why is Science so Difficult to Learn? Things are Seldom what they Seem'. *Journal of Computer Assisted Learning* 7(2): 75–83.

King, D. and Ritchie, S.M. (2012). 'Learning Science through Real-World Contexts'. In: Fraser, B.J., Tobin, K.G. and McRobbie, C.J. (eds), *Second International Handbook of Science Education*, 24: 69–80. Rotterdam: Springer Netherlands.

Klostermann, M. (2014). 'Lehr-/ Lern-Überzeugungen von Studierenden und Lehrenden im Fach Chemie im ersten Studienjahr'. PhD Thesis, Leibniz-Institute for Science and Mathematics Education, CAU Kiel.

Lee, H.-S. and Liu, O.L. (2010). 'Assessing Learning Progression of Energy Concepts Across Middle School Grades: The Knowledge Integration Perspective'. *Science Education* 94(4): 665–88.

Mahaffy, P. (1992). 'Chemistry in Context. How is Chemistry Portrayed in the Introductory Curriculum?' *Journal of Chemistry Education* 69(1): 52–6.

Mahaffy, P. (2006). 'Moving Chemistry Education into 3D – A Tetrahedral Metaphor for Understanding Chemistry'. *Journal of Chemical Education* 83(1): 49–55.

Nentwig, P. and Weddington, D. (2005). *Making it Relevant: Context based Learning of Science*. Münster: Waxmann.

Neumann, K., Boone, W., Viering, T. and Fischer, H.E. (2013). 'Towards a Learning Progression of Energy'. *Journal of Research in Science Teaching* 50(2): 162–88.

Parchmann, I., Gräsel, C., Baer, A., Nentwig, P., Demuth, R. and Ralle, B. (2006). '"Chemie im Kontext" – A Symbiotic Implementation of a Context-based Teaching and Learning Approach'. *International Journal of Science Education* 28(9): 1041–62.

Parchmann, I., Bünder, W., Demuth, R., Freienberg, J., Klüter, R. and Ralle, B. (2009). 'Lernlinien zur Verknüpfung von Kontextlernen und Kompetenzentwicklung im Chemieunterricht'. *CHEMKON* 13/3 pp.124–31.

Parchmann, I., Scheffel, L. and Stäudel, L. (2010). 'Struktur-Eigenschafts-Prinzipien'. *NiU-Chemie* 21(115): 8–11.

Parchmann, I., Broman, K., Busker, M. and Rudnik, J. (2015). 'Context-Based Learning at School and University Level'. In: Garcia-Martinez, J. and Serrano-Torregrosa, E. (eds), *Chemistry Education: Best Practices, Innovative Strategies and New Technologies*. Berlin: Wiley-VCH Verlagsgesellschaft, Chapter 10, pp. 259–78.

Schwarzer, S., Rudnik, J. and Parchmann, I. (2013). 'Chemische Schalter als potenzielle Lernschalter'. In: *CHEMKON* 20(4): 175–81.

Sevian, H. and Talanquer, V. (2014). 'Rethinking Chemistry: A Learning Progression on Chemical Thinking'. *Chemistry Education. Research and Practice* 15(1): 10–23.

Treagust, D.F. (1988). 'Development and Use of Diagnostic Tests to Evaluate Students' Misconceptions in Science'. *International Journal of Science Education* 10(2): 159–69.

10 Do we really know what science is all about?

Researchers' and students' perceptions of science

Frederike Tirre

To be able to communicate science, the first thing someone needs to clarify is: what makes science science? What is interesting to know from someone else's perspective? Seen from a practical angle, the question arises: How can you strip down a whole subject in science to a newspaper article with 1,200 characters? The master's degree in science communication that I enrolled in involved a broad set of skills. This was a challenging beginning to what was going to be a major shift in my perspective. Science communication added a new layer to my scientific thinking. It has become an instrument to investigate how research is done, in addition to doing the research. This helped me to gain insight into the scientific endeavour from a bird's eye view and to reflect on my own work and background in a field with fundamental as well as applied research. In the course of the Science Communication Masters I learned how to use mediating tools to deliver a scientific message to a targeted audience, and how these tools can be used to investigate a scientific question.

Starting the PhD journey

After I finished my studies in the Netherlands, I wondered what would come next. Peeking into so many domains of communication, such as journalism, film, museums, etc., I struggled to choose a field that I wanted to work in. One thing was clear to me: I did want to use my knowledge in a practical way, since that was what felt most natural to me. The channel and the topic mattered less than the possibility of strengthening my skills in science communication. I applied for various jobs including a job in a science outreach project on Nano Science and Technology (NST) at the Leibniz Institute for Science and Mathematics Education (IPN) in Ilka Parchmann's group, after hearing that they might need someone with my background in scientific media production and science in museums. I had met my future PhD supervisor, Professor Dr Ilka Parchmann, in a pre-university course on chemistry education (Chemistry in Context) before I started my studies in the Netherlands.

Starting at the IPN, I became a member of the scientific outreach project, where I worked with colleagues from the chemistry education department on communicating NST for the collaborative research cluster (CRC) 'Function by switching' at Kiel University. Since NST connects different disciplines such as chemistry, physics and material sciences, the challenge of this project was to be able to find the core messages of the different research projects within the cluster in order to offer a broader public insight into contemporary research.

In the beginning, this hands-on approach of communicating NST was the main part of my work. So practically, I had two foci: a) diving deep into understanding the new field of NST, by talking to colleagues and scientists, as well as reviewing all kinds of literature, and b) designing and developing scientific media such as films, apps, images, posters and experiments in order to successively set up a public exhibition and a students' lab program for secondary school students.

Identifying concerns

As one can imagine, working on a highly interesting science communication project in a totally new field is extremely time-consuming. Correcting texts for the smartphone app, researching photos for the exhibition, investigating products, communicating with and organising researchers/ students/teachers/university staff, writing scripts for scientific movies, brainstorming, cutting video material, etc., while keeping you enjoyably busy, does not, however, earn a PhD. So, the question was, how to get into science communication/education research? Basically, I did what every PhD student probably does: I tried to read myself into the field. Soon I found out that there was not very much literature on NST in education, since NST is not a field in itself but combines different disciplines. Since in many countries NST is not part of the curriculum, a lot of short exemplary teaching units exist, but only a few general approaches on how to teach NST (e.g. Lahertto 2011).

After spending some time reading and discussing with colleagues the question arose: How do we deliver the researchers' and educational messages in order to create an authentic image of NST? This question felt like step two in the process as we were already working on the communication medium before we knew what the actual message was, but this is how projects work – we had to deliver outreach results for the research cluster, and the PhD runs in parallel (and sometimes a bit behind). But in order to frame the answer to the question, other questions needed to be answered first: What exactly is Nano science? How do we as scientists and educators define it and how do others perceive and define it? What are the interests of the public? These questions lay the ground for my PhD research. Furthermore, was I interested in the public perception and opinion about such a 'hot topic'. Nano is not a new phenomenon but Nano as a research field is. This has to do with the technological development of instruments that enable scientists to look at this 'invisible dimension'. But it was rather hard to find something like a public opinion – not only based on literature but also from personal talks with friends and colleagues it seemed that most people only had a vague idea what Nano really is (except for the researchers themselves, of course). It almost seemed as if Nano as a term was as invisible as its submicroscopic structures.

Literature mainly describes two approaches to disseminate science: either from a scientist's perspective or from a school science point of view. Very seldom are these two worlds combined in order to create environments wherein science communication and education takes place. This 'shiny medal' of knowledge has two sides and having a look at both sides equally was a goal for my research. We wanted to increase the intersection between science and the public, mainly secondary school students in this case. In order to do so, we first had to find out what was going on in those two worlds.

Therefore my supervisors and I decided to carry out two different studies:

1   to investigate the perceptions of NST through the eyes of the scientists themselves on one hand, and on the other hand
2   to investigate the beliefs and conceptions about NST and science in general of 'the public', i.e. secondary students in my case.

So these two questions build the framework for my PhD thesis, shedding light on the topic of authentic NST from two perspectives.

Working on study one: the scientists' view

The first study was set up to gather first-hand information from the researchers in the field. Whilst choosing an interview format and deciding on the sort of questions that I wanted to ask the researchers, I still had to think about a way of broadcasting this knowledge. The interviews contained 16 questions about the characteristics of NST, aspects of NST to communicate, students' concepts about NST and benefits and limitations of outreach. The interviews were held in a structured manner in order to obtain as much information as possible from the interviewees. The sample consisted of eight professors working in the field of NST for several years and thus having a high level of experience in the field. The interview study was used to gather information on the researchers' side in order to answer the question: what is authentic NST science to scientists, can we give an overall definition of science and how it can be communicated to the public? Further, the scientists were asked about what should be communicated to the public.

Based on the retrieved results, alongside media and communication theories, different outreach activities were designed; the program for the students' lab targeting lower secondary school, as well as podcasts and an exhibition addressing school students and a broader public. From the interview answers, I expected to be able to draw proper definitions of NST but probably no good solutions on how to communicate them. Also I realised that the researchers themselves might not be a good source for communication since they are situated in the field of science but not in education or science communication. This issue brought me back to the literature. I needed to get to know more about different perceptions of science (Schwartz and Lederman 2008) and how scientific content can be reconstructed in such a way that it can function where it is needed (Lee 2003). This brought me deeper into the broad field of science communication.

Science communication as a tool

When we talk about science communication, it is important to take a closer look at the term itself. There seems to be more layers to it than simply talking about science; so what is this 'special communication'? From my earlier studies I already knew that science communication covers fields such as public awareness of science, public understanding of science, scientific culture, and scientific literacy (Burns *et al.* 2003; Rennie and Stocklmayr 2003; Falk and Storcksdieck 2005). The diversity of these fields within the field of science communication made it difficult to nail down a definition to refer to, especially since my PhD was situated between the communities of scientists, educational scientists and science communicators. For my further research the approach by Burns *et al.* (2003) and their vowel analogy became a guideline. They look at science communication as a tool for disseminating a message across different channels and towards different audiences, always keeping in mind the purpose of the message itself. Basically, if you try to tell someone something complicated, make sure that it grabs the attention of the person in focus. In order to do so, it is necessary to know something about the audience to which the message needs to reach out. In the meaning of 'to reach out' (or outreach in our case) science communication becomes much more than simply a translation of scientific content. It becomes the carrier of emotions, hope, knowledge, attitudes and perceptions of the natural world.

Science communication takes place in many forms; one can think of scientific writing in journalism or putting science into pictures as in documentaries or infographics. The ways of distributing knowledge are as diverse as the topics and the people working on them. The diversity was exactly one of the points I struggled with at first. Looking at the communication part of science, one has to dig a little deeper into multimedia theory (Moreno and Mayer 2007), how messages can be identified, stripped down to a core and adjusted to a specific medium. A medium can be an image in order to illustrate, for example, the inlet of a human cell.

With increasing context-complexity (for example the process of photosynthesis), media such as film (motion picture) in combination with text and audio can provide a better solution for illustrating scientific issues.

But not only is the medium important here, but, as mentioned earlier, the audience also plays a key role. Identification of the audience is the first step; analysis of the usability of the medium forms step two. If you build a smartphone application simulating the function of a cell and how to alter cell processes, it might be a great idea design wise but maybe not everyone uses a smartphone. No less important is the message itself: there needs to be a main message that can be understandable by the audience. Once the core is identified, text and images (video material, sound, etc.) need to be placed in balance (for example explaining text next to figure of interest) in order not to confuse the audience, here the secondary school students, but to help them understand.

Challenge: combining project tasks with research

After this second literature review, the research was clearer to me. When we talk about science communication, we have to keep three things in mind: the message itself (content), the medium and the audience. One of the project aims was to design an exhibition on NST that would reach a broad audience and could be displayed in, for example, a shopping mall. With that in mind, our project team thought about possibilities for creating this but at the same time making it empirically testable. However, there was one major problem to deal with: 'the public'. Several attempts to define the public as a whole have been made (Burns *et al.* 2003) but lead us to the conclusion that this is a difficult task since there are too many factors influencing an audience with such an extremely wide range of background knowledge, interests, attitudes, etc. In order to reduce the undertaking to a scale manageable in a PhD thesis, we needed to limit the sample size, and my plan of creating and testing an interactive exhibition on NST in a shopping mall vanished. From an outreach perspective the shopping mall was the perfect place to attract the attention of people who did not even know that NST might be of interest to them. From a research point of view, this seemed to be 'uncontrollable'. So we decided to keep the exhibition as an eye-catcher that disseminates information and activates awareness about NST in the public, but to focus on the student lab for empirical research.

Refining the research questions

In order to be able to compare researchers' and students' perspectives, it is necessary to elaborate both sides of the coin. That channels the research and the design of out-of-school learning environments (students' lab, exhibition) together with its multimedia learning tools (podcast, app, presentations, etc.) in a constant flow of evaluation back and forth.

Generating and discussing research questions over and over again, from all those questions lying on the table, finally I could pin down the following basic research questions for my PhD:

1   Which aspects of authentic (Nano) science are pointed out by researchers?
2   How do they match or contrast beliefs of students?
3   Which effects on students' beliefs can be measured by different means of science communication?

But with this process going on, and month after month quickly passing by, the challenges of my own PhD project became clear and can be summarised as a package of several general components: a) Keep the goals and aims of the outreach project in mind, b) find a structure for the PhD project that includes the personal research interests, c) gather a theoretical background of research (literature), and d) create a test instrument to gather empirical data for later analysis. But probably most important: make an organised project plan, set deadlines and stick to it!

Working on study two: the public's/students' views

For the second study, an authentic environment had to be developed for training and testing the students, giving them an idea of what Nano science is like, in terms of scientific content, Nature of science (NOS) and Nature of scientists (NoST).

Authentic science – what is that?

Braund and Reiss (2006) carved out five characteristics of science that should be communicated in out-of-school settings like students' labs and that can be applied to NST in order to give an authentic image of NST: First, basic concepts of NST should be developed and integrated into the learning activity, next to the extended and authentic practical work that students carry out themselves. The lab should be a place with social outcomes such as collaborative work and responsibility for learning (Braund and Reiss 2006). What makes out-of-school settings like student labs unique and thus necessary for understanding NST is the access to rare material and to contemporary science. Rare materials in this case are instruments or substances that are used in particular contemporary research and not a simplified experimental set-up as in school.

Besides the NST content (as Stevens *et al.* [2009] defined) we wanted to disseminate the hows and whys of research in order to contribute to a more authentic experience for the students in the lab. Yet few people even know what research is being conducted, much less understand why it is being done and what the potential implications may be. This is a critical shortcoming of our public information system. Given the frenetic pace of science research in multi-disciplinary fields, it is increasingly vital that the public are made aware of new findings in a coherent manner (Field and Powell 2001). So the communication of NST should also present an authentic perspective of science and what it really is in order to build a generation of scientific literate citizens.

Development of a students' lab program on NST

Those findings in the literature motivated me to pull out the idea of an out-of-school students' lab program that was built for lower secondary school students, since most of them had little or no contact with scientific topics. These 'rough diamonds' could be shaped by bringing them into contact with science in a manner they would enjoy. Looking back at my own experiences with science in school, raising curiosity and interest became a personal mission during the development of this program.

Meanwhile I had developed my own perception of authenticity that included aspects of authentic out-of-school learning (Braund and Reiss 2006) together with multimedia theory and scientific content of the Collaborative Research Center. I also saw the emerging need for visits to out-of-school learning environments for schools since they provide another stimulus for scientific interest (Lucas *et al.* 1986). Those visits allow student learning to happen in a natural way, that is, by allowing personal interest and curiosity to drive the students' learning, not only will students be gaining more from their excursion, they have the opportunity of practicing scientific investigative processes (Griffin 1998). The latter became one of the foci during the research – showing secondary school students how science really works!

When you hear that something is authentic, it means something positive, that something is not fake. I have read a lot on authenticity – but bringing the big ideas back to the practical floor of a student lab is challenging: can a person be authentic? Or a thing? Is authenticity a subjective perception of a person or is it something that everybody agrees on? I could not stop asking myself these questions because I found it hard to juggle scientific content, the nature of science and the perceptions of the students, trying to make it look as something recognisable to kids who may not have thought about science yet. How could I combine scientific methods/results in NST with NOS aspects as validity of science and personal skills in order to give the students insight into science as an endeavour?

These questions led me to more fundamental thinking about the intentions of my work and my personal aims in this journey. I realised that I not only want to carry out the research, but remind myself of what brought me into this field of science – the urge to be a communicator between different worlds. While designing the student lab program I realised that I had to step back from my analytical work on the research side and think myself into the minds of the students visiting the lab, participating in my program and (hopefully) getting some of the ideas I wanted to teach them – and thus in the end help me gather reasonable data for my study.

It took me a while to combine the findings on the characteristics of NST and the core content necessary to teach NST in out-of school settings with the specific research projects of the CRC. The next step, to didactically reconstruct this content and process it into fitting media for the setting of students' labs, was almost as demanding as the first.

Empirical framework and study design

For knitting the loose ends together and trying to fit the project aims into my research interest, I still needed a model that could combine all these aspects. The difficulty here was the variety of aspects that needed to be covered. We had science communication aspects (the how-to) as well as aspects defined by the setting (the where-to) in order to design out-of-school learning environments, we had the scientific content and we wanted to build on the public's perception of NST. Models for each category could be found but only the Model of Educational Reconstruction (MER) by Duit *et al.* 2012 seemed to merge all these aspects. Literature research and talks to experts both in NST and science education showed that the MER could serve as a suitable framework where all aspects could be covered. Also in the context of NST, the MER had proved effective as a foundation in teaching NST to students.

The MER combines three different domains:

1   the scientific clarification
2   the comprehension of students' perspectives
3   the design of learning environments.

Since the MER is used for both – the construction of outreach content and activities, and research – the three domains are in a constant back and forth flow in order to create and maintain scientific correct and up-to-date information on NST (Figure 10.1). If we look at the different sections of the model, we have the two perspectives mentioned earlier: the interviewed researchers [left] reflect the scientific clarification and students [right] reflect the students' comprehension of the scientific context. The knowledge gathered on these two sides is based on empirical research. From the results gathered in both studies, learning environments such as the students' lab and the exhibition have been built. This latter section represents the outreach content and activities.

Applying the model to the outreach project, the scientific clarification side of the model represents the experts' views, in my case the views of the researchers on NST. This side has been investigated by my first study (study one, see above) interviewing researchers at Kiel University and at the University of Helsinki.

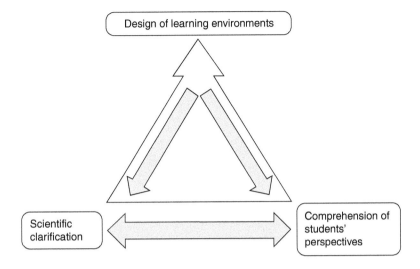

Figure 10.1 Model of Educational Reconstruction (MER), representing a constant flow of knowledge and adaptions between the three dimensions

Comprehension of students' perspectives

The questionnaires for testing the students' comprehension were built using scales from existing instruments in order to test for the NOS-comprehension of the students. The written task assessments at each working station and the working stations in the lab were influenced by the practical experiences on the topics used in the 'Klick!-Lab' for upper secondary school students. I transformed the content to a more understandable level for younger children and applied the NOS aspects from literature, such as validity (Urhahne *et al.* 2011) and relevance of sciences (Frey *et al.* 2006), skills and tasks of researchers (Wentorf, Chapter 8, this book) and communication and goals of research (Urhahne *et al.* 2011).

Design of learning environments

Before I could test the perceptions of the students, the lab program had to be designed and tested. The existing lab program for upper secondary school students (grades 11–13), the 'Klick!-Lab', demanded a high level of self-sufficient work. The program designed for my study is designed for lower secondary school students, (grades 8–10) and given a new name: the 'Junior-Klick!-Lab'. Due to a younger target group with a lower scientific knowledge, the program was structured differently with a higher interaction between students and explainers at each work station. The program contains seven working stations where the students experiment themselves and learn about NST, methods, content and technique, but also about the NoS. What does it mean to be a scientist? How do they work? The working stations reflect ongoing research in the CRC and use similar techniques such as an Atomic Force Microscope (AFM) which is frequently used in NST analysis. The classes visited the laboratory for half a day, with students rotating through experimental and non-experimental work stations in a given order, so every student completed all seven stations. The students' perceptions were evaluated with a paper-pencil test before and after the lab visit and lay the foundation for quantitative results in the second study of my PhD.

Analyses of students' perspectives before and after a visit to the Junior-Klick!-Lab

The questionnaire was designed with a 4-point-Likert-scale and included items on NoS, the validity of scientific methods and results, and beliefs on skills and characteristics of scientists (NoSt). Some items were newly developed, whereas others had been taken from existing instruments, like the beliefs on NoS. Questions targeting the NoSt aspects have been used from Wilfried Wentorf's study on 'Planspiel Wissenschaft' (see Chapter 8 of this book). Those questionnaires are currently analysed quantitatively. Additionally, the students filled in a written work assessment at each working station, containing two questions: one on the content, and one on the displayed aspect of NoS. These will be analysed qualitatively by Masters' student research projects.

Since study organisation is a topic not usually mentioned in research papers, I briefly want to address this issue here – since this also takes a significant amount of your PhD working time. It takes a lot of preparation to gather data in an intervention study as presented here: I needed seven student-explainers for each visit, including myself, who would survey one working station each and help to carry out the experiments with the students. In order to test a representative sample, I needed between 150–200 students, which resulted in seven classes ranging in size from 16–31 students. After having contacted the teachers at schools throughout the area of the state, a date needed to be found for both, the teachers and the lab side. Once I had the confirmation of both, I started 'hiring' the teacher-students, which meant large mailing lists and constant recruiting during seminars at the IPN and private canvassing. Here the problem was that the student-explainers helped me because they were nice or because they wanted to gather some more experience with children outside the school. But they did not get anything in return such as credit points for their study. I was dependent on their good will and their flexibility with spontaneous dates which I am still very grateful for! If 'my students' were not already old hands at it, I needed to meet and brief the new recruits before each visit and give them a tour through the lab and background information on their working station, instructing all of them the same way so they would be coherent in their explaining, leading to steady research conditions. Last but not least, the visiting classes need to be kept under control during their visit in order to participate in the research. I also had to obtain permission from the government, the school headmasters and the parents.

Outlook and conclusions for practice

Developing research results into outreach activities

Ultimately, the results from the interviews combined with theories on Multimedia and Museology together with some preliminary results of the students' beliefs on NoS, built the base of an exhibition on Nanoscience and research in a shopping mall in Kiel, the podcasts on Nanoscience in the CRC, as well as the 'Junior-Klick!-Lab' for lower secondary students. One should note that, as mentioned earlier, the three perspectives of the MER and thus for the different aspects of the outreach project itself are not evolving linearly but influence and interact with each other. This creates a dynamic field that allows knowledge and action to be in perpetual movement. The model has proved to be well fitted for the aim of this project and will be used in future outreach work.

Making research results available for the scientific community

Concerning my own research, I am currently writing an article on the results of the interview study which had been analysed further after the development of categories for the outreach measures, based on a framework of the Qualitative Content Analysis. The next step will then be the quantitative analysis of the student questionnaires, resulting in a publication on students beliefs on NST.

My personal conclusions

Ultimately, the question arises: What is all this for? Why is it so important to connect science and society in a more active way? The answer is simple: Science is awesome! And science is an essential part of our life no matter if we are interested in it or not. Every scientist, regardless of which field he or she is working in, will agree with that. But what about the rest of the world? What if they don't know it yet? And what if this is not due to a lack of 'nerdiness' but just due to an incorrect and dusty image of science? Those questions highlight even more the need for communication and outreach on highly relevant scientific topics from all fields of science. Outreach steps in where school ends, trying to broaden horizons and inform the public (including school students) about ongoing research. It offers citizens an opportunity to keep pace with rapidly developing science and supports the constant growth of a scientific literate society. So hopefully, this research can contribute to connecting worlds, science and the public and stimulate a broader interest in and motivation for NST and science in general.

Acknowledgement

Funded by the German Research Foundation, the Federal Government of Education and Research.

References

Braund, M. and Reiss, M. (2006). 'Towards a More Authentic Science Curriculum: The Contribution of Out of school Learning'. *International Journal of Science Education* 28(12): 1373–88.

Burns, T., O'Connor, D. and Stocklmayer, S. (2003). 'Science Communication: A Contemporary Definition'. *Public Understanding of Science* 12: 183–202.

Duit, R., Gropengießer, H., Kattmann, U., Komorek, M. and Parchmann, I. (2012). *The Model of Educational Reconstruction – A Framework for Improving Teaching and Learning Science.* Rotterdam: Sense Publisher.

Falk, J. and Storksdieck, M. (2005). 'Using the Contextual Model of Learning to Understand Visitor Learning from a Science Center Exhibition'. *Science Education* 89(5): 744–78.

Field, H. and Powell, P. (2001). 'Public Understanding of Science Versus Public Understanding of Research'. *Public Understanding of Science* 10(4): 421–6.

Frey, A., Taskinen, P. and Schütte, K. (2006) *PISA Skalenhandbuch–Dokumentation der Erhebungsinstrumente.* Münster: Waxmann-Verlag.

Griffin, J. (1998). 'Learning Science through Practical Experiences in Museums'. *International Journal of Science Education,* 20(6): 655–63.

Laherto, A. (2011). 'Incorporating Nanoscale Science and Technology into Secondary School Curriculum: Views of Nano-trained Science Teachers'. *Nordic Studies in Science Education* 7(2): 126–39.

Lee, H.-S. and Butler, N. (2003). 'Making Authentic Science Accessible to Students'. *International Journal of Science Education* 25(8): 923–48.

Lucas, A.M., McManus, P. and Thomas, G. (1986). 'Investigating Learning from Informal Sources: Listening to Conversations and Observing Play in Science Museums'. *European Journal of Science Education* 8(4): 341–52.

Moreno, R. and Mayer, R. (2007). 'Interactive Multimodal Learning Environments. Special Issue on Interactive Learning Environments: Contemporary Issues and Trends'. *Educational Psychology Review* 19(3): 309–26.

Rennie, L. and Stocklmayr, S. (2003). 'The Communication of Science and Technology: Past, Present and Future Agendas'. *International Journal of Science Education* 25(6): 759–73.

Schwartz, R. and Lederman, N. (2008). 'What Scientists Say: Scientists' Views of Nature of Science and Relation to Science Context'. *International Journal of Science Education* 30(6): 727–71.

Stevens, S., Sutherland, L., and Krajcik, J. (2009). *The Big Ideas of Nanoscale Science and Engineering.* Arlington, VA: NSTA Press.

Urhahne, D., Kremer, K. and Mayer, J. (2011). 'Conceptions of the Nature of Science – Are they General or Context Specific?' *International Journal of Science and Mathematics Education* 9(3): 707–30.

11 Finding and elaborating frameworks for analysing context-based chemistry problems

Karolina Broman

The opportunity to set out on the research journey reported in this chapter began when funding became available from the Faculty of Teacher Education at the university to support doctoral research for teacher educators, something requested from the Swedish National Agency for Higher Education. As a teacher and teacher educator of chemistry, this funding offered me the possibility to explore and investigate interesting issues that had arisen in the course of my career. Even as a university student, I had noticed the disparity between those, like myself, who were interested in chemistry, and those who found the subject boring and difficult. When starting as a PhD student, I began to engage in the literature, and I found several publications describing students' opinion of their school chemistry as something boring, difficult, meaningless, not interesting and irrelevant for the individual's future (e.g. Osborne *et al.* 2003; Osborne and Dillon 2008). This extremely negative picture was not something I had observed as a teacher in upper secondary school and I found it depressing to read so much that focused on problems in science education. The literature made me curious and I wanted to investigate the situation from another perspective. My experience as a chemistry teacher had been more positive and therefore it seemed useful to find out and share more about what upper secondary school students think about their chemistry education from a research perspective. The choice to investigate upper secondary students was primarily made as I had experience from this level as a practitioner. Furthermore, investigating the ideas from the group of potential future scientists seemed important as this group of students form the pool of those applying for university studies within natural science, and understanding their views and increasing their interest is an issue important to society (Osborne and Dillon 2008).

Developing a research focus

The early readings of literature suggested that both cognitive and affective aspects of chemistry are important in students' learning experiences, and in line with these ideas I began the research process by conducting a small empirical study using a questionnaire (Broman *et al.* 2011). I used this survey to explore students' thoughts about content areas being more or less interesting and more or less easy, about working methods in class, and about students' opinions about how to improve school chemistry to make it more meaningful. From this survey and from a follow-up questionnaire (Broman and Simon 2014), I found that upper secondary school students and their teachers were quite satisfied with their chemistry education experience, however students asked for more laboratory work and more connections to everyday life, a result in line with the literature (e.g. Osborne and Collins 2001).

With this result in mind I continued reading about chemistry teaching and learning, and was particularly interested by the *International Journal of Science Education* (*IJSE*) special issue featuring context-based learning (CBL) approaches (Pilot and Bulte 2006a). The projects reported in that special issue came from the UK, US, Netherlands, Israel and Germany and have been influential in guiding my work. In the beginning, I used the authors' names to find more to read, and also decided to go to conferences to listen to the people behind the research. This made it possible to find an international arena for my future work. From that special issue, I also followed up references to build a theoretical background and to broaden my reading. One example, a book on CBL called *Making it Relevant* (Nentwig and Waddington 2005) provided a broader and more diverse description of different CBL projects. From this I have understood both the benefits as well as the difficulties when doing research on CBL approaches, as one underlying problem is the definition of CBL, and the notion of what context really stands for.

I learned about the difficulty of switching between the broad perspective of a teacher and the focused perspective of a researcher, which has not always been easy to handle. Even though my supervisors tried to guide me into thinking as a researcher, my teacher background made me ask many incoherent questions, mainly since I was interested in students' opinions about totally divergent areas, for instance their ideas about chemistry teachers, their school chemistry, their educational choice and their chemistry content knowledge.

The construction of research questions was a difficult task; my teacher background made them very broad. To think as a researcher and be focused and structured has been challenging, since this forced me to leave aside questions I found interesting but were, however, too broad to investigate. One of the first research questions I asked was for a comprehensive picture: how does a context-based approach influence teaching and learning chemistry in Swedish upper secondary school chemistry classrooms? Only further on in the process, the questions have been narrowed down and specified to make them researchable (see Bounce and Cole 2008).

In developing a research focus when starting off as a teacher and teacher educator, I also noticed that words like attitude, motivation and learning I had used in everyday life as a teacher began to imply more explicit things. In the beginning I struggled with these words, for instance, I found it problematic using the word 'attitude' in my first two exploratory studies (Broman *et al.* 2011; Broman and Simon 2014) since I know there are so many ideas about what this word means and how it relates to several theoretical frameworks (e.g. Fishbein and Ajzen 1975). The Swedish translation 'attityd' is used in everyday life as something more general and broader. However, reading and talking about research also made me aware of the importance of clarifying what I mean by the terms I use. In my project, the notion of 'context' is very important to explicitly define and use in a stringent way. Since this is a very common word in research implying different things, the reading of other research literature sometimes made me insecure about the interpretation of the term. The reading of CBL literature has provided me with two definitions of context that I use in my research project. Both definitions emphasise the need for applying the chemistry content in everyday life: 'a learning context requires relating learning to an *application* in the real world' (Whitelegg and Parry 1999: 68), and the context 'is the red thread along which the investigation of the issue in the question develops' (Nentwig *et al.* 2007: 1441). These definitions have been in my mind when designing my studies to make sure that the context is not only a shallow decoration added to the 'real' chemistry.

Specifying the research focus from further engagement in the literature

After acquiring a broad background picture of the research field of CBL, I went back to the *IJSE* special issue to find more concrete ways to move forward. Of particular interest was the final paper in the issue (Pilot and Bulte 2006b), which was a review with an outlook suggesting areas for future research and where I could see value for my project ideas. There are two aspects specifically important from these authors' point of view that I have emphasised in my research: 1) Knowledge about items for assessment and the design of adequate tasks, and how to analyse students' response to these tasks. This knowledge is necessary to make assessment in accordance with new higher order learning aims (Pilot and Bulte 2006b: 1107); 2) Knowledge about what contexts are appreciated by students and how the settings relate to conceptual learning of chemistry (Pilot and Bulte 2006b: 1109). This final paper was a concrete example of reading that really foregrounds my research, helping me to describe my issue and to move further, developing a more fine-grained theoretical and analytical framework.

From reading research papers on CBL approaches, I understood that these approaches have been introduced as a way to both raise students' interest as well as offering ways to connect different content knowledge by combining relevant areas into an entity from where the teaching emanates, i.e. the context. Previous research highlights positive impact regarding students' interest, attitudes and motivation, whereas results on students' cognitive learning outcomes are more ambiguous to interpret (Bennett *et al.* 2007). One focal point is that CBL sets a demand for higher order thinking as the subject-matter knowledge is embedded in different contexts. As a consequence, the learners have to identify the chemical aspect within an often more complex problem and also have to apply chemical knowledge to solve a certain task. This understanding has led me to appreciate the methodological demands of problem-solving strategies and task demands in general, and led me to explore the specific challenges of CBL. I have used frameworks for systematising these demands as the foundation for subsequent empirical studies; my research consists of two parts relating to the two aspects from the *IJSE* special issue. The first aspect concerns cognitive parts regarding design of context-based problems aiming for higher order thinking and analysis of students' responses to these tasks. In this chapter I will present my work elaborating frameworks possible for use in the analysis of students' responses on context-based problems. The structured design of more context-based tasks, analysis of the problem-solving process using think-aloud interviews, and the affective parts mentioned in the second aspect discussing students' perceived interest, relevance and difficulty regarding these context-based problems are previously published (Broman and Parchmann 2014; Parchmann *et al.* 2015; Broman *et al.* 2015).

How to investigate problem-solving strategies? Elaborating a methodological approach

When taking PhD courses, there was much discussion about methods, and I realised that it was important to learn more about different methods as a PhD student. Therefore I wanted to practice doing more in-depth research, something besides questionnaires. In the planning of my first problem-solving study, I focused on finding more qualitative ways to investigate upper secondary school chemistry to get an overview of a larger cohort of students. The results of my two exploratory studies (Broman *et al.* 2011; Broman and Simon 2014) and my reading on CBL approaches led me to the idea of observing CBL before investigating it any further, so I asked two teachers who agreed to bring CBL approaches into the classroom. They were willing to have me there doing observations and interviews, one class in the autumn semester, the other in the spring. The idea was to see what happens in the classroom when a new approach focusing on everyday life is implemented.

To introduce the CBL approach, I applied for a grant to buy context-based textbooks for all students, the Swedish Salters' version (Engström *et al.* 2001), and started observing the first class. I stayed there for two and a half months for all chemistry lessons involving the content area of organic chemistry. The observation part was very interesting, perhaps mainly since I used to teach exactly the same course when I worked as a teacher.

However, even though the teacher was very competent and appreciated by the students, I realised that the teacher taught as she always had done; there was nothing explicitly context-based. The Salters' book was not used substantially and the connection to everyday life was no more obvious than earlier. In interviews afterwards, the teacher agreed that it was difficult to do something new without more guidance. As a consequence, there was little to investigate from the classroom observations, as not much context-based focus was observable. As a former chemistry teacher, this was an understandable result; to change teaching when you are an experienced teacher needs more guidance than someone asking for a change. As a researcher, it was nevertheless unsatisfactory to understand that my observations and my field-notes had been a time-consuming part of my study from which it was impossible to draw many conclusions. However, the time spent in the classroom was not wasted; it was important to take part in a chemistry classroom as an observer, not as a teacher or teacher educator. This complex and broad view of the classroom situation has been helpful for me to look at chemistry education in a more objective way, not simply relating my picture of school chemistry to my own experience.

My original research question as mentioned earlier (i.e. how does a context-based approach influence teaching and learning chemistry in Swedish upper secondary school chemistry classrooms?) was too broad; however at that time, I was not aware of the problem. To pose researchable research questions after a long background as a teacher has perhaps been one of the most difficult parts in the doctoral process, it was only after collecting the data and starting the analysis that it became apparent that the question was too broad.

A first change in direction

In the outlook paper of the *IJSE* special issue (Pilot and Bulte 2006b) and in a qualitative in-depth review about CBL (Bennett *et al.* 2007), an upcoming concern was that there was a need for research in terms of learning outcomes related to assessment, as most of the studies reviewed were conducted in countries with more conventional assessment in national tests and where students performed better on test items resembling the style of the course they took. Since Swedish upper secondary schools have no national tests in chemistry, there was a possibility to continue my research and work with teachers who could adjust their assessment. When there was time for the test in organic chemistry in the class I had observed, the teacher agreed to bring in ten context-based problems I had developed. These problems are not simple algorithmic tasks; they are broad and open and demand higher order cognitive skills, i.e. more than just rote memorisation and recall (Salta and Tzougraki 2011). This gave me students' written answers on 38 test items, both more conventional tasks as well as context-based problems (Broman *et al.* 2015).

After reading the written answers through, I found one of the context-based problems, considering the medical drug Tamiflu, worth working with further. The specific context-based problem dealt with swine flu, very much reported on in media at the time of collecting data (in the school year 2010–11). The problem consisted of a molecular structure of Tamiflu and was asking for both a description of the molecule and its chemical properties, and an explanation of why the drug spreads in the environment. The reason for selecting this task was that the students' responses were broad, diverse and various, not only presenting simple recall of memorised facts. In retrospect, this choice to only continue analysing one of the ten context-based tasks limited the following analysis since there are difficulties when drawing general conclusions from only one task.

From the students' written responses, I decided to go further and to interview nine students from the class two weeks after the test about how they solved this specific task. When compared to students' written responses, the interview data gave in-depth information on the process of problem-solving, both on how the students themselves tackled the task, and how hints from the interviewer can help students develop their problem-solving competence. Moreover, to compare the students' problem-solving strategies with experts, five chemistry professors were also asked to solve the Tamiflu task. These interview results are previously published (Parchmann *et al.* 2015).

Unfortunately, in the Christmas holiday, the second teacher who I was going to observe contacted me and informed that he was going to leave his job, making it impossible to investigate the second class. This changed the prerequisites, and I had to think of new alternatives. The ability to adjust the research plan has been an important aspect to handle as a PhD student; when you work with people as you do in the educational sciences, many things can happen to disrupt the plan. This has sometimes felt frustrating, especially when empirical data has become difficult to use. On the other hand, this gave me the opportunity to reconsider the project together with my supervisors, something now in hindsight I find favourable.

Since the cognitive domain of learning has always interested me, I started reading about problem solving and the idea to continue with in-depth analysis of the Tamiflu task and scrutinise it further felt appealing. From this representative context-based problem I had the opportunity to elaborate both a framework for analysing student responses and also to develop new context-based tasks designed with a clear structure for use in the subsequent study (Broman and Parchmann 2014).

Refining the focus on problem solving

To supplement the written answers of the Tamiflu task from 26 students in one class, other teachers were asked to append the task to their examination. This gave me more empirical data (i.e. 236 written answers, nine student interviews, five expert interviews and the ordinary test with answers from the class I observed) to analyse. By continuous reading about problem solving, and consulting with my supervisors, the decision was to elaborate an analytical problem-solving framework, possible to use when analysing context-based problems. Thus a framework was elaborated step-by-step (Broman *et al.* 2015) which was possible to use both for designing new tasks as well as analysing students' responses to the tasks (Broman and Parchmann 2014). During this process, my own picture of what a framework actually *does* for research has evolved, and the awareness of the need for having a suitable framework to construct researchable questions has been influential.

From both my experience as a chemistry teacher and from in-depth reading of literature regarding problem solving, it is clear that problem solving is a fundamental part of chemistry education. Since the beginning of science education research, the area of problem solving has been challenging for researchers since students show several difficulties in the area. Students tend to apply algorithmic approaches when solving problems (Cartrette and Bodner 2010) and find it problematic to transfer their common algorithmic problem-solving strategies to unfamiliar conceptual problems (Salta and Tzougraki 2011). This made me aware of the relationship between different skills used in the problem-solving process, and made me search for frameworks describing different kinds of skills.

In addition to the skills students need to solve the problem, the problems in themselves need to be analysed. Since these context-based problems connect different content areas, in this case organic chemistry and chemical bonding, it was important to investigate how students transfer content knowledge from one area to another. To transfer, in other words to apply knowledge and skills in new learning contexts, is considered difficult for students (Zoller and Levy Nahum 2012). The difficulties of transferring knowledge and the use of varying contexts for the application of knowledge sets high demands on students, even though these concerns are not specific for CBL approaches. Hence, the focus in my doctoral project is to explore frameworks possible to use to analyse both the demands of different tasks and of different strategies that students apply to solve problems in general, or context-based tasks in particular.

Finding and elaborating frameworks for problem solving and transfer

In my own teacher education, I encountered some broad frameworks for learning, such as Bloom's taxonomy, that have been applicable when working as a teacher and teacher educator. When emphasising research, it was important to find frameworks suitable to explicitly analyse context-based problems, both regarding the tasks in themselves, as well as students' responses. When studying as a PhD student, more focused frameworks like the Higher Order/Lower Order Cognitive Skills (HOCS/LOCS) taxonomy or the Model of Hierarchical Complexity in Chemistry (MHC-C) have been explored.

The HOCS/LOCS framework by Zoller and Dori (2002) can be derived from Bloom's taxonomy to classify learning objectives within cognitive processes (i.e. remember, understand, apply, analyse, evaluate and create). The first three cognitive processes are defined as LOCS, whereas the three last cognitive processes are HOCS. Common LOCS are traditional rote memorisation, recall and algorithmic teaching which give students the idea that every chemistry question always has 'one correct' answer (Leou *et al.* 2006), something I often reflected on as a practitioner. My previous students had often commented that chemistry tasks had correct answers given in the solution pages at the end of the textbook. This idea of chemistry as a subject with only correct or incorrect responses to problems fits badly with chemistry as a research area (Smith 2011). Problem solving and transfer are examples of HOCS (Zoller and Levy Nahum 2012) and since HOCS are a challenge for students, they need to be practiced as students are not used to applying HOCS as often as LOCS. Avargil and colleagues (2012) illustrate the benefits for students by combining CBL approaches with HOCS.

Besides the skills students need to solve the tasks, a framework for analysing the complexity of tasks has been explored: the MHC-C (Bernholt and Parchmann 2011). This framework gave me new ideas on how to proceed with the analysis since the model reflects fundamental aims of science education, for example to explore how students are able to describe and explain scientific phenomena. In the MHC-C, five levels of hierarchical complexity have been defined for school chemistry: everyday experiences, facts, processes, linear causality, and multivariate interdependencies (Bernholt and Parchmann 2011). Compared to the HOCS/LOCS-dichotomy, the MHC-C offers a system of categories to describe task demands in a more fine-grained and content-bound way, and I found this framework suitable to elaborate further in combination with the HOCS/LOCS framework. Regarding context-based problems and related students' problem-solving strategies, both the differentiation between HOCS and LOCS, and the MHC-C seemed to be promising frameworks for analysing students' more or less successful approaches to solve context-based problems in a systematic way.

Furthermore, I also had to relate the analysis to the chemistry syllabus (Swedish National Agency for Education 2000) since the content-side of the task demands had to be considered. Even though both the HOCS/LOCS and the MHC-C frameworks comprise the range from correct to incorrect, students might solve the problem on a high cognitive level and show complex causal reasoning, however the answer is totally wrong from a scientific point of view. As a consequence, the analysis of students' responses had to be done in three steps: according to the syllabus for content knowledge, according to HOCS/LOCS for students' skills and the quality of the process, and according to MHC-C for an integration of cognitive aspects from the content of subject matter and of the context (Broman *et al.* 2015).

The emerging research questions and refined methodology

When elaborating frameworks possible to use for identifying and characterising students' approaches to solving one exemplary context-based problem, the research questions had to be refined to fit the aim of my doctoral work. At this time I had narrowed my original research question to one focusing on students' solving of context-based problems and their movement from lower to higher order thinking. By refining the issue investigated, the methodology also had to be refined.

The subsequent investigation was carried out in Swedish upper secondary schools with students (aged 18–19 years old) at the end of the Natural Science Programme. The programme has compulsory chemistry courses preparing students to continue chemistry training at university level; in other words, possible future scientists. It was a positive experience to go back and meet similar students to those I worked with as a teacher, even though this time I had to think like a researcher, not a teacher. The teaching supplied students with content knowledge but did not give them regular opportunities to apply that knowledge in different contexts, as shown from the aforementioned classroom observations. However, there was a very positive classroom environment with a dedicated teacher and satisfied students.

Conclusions from the Tamiflu study

To completely solve the Tamiflu task, both description and reasoning was requested from the students; however the analysis mainly shows LOCS-focused description strategies and the two lowest MHC-C levels. Even though the empirical data contained 236 written responses to the context-based task, and the responses were highlighting scattered solutions, it was apparent that the study had evident restrictions. When summarising students' written answers to the Tamiflu task (Broman *et al.* 2015), it was obvious that this empirical explorative study was too limited to draw conclusions on students' problem-solving strategies, although it did give me ideas on how to proceed in my next study. First of all, one item was not enough and therefore 15 new context-based problems have been systematically designed (Broman and Parchmann 2014). Second, to investigate the problem-solving process, in-depth semi-structured interviews using think-aloud techniques with my teacher experience as an interviewer would get a more in-depth picture of the process (Parchmann *et al.* 2015). Finally, to combine cognitive and affective parts to both investigate students' perceived interest, relevance and difficulty in combination with their problem solving is a way to hopefully get a more comprehensive picture of CBL.

When analysing items from a chemistry test and students' responses to one representative context-based problem, I have reflected on many parts. When looking at the empirical data from the Tamiflu study, it has been obvious that students show difficulties transferring their chemistry content knowledge when asked to answer more open problems with an everyday life context. There are probably several reasons for this, principally that to remember factual knowledge is a skill students are familiar with from many years in school. From the analysis of all items in the test, it was apparent that the focus is on LOCS questions; this is what students are accustomed to. When students get a task where they cannot give the correct answer at once, they try to remember something from the textbook or something the teacher has said. This emphasis on LOCS makes it problematic for students to deal with context-based problems like the Tamiflu task. From my teaching experience, this focus on LOCS and factual knowledge is nothing new; however, when looking at this from a researcher's perspective, it is not enough to just claim there is a need for a paradigm shift from LOCS to HOCS. Both teachers and students require assistance on concrete ways to make this change in school chemistry. Hopefully, my experience as both a teacher, teacher educator and PhD student can be applicable in assisting school chemistry to develop into a subject, both relevant to students and with a focus on students' higher order thinking, not just on rote memorisation of factual knowledge.

Reflections on shifting from practitioner to researcher

When reflecting on the shift from being a teacher to becoming a researcher and to summarise my PhD journey, it is evident that the transition is not without resistance. In the beginning everything felt interesting and I wanted to investigate so many different parts of chemistry education. I asked questions related to many different areas; I wanted to get a comprehensive picture and was unfortunately not systematic and focused enough. Both the theoretical and analytical frameworks are essential parts of research and are underlying the work with constructing good and researchable questions. I first have to pose the questions to myself, find the important focused issue, and thereafter I can do the research. In the beginning I was too eager to go out and collect data that has proven difficult to handle mainly since I was not systematic enough. The planning phase is more important than I ever thought at the beginning of my time as a PhD student. Therefore, I feel much more confident with my second CBL-study since I have been working in a much more structured way and have been systematic in the planning phase, also finding a more narrow focus of my study. This makes me hopeful to finalise my PhD student journey from being a teacher to becoming a researcher, even though I still hope to use my teaching experience both as a teacher educator as well as a researcher.

References

Avargil, S., Herscovitz, O. and Dori, Y.J. (2012). 'Teaching Thinking Skills in Context-based Learning: Teachers' Challenges and Assessment Knowledge'. *Journal of Science Education and Technology* 21(2): 207–25.

Bennett, J., Lubben, F. and Hogarth, S. (2007). 'Bringing Science to Life: A Synthesis of the Research Evidence on the Effects of Context-based and STS Approaches to Science Teaching'. *Science Education* 91(3): 347–70.

Bernholt, S. and Parchmann, I. (2011). 'Assessing the Complexity of Students' Knowledge in Chemistry'. *Chemistry Education Research and Practice* 12(2): 167–73.

Bounce, D.M. and Cole, R.S. (2008). *Nuts and Bolts of Chemical Education Research.* Washington DC: American Chemical Society.

Broman, K. and Parchmann, I. (2014). 'Students' Application of Chemical Concepts when Solving Chemistry Problems in Different Contexts'. *Chemistry Education Research and Practice* 15(4): 516–29.

Broman, K. and Simon, S. (2014). 'Upper Secondary School Students' Choice and Their Ideas on How to Improve Chemistry Education'. *International Journal of Science and Mathematics Education.* doi: 10.1007/s10763-014-9550-0.

Broman, K., Ekborg, M. and Johnels, D. (2011). 'Chemistry in Crisis? Perspectives on Teaching and Learning Chemistry in Swedish Upper Secondary Schools'. *Nordic Studies in Science Education* 7(1): 43–60.

Broman, K., Bernholt, S. and Parchmann, I. (2015). 'Analysing Task Design and Students' Responses to Context-based Problems through Different Analytical Frameworks'. *Research in Science & Technological Education.* 33(2): 143–61.

Cartrette, D.P. and Bodner, G.M. (2010). 'Non-mathematical Problem Solving in Organic Chemistry'. *Journal of Research in Science Teaching* 47(6): 643–60.

Engström, C., Backlund, P., Berger, R. and Grennberg, H. (2001). *Kemi B. Tema & teori. [Chemistry B. Theme & Theory].* Stockholm: Bonnier Utbildning.

Fishbein, M. and Ajzen, I. (1975). *Belief, Attitude, Intention and Behavior: An Introduction to Theory and Research.* Reading: Addison-Wesley Publishing Company.

Leou, M., Abder, P., Riordan, M. and Zoller, U. (2006). 'Using "HOCS-Centered Learning" as a Pathway to Promote Science Teachers' Metacognitive Development'. *Research in Science Education* 36(1–2): 69–84.

Nentwig, P., Demuth, R., Parchmann, I., Gräsel, C. and Ralle, B. (2007). '*Chemie im Kontext:* Situated Learning in Relevant Contexts while Systematically Developing Basic Chemical Concepts'. *Journal of Chemical Education* 84(9): 1439–44.

Nentwig, P. and Waddington, D. (eds) (2005). *Making it Relevant: Context-based Learning of Science.* Münster: Waxmann.

Osborne, J. and Collins, S. (2001). 'Pupils' Views of the Role and Value of the Science Curriculum: A Focus-group Study'. *International Journal of Science Education* 23(5): 441–67.

Osborne, J. and Dillon, J. (2008). *Science Education in Europe: Critical Reflections. A Report to the Nuffield Foundation.* London: King's College.

Osborne, J., Simon, S. and Collins, S. (2003). 'Attitudes Towards Science: A Review of the Literature and its Implications'. *International Journal of Science Education* 25(9): 1049–79.

Parchmann, I., Broman, K., Busker, M. and Rudnik, J. (2015). 'Context-based Learning on School and University Level'. In: Garcia-Martinez, J. and Serrano-

Torregrosa, E. (eds), *Chemistry Education: Best Practices, Innovative Strategies and New Technologies*. Weinheim: Wiley-VCH, pp. 259–78.

Pilot, A. and Bulte, A.M.W. (2006a). *International Journal of Science Education Special Issue: Context-based Chemistry Education*. Abingdon: Routledge.

Pilot, A. and Bulte, A.M.W. (2006b). 'The Use of "Contexts" as a Challenge for the Chemistry Curriculum: Its Successes and the Need for Further Development and Understanding'. *International Journal of Science Education* 28(9): 1087–1112.

Salta, K. and Tzougraki, C. (2011). 'Conceptual Versus Algorithmic Problem-solving: Focusing on Problems Dealing with Conservation of Matter in Chemistry'. *Research in Science Education* 41(4): 587–609.

Smith, D.K. (2011). 'From Crazy Chemists to Engaged Learners through Education'. *Nature Chemistry* 3(9): 681–4.

Swedish National Agency for Education (2000). 'Chemistry Syllabus for Upper Secondary School'. Stockholm: The Swedish National Agency for Education.

Whitelegg, E. and Parry, M. (1999). 'Real-life Contexts for Learning Physics: Meanings, Issues and Practice'. *Physics Education* 34(2): 68–72.

Zoller, U. and Dori, Y.J. (2002). 'Algorithmic, LOCS and HOCS (Chemistry) Exam Questions: Performance and Attitudes of College Students'. *International Journal of Science Education* 24(2): 185–203.

Zoller, U. and Levy Nahum, T. (2012). 'From Teaching to KNOW to Learning to THINK in Science Education'. In: Fraser, B.J., Tobin, K.G. and McRobbie, C.J. (eds), *Second International Handbook of Science Education*. Berlin: Springer, pp. 209–29.

Part III

Practitioner-led design-based research

12 From 'what' to 'how'

Researching students' meaning-making in sustainability dilemmas

Katarina Ottander

The aim of this chapter is to illustrate the process of designing a research project based on my experience of teaching biology and environmental science in upper secondary schools in Sweden. Attention will focus on the challenges of finding a suitable theoretical framework to explore the empirical material that is appropriate to the research questions. It is a reflective text about my research project, which arose from 15 years of teaching experience.

One of the biggest challenges I had, as a teacher working in upper secondary school, was when teaching within a general science course. Students came to me at the beginning of the course and told me 'I cannot do science, it's too difficult'. They did not believe themselves to be able to take part in scientific discourse. I felt that these students had lost or not gained a sense of confidence about doing science and taking part in socioscientific discourses. Another concern I had was when the students were engaged in working with socioscientific issues in the classroom, such as sustainability issues. My concern was related to whether scientific knowledge really was involved as they worked with the issues. Furthermore, science was sometimes used in a different manner to that which I had intended.

Sustainability issues can be seen as based on values and political socioscientific issues, closely associated with norms about how to behave, which makes teaching about them difficult. How should politics and values be dealt with within the science classroom? I was concerned that *if* the value-based and political dimension in these issues affect how scientific knowledge is used, and *if* the political aspects affect students' use of scientific knowledge, then it is important to gain knowledge about this process. This is because, when we bring socioscientific issues into the science classroom, we *per se* bring in politics. Therefore, when I had the opportunity to do research I wanted to dig deeper into these questions. I wanted to understand the students' way of expressing natural science in sustainability issues. What did they use it for? What role did it have?

Developing a research focus from engagement in the literature

There is much research focusing on the concerns I had as a teacher, both in the field of socioscientific issues and in scientific literacy. One goal in science education is for all students to develop scientific literacy in order to be able to participate in social dialogues concerning socioscientific issues (Millar 1996; Roberts 2007; Osborne and Dillon 2008; Sadler 2009). One rationale for this is to work with situations that students may face as citizens where considerations other than scientific ones have to be taken into account (Roberts 2007). Socioscientific issues are said to be relevant and can act as a bridge between school science and students' lived experiences (Sadler *et al.* 2007). It is assumed that learning within socioscientific issues can promote democratic citizenship in science education.

On reading research from the field of environmental and sustainability education, I found the normative and political aspects of these issues needed to be taken into consideration. Three selective teaching traditions within environmental and sustainability education have been identified in Sweden: *fact-based*, *normative* and the *pluralistic* traditions (Öhman 2004; Borg 2011). These three traditions express different goals with sustainability education that take the normative and political aspects into account in different ways. In the fact-based tradition, the focus is on content knowledge, which here is seen as most important for understanding environmental problems. Environmental problems are seen as ecological issues, which have scientific and technological solutions. However, the traditional science-oriented approach to environmental education has been criticised for leading to knowledge about the existence of environmental problems without addressing the societal perspectives of these questions (Jensen and Schnack 1997; Scott and Gough 2003; Osborne and Dillon 2008; Gough 2010). In the normative tradition, the aim of education is to support an environmentally friendly transformation of society. Students shall learn environmentally friendly values and attitudes. Some argue that it is not the task for education to solve societal issues (Jensen and Schnack 1997) and that this could contradict an education where students learn to think for themselves and become autonomous individuals (Jickling and Wals 2008). As a response to problems associated with the fact based and normative traditions, the pluralistic tradition has developed. In the pluralistic tradition, environmental problems are seen as conflicts between people's different interests. It is viewed as important that students learn to critically examine different perspectives on environmental and sustainability issues. However, in the pluralistic approach to science education, studies show that students do not bring much science into discussions about socioscientific issues (Ratcliffe and Grace 2003; Nielsen 2011). Attention paid to canonical science content lessens when the scientific information becomes more uncertain and the context of instruction becomes more emotional (Aikenhead 2006).

From reading this literature, I realised that science education researchers had different ideas about what was important for students to learn. Differing research traditions also gave scientific knowledge different roles in relation to socioscientific issues that were not necessarily obvious for the students, who could have other ideas about what scientific knowledge could be used for. I sought for knowledge that clarified how students used science and, moreover, which roles they gave to science when they were discussing pluralistic formulated sustainability tasks in small groups. My thinking was that students do what they find relevant to do in different school situations and, by gaining knowledge about how students actually engage in different school activities, we can learn things that can inform science education. I wanted to understand the students, their talk and their participation; I wanted my research to capture their voices. When knowing more about that, we are in a position to discuss the consequences of teaching and to problematise what it is to be scientifically literate. The first aim with the thesis was thus to investigate what skills and knowledge students actually use in discussions related to sustainable development and which roles they give to science. On the basis of this aim I designed the methodological approach.

Developing a methodological approach

Since my research aim was to focus on what skills and knowledge students use in sustainability discussions in science education, I decided to conduct classroom studies. Through studying students' talk in situ, I did not have to think of whether and how students' talk differed from one situation (interview) to another (in classroom). I found small group discussions relevant for study because, in Sweden, group discussions together with interactive lessons were the most common teaching method in relation to sustainability in science education (Borg *et al.* 2012).

At the time of the data collection, all students in Sweden had to attend a general science course, *Science Studies A*, in the upper secondary school in both vocational and theoretical programs. The Swedish syllabus (Swedish National Agency for Education, 2000) stated that *Science Studies* is an interdisciplinary subject in which scientific questions can be viewed from different perspectives. The course aim is that the students should construct scientific knowledge required to take a stand on issues that are important to the individual and society, such as sustainable development and energy consumption. I found that the general science course was appropriate for my research aim. The research was conducted in the social science programme because I wanted to do research in programmes that did not have the natural sciences as major subjects. I considered it more relevant to study classes where, maybe, a scientific discourse was not easily available for all students. The challenge of getting *all* students to see themselves as legitimate users of science may not have been achieved if I had conducted the study in natural science and technology programmes.

Initially an exploratory study, where students discussed ecological footprints, was conducted in a class with both social science students and hairdressing students. The ecological footprint measures the amount of biologically productive land and water area required to produce all the resources an individual, population, or activity consumes, and to absorb the waste they generate, given prevailing technology and resource management practices (global hectares) (Ewing *et al.* 2008). The group discussions were audio recorded and transcribed and a content analysis was undertaken, because I was concerned to know what students talked about.

Classroom studies have subsequently been conducted in three social science classes with different teachers. All classes were in their first year in upper secondary school and attended the general science course, *Science Studies A*. In this main study there were 84 students, 29 male and 55 female. The data collections consisted of three different methods, audio-recorded small-group discussions, classroom observations and interviews with selected groups. The focus was on the small-group discussions since I wanted to gain knowledge about students' use of science in value-based sustainability issues. Students were audio recorded three times when they were working in small groups, discussing issues related to sustainable development. I designed three different tasks to focus on the potential dilemma between social justice and the demand and supply of natural resources. In these tasks, science could be useful in conjunction with, for example, the social, ethical and economic aspects.

The main purpose of the tasks was to get students to talk about and discuss sustainability issues and thus feel involved in societal discussions, which involve science. The design of the tasks was made so all students would feel that they could contribute to the discussions. Another aim with the tasks was that sustainability issues should be illuminated from different perspectives, which is seen as an important goal in a pluralistic teaching tradition. The tasks and the teacher did not specify areas within science to be involved in the discussions. Instead, students used the science they found relevant to create meaning about the sustainability issue in their discussions. The tasks were: *Earth at night*, focusing on the world's energy supply, *Ecological footprints*, focusing on the world's resources, and *Do we have enough food?* focusing on the world's food supply.

The reason for making observations was to acquire a description of the educational context and the classes, because I thought that the different characters of the classes could generate a different kind of engagement in the small group discussions. Different classrooms can have different permissive climates for discussions or different teaching traditions. In Sweden, 40 per cent of the upper secondary school science teachers teach within the fact-based teaching tradition when educating about sustainability, 16 per cent of the teachers teach within the normative teaching traditions, and 25 per cent teach within the pluralistic tradition (Borg *et al.* 2012). Therefore, I found it important to have information about the classes and their education and so field notes were taken. Additionally, group interviews were undertaken in order to have students' view about the tasks, the discussions and science education. The interviews were audio recorded and notes were taken. However, the main empirical material consisted of the audio-recorded group discussions. The transcribed group discussions could be used to explore students' use of science and the roles they gave to science. The classroom observations and the focus interviews were made to add information to the small group discussions.

Searching for analytical tools

While I was working on an article based on the exploratory study, I was concurrently analysing the empirical material from the large data collection and in doing so experienced several difficulties. In the exploratory study, students' discussions were categorised based on what they talked about. I developed a coding scheme and the students talk was categorised into five categories: social dimension, science dimension, economical dimension, environmentally friendly activities, and personal experiences. In the discussions, knowledge from different categories was intertwined in arguments and statements so the talk was categorised into the dimension that was dominating the discussion. I felt that the analytical procedure was rigorous – strictly following a coding scheme – and the categorisation was repeated after several months with a high level of agreement. At this point I felt that the analysis gave an incorrect impression of the students' discussions because I found that students' talk was interwoven and my categorisation did not show this. One of the strongest characteristics of the students' discussions was hidden. Students drew on environmental discourses in one utterance and then economical discourses in the next and so on.

Another dimension of analysing students' discussions was in relation to the factual and value based aspects. In research about socioscientific issues it has been shown that students draw on both when discussing societal issues (Christenson *et al.* 2012; Ekborg 2005). In my analysis I was concerned that the fact and value distinction was blurred, which raised questions about the ends to which the students used factual and value-based aspects in their discussion, and so I started to ask these questions of the transcripts. The analysis could not be fulfilled because the factual aspects and value-based aspects were inseparable in students' talk. The excerpt shown below is an example of this. The students are discussing the task *Do we have enough food?* and the group begins to discuss whether what we eat matters. They focus on pigs to get an understanding of the issue; the group's idea is that pigs eat human leftovers. Only by looking at the words the students use for leftovers can we see that they involve values. Birgitta also uses the adjective disgusting. Then Ritva in her utterance includes economics. She does state that it will cost money, which could be seen as a factual statement, but through that being said a value is included – that economics is important. Otherwise, the statement would not have been uttered. The same goes for Rosa's last statement; by being said it expresses the view that eating others of the same species is strange.

Berit: pigs they eat like, like garbage
Birgitta: the disgusting thing is that usually pigs eat our slop
Rosa: then you can, then you can give them leftovers
Ritva: but that will cost [money]
Rosa: give them the food we haven't eaten
Ritva: garbage, compost
Rosa: then they will eat themselves

My research question focused on students' use of scientific knowledge. In the analyses, it therefore became important to judge what was scientific in the discussions and to discriminate between a correct and incorrect use of scientific knowledge. My approach involved a view of knowledge as 'solid' with right and wrong answers and did not capture the students' way of expressing themselves. In this excerpt, students' knowledge is that pigs eat leftovers. How should that be judged, from a science education perspective? The analyses became a top-down perspective on students' talk, investigating whether the students expressed what could be expected from a science education perspective but missing the nuances of what the students actually said. Students' voices were not captured, since the students used their everyday language, which portrayed them as non-knowers. This was not my intention with my research; I wanted to understand the students, their talk and their participation. Hence, the analytical process became challenging in many ways. These challenges forced me to look for theoretical perspectives that took the problems mentioned above into consideration, and could provide analytical tools that helped to answer the research questions in the main study. The analyses should explore the students' talk in a holistic way and stay close to students' voices/perspectives. I needed a theory that could help me through the analytical process.

Theoretical changes

An important theoretical shift concerning my research questions was to start asking questions about 'how' students talk, instead of asking questions on 'what' the talk is about. The analytical object changed from the individual (and her or his thinking) to the conversation. Instead of studying students' use of knowledge I became more concerned with students' meaning-making. Through this, I did not have to separate what belonged to science from what did not, nor did I have to separate factual expressions from value expressions, nor right from wrong. The theory was based on the interwoven aspect of talk and so I had to reformulate the aim of my thesis, though it still captures my original intentions with the research.

Discursive psychology (Potter and Wetherell 1987; Edley 2001; Wiggins and Potter 2008) provided a theoretical framework that could contribute to understanding students' meaning-making concerning sustainability, through the concepts of interpretative repertoires and subject positions. Potter and Wetherell describe an interpretative repertoire as constituted through a limited range of words used in particular stylistic and grammatical construction: 'Interpretative repertoires are recurrently used systems of terms used for characterizing and evaluating actions, events and other phenomena' (Potter and Wetherell 1987: 149). One purpose of discursive psychological analysis is to study how people strategically use interpretative repertoires to portray themselves or 'parts of the world' in social interaction and to discuss the social consequences arising from that repertoire. For example, the students in my study talk from the position of living in Sweden, being a student and participating in a school activity within science education. They can position themselves or others as, for example, being environmentally sensitive or insensitive.

A discursive psychological approach focuses on how people construct meaning; this focus made it possible to explore how students used *their* knowledge and the meaning *they* put into it. Discursive psychological analysis is an interpretative analysis, which implied that I needed to think differently. I struggled with my role as a researcher: how could *I* interpret students' meanings and meaning-making from their talk? I still had the individual as the analytical object and it was difficult to change focus to the conversation as the analytical object.

Realising that it was patterns within the conversation (interpretative repertoires), and the meanings these interpretative repertoires carried with them that were being analysed (not individuals' thinking), was difficult. I asked analytical questions about which function and consequences the interpretative repertoires had in the conversations and found that they carried different meanings; also different subject positions were constructed through the talk. The framework could provide a contribution to understanding students' meaning-making about sustainability in science education classrooms. The informants in the study also become portrayed as knowers, which was important in recognising their status as participants in socio-scientific discourse.

Problems with my data collection because of the theoretical change

Discursive psychological analysis includes close and detailed reading of the transcripts; therefore it is recommended to limit data collection and focus on 'real-life situations' (Wiggins and Potter 2008). I had collected 58 audio-recorded group discussions, eight audio-recorded focus groups interviews, and field notes from 29 lessons. I was drowning in my empirical material; it was too much to get an overview, so I had to limit the empirical material for analysis. At first the focus group interviews were excluded and only the field notes were used for describing the different characters of the classes. Then I decided to only use questions in the tasks that made the students talk openly. Finally, every second group discussion from two tasks was used for analysis. After I had reduced my empirical material, it felt more manageable. In the group discussions, students seldom expressed more than one sentence as an utterance. They did not express themselves in detail, which made it hard to do an interpretative analysis. Although I saw patterns in the way students talked within the groups and between the groups, after several readings I found that different interpretative repertoires expressed different 'views of the world'. Today, I would have limited my data collection to fewer group discussions and make some effort to encourage the students to talk more.

Results from the students' discussions

The school tasks in this study present potential dilemmas for the students between social justice and the demand and supply of natural resources. In reformulating my analysis I focused on how students constructed meaning in relation to the dilemmas presented to them. I analysed how meaning was created, took shape and sometimes settled into 'accepted truth' (Wetherell *et al.* 2001). Different interpretative repertoires brought different meanings to the small-group discussions or, in other words, beliefs about the world. Within the discussions, students thus met different meanings that the interpretative repertoires carried with them. Students negotiated different meanings in the discussions. My results show that when students are introduced to sustainability dilemmas in a task, different perspectives – interpretative repertoires – are often presented. The students face different dilemmas and negotiate between various perspectives. This is one important aim in a pluralistic approach to sustainability education. My results also show that the discussions are highly culturally embedded; a western society is the norm. Pluralism of perspectives occurs *within* an ideological and cultural frame.

The students construct different subject positions through their use of the interpretative repertoires, and they often create positions where it is possible to live in a western lifestyle, have social justice and the environmental problems are solved. Different dilemmas put the students first in a troubled subject position, and then through talk they create an untroubled subject position. Students use strategies, probably unconsciously, that make the dilemma invisible, avoid the dilemma or solve the dilemma through compromises between interpretative repertoires.

One example of how two different interpretative repertoires collide and create a troubled subject position and how this becomes an untroubled subject position in the discussion, is shown below. This is from one group who is discussing the satellite picture over earth at night where they can see light in different places and darkness in other places. From the group discussions about the satellite picture I identified different interpretative repertoires. In my example, there are two interpretative repertoires at work. One interpretative repertoire is the 'limitation repertoire'; in this interpretative repertoire the students' speech draws on the idea that there are limited resources on earth. Students say, for example, that we will have to save energy or that we cannot continue to waste energy. Another interpretative repertoire is 'equity with western society as a norm'. In this repertoire, the consequence of students' talk is that a desirable society to live in is a western society. Students say things such as that it is boring in places where it is dark and that, for example, Africa will catch up or be upgraded.

In the example below, the students discuss whether it is desirable that the satellite picture becomes brighter as they thought this was the most reasonable scenario. They say that it would be better if it was dark at more locations because then less energy is used, the limitation interpretative repertoire. But, at the same time, the students express the view that it will cause problems because 'there are open places [who need light] at night'. The students find themselves in a troubled subject position if they want humans both to live within the earth's limited resources and, at the same time, want people to experience light as in a western society. The dilemma the students are facing is solved through limited energy consumption by 'switching off advertising' and 'turning off all lights at home' while 'the lights are blazing in the hospital' and such like.

Lotta:	if we think it is good [that the satellite picture will become brighter in the future]
Mona:	No, it is not, or
Lotta:	… NO, NO
My:	it should almost be completely dark … it should be much … it should be darker in more places (Everyone except Alex starts talking)
Lotta:	because it is night, then it should be like totally dark
My:	yes but it is, it is still places that are open on nights
Lotta:	yes, but they can use other ways
My:	yes, but what, … shall they light candles, or (laughs)
Lotta:	yes, why not (laughs)
Lotta:	they can walk with torches (laughs)
Lotta:	yes but, yes but they need, it is
Alex:	they can start with switching of advertisement at night

Everyone:	YES
Alex:	and have lit like where it is open
Lotta:	yes but, yes but, so, all homes, so, it can just
My:	all homes will also be dark, but anyway, it should be lit in hospitals and stuff, because there's still a few spots that need to be [lit]
Lotta:	yeeeas

In this part of the discussion, the troubled subject position is changed to an untroubled subject position by reducing unnecessary energy consumption while still continuing to use energy at hospitals and other important places. The speech thus results in a compromise between the two interpretative repertoires and, through talk, the dilemma is solved, although in the talk there is no actor who will make these changes.

I interpret this as a human endeavour; how people through language solve troubled subject positions and turn them into untroubled subject positions. Talk becomes both a weapon and a shield to portray our 'reality' and ourselves as at least okay. This is an important consideration when teaching about sustainability issues and other socioscientific issues, because when students are put in situations where they are supposed to act politically, which is inherent in sustainability issues, they might find themselves accused of not living environmentally enough. How shall this be dealt with in education? Sustainability tasks also run the risk that some views of the 'world' are sustained if we, as teachers and researchers, are not aware of them. For example, in my research, the interpretative repertoire *equity with western society as norm* excludes alternative ideas of societies. One part of the interpretative repertoire is the talk about Africa as a poor continent, with few resources and lack of knowledge. Consequently, there is a risk that these views of Africa will be sustained if this talk dominates the students' discussions and is not challenged by teachers.

My first theoretical framework gave the impression that students' talk was unscientific, as they used scientific knowledge to a tiny extent in their discussions, because there were few science concepts used and the reasoning did not seem based on science. With my new theoretical framework, where I see school science as a discourse, my results show that the students use science in their meaning-making. School science as a discourse means that parts of students' speech are based on *their* interpretations of: conceptions and beliefs found in science teaching; conceptions and beliefs that science has created (science products); and conceptions and beliefs about the nature of science. The students use their everyday language but they draw on scientific views of the world; an example of this is the 'limitation repertoire' presented in the example above. The analysis suggests that the students' speech itself does not need to contain scientific concepts and theories and that the accuracy of the scientific knowledge is not judged. It is the students' speech and their use of natural sciences that are being analysed. Defining school science as a discourse thus differs from studying students' use of concepts where science becomes something that is solid, with right and wrong answers.

Conclusion

Reflecting on my methodological journey has shown the importance of learning how theory works throughout the thesis. I undertook a large data collection that was sound from the practitioner perspective with regard to the needs of the research, but my initially theoretical framework did not succeed with this. I needed another theoretical framework that would inform the analytical perspective that would be true to the original intentions of the research; an analytical perspective that captured students' voices. This dilemma has caused different problems when working with my thesis that have forced me to make unexpected choices concerning my empirical material. Ultimately, I feel that through the work with my thesis I have gained knowledge about the challenges students face when they are engaging in sustainability issues within science education. These challenges affect students' meaning-making about the issues, which is crucial for teachers and researchers to be aware of. Finally, how the students were portrayed from my research has also been important. It has been important for me to do them justice, and I realised that the theoretical perspective I chose in my research affected how students and their knowledge were portrayed.

References

Aikenhead, G. (2006). *Science Education for Everyday Life: Evidence-Based Practice.* New York: Teachers College Press.

Borg, C. (2011). 'Utbildning för hållbar utveckling ur ett lärarperspektiv: Ämnesbundna skillnader i gymnasieskolan'. Licenciate thesis, Karlstads universitet, Karlstad.

Borg, C., Gericke, N., Höglund, H.-O. and Bergman, E. (2012). 'The Barriers Encountered by Teachers Implementing Education for Sustainable Development: Discipline Bound Differences and Teaching Traditions'. *Research in Science & Technological Education* 30(2): 185–207.

Christenson, N., Rundgren, S.-N. and Höglund, H.-O. (2012). 'Using the SEE-SEP Model to Analyze Upper Secondary Students' Use of Supporting Reasons in Arguing Socioscientific Issues'. *Journal of Science Education and Technology* 21(3): 342–52.

Edley, N. (2001). 'Analysing Masculinity: Interpretative Repertoires, Ideological Dilemmas and Subject Positions'. In: Wetherell, M., Taylor, S. and Yates, S. (eds) *Discourse as Data: A Guide for Analysis.* London: Sage, pp. 189–228.

Ekborg, M. (2005). 'Is Heat Generated from a Crematorium an Appropriate Source for District Heating? Student Teachers' Reasoning About a Complex Environmental Issue'. *Environmental Education Research* 11(5): 557–73.

Ewing, B., Reed, A., Rizk, S.M., Galli, A., Wackernagel, M. and Kitzes, J. (2008). *Calculation Methodology for the National Footprint Accounts, 2008 Edition.* Oakland: Global Footprint Network.

Gough, A. (2010). 'Mutualism: A Different Agenda for Environmental and Science Education'. *International Journal of Science Education* 24(11): 1201–15.

Jensen, B.B. and Schnack, K. (1997). 'The Action Competence Approach in Environmental Education'. *Environmental Education Research* 3(2): 163–78.

Jickling, B. and Wals, A.E.J. (2008). 'Globalization and Environmental Education: Looking beyond Sustainable Development'. *Journal of Curriculum Studies* 40(1): 1–21.

Millar, R. (1996). 'Towards a Science Curriculum for Public Understanding'. *School Science Review* 77(280): 7–18.

Nielsen, J.A. (2011). 'Co-opting Science: A Preliminary Study of how Students invoke Science in Value-laden Discussions'. *International Journal of Science Education* 34(2): 275–99.

Öhman, J. (2004). 'Moral Perspectives in Selective Traditions of Environmental Education'. In: Wickenberg, P., Axelsson, H., Fritzén, L., Helldén, G. and Öhman, J., (eds), *Learning to Change our World.* Lund: Studentlitteratur, pp. 33–57.

Osborne, J. and Dillon, J. (2008). *Science Education in Europe: Critical Reflections. A Report to the Nuffield Foundation.* London: Kings College.

Potter, J. and Wetherell, M. (1987). *Discourse and Social Psychology: Beyond Attitudes and Behavior.* London, Thousand Oaks, CA and New Dehli: Sage Publications.

Ratcliffe, M. and Grace, M. (2003). *Science Education for Citizenship.* Maidenhead: Open University Press.

Roberts, A.D. (2007). 'Scientific Literacy/Science Literacy'. In: Abell, S.K. and Lederman, N.G. (eds), *Handbook of Research on Science Education.* Mahwag, NJ: Lawrence Erlbaum Associates, pp. 729–80.

Sadler, T.D. (2009). 'Situated Learning in Science Education: Socio-Scientific Issues as Contexts for Practice'. *Studies in Science Education* 45(1): 1–42.

Sadler, T.D., Barab, S.A. and Scott, B. (2007). 'What do Students Gain by Engaging in Socioscientific Inquiry?' *Research in Science Education* 37(4): 371–91.

Scott, W. and Gough, S. (2003). *Sustainable Development and Learning: Framing the Issues.* London: RoutledgeFalmer.

Swedish National Agency for Education (2000). Kursplaner 2000. SKOLFS 2000:9. www3.skolverket.se/ki03/front.aspx?sprak=SV&ar=0607&infotyp=5&skolform=2 1&id=3203&extraId= (accessed: 28 November 2011).

Wetherell, M., Taylor, S. and Yates, S.J. (2001). 'Introduction'. In: Wetherell, M., Taylor, S. and Yates, S. (eds), *Discourse Theory and Practice, A Reader.* London: SAGE Publications Ltd, pp. 1–8.

Wiggins, S. and Potter, J. (2008). 'Discursive Psychology'. In: Willig, C. and Stainton-Rogers, W. (eds), *The SAGE Handbook of Qualatative Research in Psychology.* London: SAGE Publications Ltd, pp. 73–90.

13 Line graphs in mathematics and science

The use of different learning approaches

Elizabeth Wady

The focus for my study began when working as a science teacher in secondary schools preparing students for national examinations at age 16. I noticed consistently that students of all academic abilities found drawing and understanding graphs difficult. As an above average student myself who had attended a selective school from age 12, I had never found graphical work a challenge. I have a medical condition that means I have a tendency to focus upon details to a greater extent than most individuals. It always surprised me at school that many students found graph plotting so difficult, though they had all passed the selection process at age 12. As a teacher I decided to look more closely at the problem by undertaking doctoral research that could possibly assist teachers to improve students' graphical comprehension. A vast amount of information is encountered in society which, the more graphical ability one possesses, the better one is likely to comprehend. Thus graphical competence is important and my view was that learning graphs warranted closer scrutiny from a research perspective.

The design for my research involved studying students' approaches and behaviours whilst they engaged in graph work during science and mathematics lessons, which suggested a classroom observation study with opportunities to follow up observations of performance with interviews. In order to do this I chose to become an observer-researcher rather than a teacher. This choice required me to work with other teachers who would be willing to accommodate me as an observer whilst they taught graphical lessons. Engagement with the literature on research into graphical difficulties led me to design some lessons that would cover a range of difficulties. This chapter focuses on how I set up my study in order to collect observational and interview data from students, and how I drew on theoretical perspectives on learning approaches (Marton and Booth 1997) to analyse how students performed when experiencing a range of teaching strategies and using different resources.

Research context

At the outset of my study I had one research question: what do students find difficult about graphs? Whilst reading literature concerning graphical learning I found that researchers consider graphical comprehension to be of value; for example, Norman (2011) identified six purposes: decoration, representation, organisation, interpretation, transformation and extension. Glazer also points out that there is much daily information that needs to be understood in media reports, weather, sports, health, environment and political reports (Glazer 2011). Consequently Norman's skills would be helpful in daily life, as well as in education.

Student misconceptions regarding graphs do vary between different research reports, for example, Leinhardt *et al.* (1990) classify errors into four categories: confusing slope and height, confusing an interval and a point, considering a graph as a picture and viewing graphs as made from discrete points rather than continuous ones. Another misunderstanding is misreading the scales (Swatton and Taylor 1994). Students also have great difficulty in drawing a line of best fit and calculating its gradient using hand methods (Forster 2002). Twelve misconceptions found by Preece (1983) include 1) reading and plotting points; 2) inability to read relative values; 3) interpreting intervals as points; 4) variable concepts not understood; 5) world knowledge interferes with interpretation; 6) pronounced graphical features distracts the pupil; 7) misinterpreting a symbol; 8) confusion from too many variables; 9) only one curve on multiple curve graphs is interpreted; 10) not transferring information between graphs; 11) gradient is confused with maximum and minimum; 12) the graph is interpreted iconically.

Despite all these student misconceptions I have found just one book and two articles concerning methods of teaching that tackled some of the difficulties of secondary school students (Goldsworthy *et al.*, 2000; Swatton and Taylor 1994; Beckmann 1989). Hence, I designed my own graphical lessons which covered all the graphical difficulties I had observed in classrooms and found in academic literature.

Having designed the kind of graphical lessons that would be useful I needed to make decsions about who should teach the lessons, and what age students to observe. Though I would like to have taught the lessons myself to ensure that the tasks would be presented as I imagined them, I needed to be an observer, and also have opportunities to work with students other than my own. I therefore decided to ask other teachers if I could attend lessons they taught whilst I observed and filmed the students. Unfortunately not all the teachers who consented to my research were willing to let students of the age I had selected participate in this way. Therefore I had to abandon my lessons in favour of observing graphical lessons designed by teachers themselves as part of the normal school curriculum. I chose to include students preparing for national examinations at age 16 as this was the focus of my original interest and younger students have fewer opportunities to study graphs. Students in their final year of taking examinations were not included as teachers would be unwilling to let such students participate, which left students aged between 14 and 15, in the first year of study for their examinations.

Developing a theoretical framework and observation focus

It took me a long time to realise what a theoretical framework actually is. Much of the work on student approaches to learning broadly comprised either descriptive accounts of conversation and lesson context or quantitative analysis of learning inventories. These inventories were frequently used to monitor students' self-assessment of their learning approach with a statistical analysis. Consequently I decided that my work would involve both quantitative and qualitative analyses of graphical learning which differ from those found in the literature. The statistical analyses I read about did not fully explore students' perspectives, hence consideration was also given to students' perceptions of their graphical learning and how classroom contexts affect such learning. I felt that use of only one analytical method would not convey the subtlety of learning approach phenomena but combining quantitative and qualitative observation with data from students may portray a picture closer to reality.

Having decided to observe ways in which students engaged with graphs in tasks designed by teachers in normal lessons, I needed an analytical process for investigating that engagement. Learning approaches featured greatly in my reading; these are ways in which the learning situation is experienced and the ways in which it is handled (Marton and Booth 1997). Other scholars also describe a student's relation to a learning task in terms of their motives and their strategies (Biggs 2001; Byrne *et al.* 2004). Thus a learning approach includes not only how students tackle learning but the reasons why they use a particular learning process. Recognising learning approaches and their associated behaviours from my teaching experience I realised they provided a way of analysing students' learning in graphical contexts. I synthesised a range of learning approach behaviours (LAB) from reading a range of literature sources (Bain 1994; Biggs 2003; Byrne *et al.* 2004; Chin and Brown 2000a, 2000b; Entwistle and Marton 1984; Entwistle 1987; Kember *et al.* 2004; Nolen and Haladyna 1990; Postigo and Pozo 2004; Sternberg and Zhang 2001). Essentially, three main learning approaches are identified in the literature: surface, deep and strategic. Within each learning approach are a range of associated behaviours that I summarised in such a way that made them identifiable to an observer (Table 13.1). Observation was not regarded as providing more accurate information compared to other data collection methods, merely giving a different understanding. Memories and impressions can be useful in the right context and the latter were in fact obtained. Prior to a pilot study being undertaken it was realised that visual observation alone may not

Table 13.1 Learning behaviours associated with the three learning approaches

Surface approach	Strategic approach	Deep approach
Rote learning selected content	Following up suggested readings	Reading widely
Listing points not addressing an argument	Being neat and systematic	Inter-relate new and previous knowledge
Focusing on isolated facts, treating items independently of each other	Organising time, working space and syllabus coverage efficiently	Focus on underlying meaning as well as patterns and details
Describing only visible things	Planning ahead	Discussion with others
Explanations are reformulations of the question and are vague	Allocating time to tasks in proportion to their importance	Forming hypotheses
Questions refer to factual or procedural information and are often closed	Working consistently	Relating evidence to conclusions and examining the logic of their argument
Unthinking use of procedures	Outlining and note-taking	Venturing ideas spontaneously
Reliant on peers/teachers for ideas	Ensuring conditions and materials for studying are appropriate	Questions focus on explanations, causes or resolving discrepancies in knowledge
Reproducing tasks or procedures		Persistence in tasks/commitment to work
Failing to distinguish principles for examples		Generating ideas on their own
Associating facts and concepts unreflectively		Predicting outcomes
		Generative thinking
		Elaboration and integration strategies

permit sufficient understanding of LA use in graphicacy. This would be particularly true if sounds were of too low a decibel rating to be captured on film. Accordingly, sound recording was implemented throughout pilot and main studies so that, as long as the classroom was not excessively noisy, few verbal productions were lost (Bucher *et al.* 2003).

The synthesis of an observable list of LAB led me to decide that film and audio recordings of LAB would illustrate when students used such behaviours in graphical lessons. I therefore collected data using film and audio, and analysed these data for frequency of different LAB. In the pilot study I filmed and audio recorded two mathematics and two science classes for preliminary analysis using the LAB. The majority of learning approach behaviours were categorised according to criteria laid down by multiple authors, as cited above, however, as well as LAB reported in the literature some novel behaviours were also exhibited during graphical lessons (first observed in the pilot study). Construction of definitions for these novel behaviours was thus necessary. Firstly, it became apparent that 'students asking procedural questions' was insufficient for accurately describing student talk concerning procedures, thus a new term, procedural talk, was introduced. Procedural talk concerns how to perform a task and may include procedural questions in addition to other material. Definitions of procedural-like talk largely describe what it is not, such as neither precise nor explicit (Moschkovich 2003). The lack of explicitness is exemplified by Pimm (1987) who found procedural talk to include many indefinite words such as 'thing' and 'it'.

Note-taking, another novel behaviour, was construed as paraphrasing information presented (a strategic behaviour). Later on in lessons, without prompting or instruction, students would write down either what the teacher said or information presented to them. It is this writing without being instructed to do so that causes behaviour to be categorised as note-taking. Students sometimes deemed certain information as worthy of note and organised their time in writing it down. As such, note-taking represents an efficient management of time so it is deemed a strategic behaviour as well as a deep one. Also, attention whilst on graphical tasks was categorised as a deep and strategic behaviour. Attention was observed in the pilot study as being directed towards teachers speaking and to texts they had to read. The analysis resulted in extra behaviours that were deep and strategic (note-taking, sustained effort, attention to the teacher or text), which were then noted when observing the films.

Student perspectives

In addition to the observation study I used a questionnaire early on to investigate student perspectives on graphical lessons. I developed a modified Learning Process Questionnaire (LPQ) (Biggs 1993) to assess students' perceptions of their use of learning approaches in graphical tasks in order to see what extent this agreed with their actual behaviours. Modifications comprised making statements specific to graphs. For example, LPQ statement one is 'I find the only way to learn is to memorise facts by heart'. This was altered by adding 'about graphs' in-between the words 'learn' and 'is to memorise'. Students then had to select from five rankings how far the statements applied to themselves. The purpose of the questionnaire was to obtain self-inventories of learning approach use to compare with visual and audio data. Prior to the pilot study, this questionnaire had been tested with a class known to the researcher, analysis of results (using interview and observation data) indicated that students had accurate perceptions of their graphical learning approaches and comprehended the skills required in this area. These findings were corroborated by inter-rater agreement of the two other science teachers for this class. Consequently it was expected that the questionnaire would yield valid and reliable data in the pilot study.

In the pilot study students completed my modified LPQ. Despite earlier measures of reliability it became apparent that questionnaires gave an inadequate sense of students' perceptions of their learning approaches. Firstly, students perceived themselves to use one learning approach during a task whereas observational data indicated they used several. For example, a common occurrence whilst completing a task was to find students making deep learning approach (DLA) statements in the midst of procedural talk (surface learning approach, SLA) during a period of sustained effort (deep-strategic learning approach, DSLA). Questionnaires did not therefore capture the complexity of students learning approach behaviours. Secondly, students greatly underestimated their use of the SLA in comparison with observational and interview data. Appreciation of this situation led to interviewing students in addition to using a questionnaire. Interview data were found to correspond with observed student behaviours and provided greater insights regarding perceptions than did questionnaires. Accordingly, the adapted LPQ was discontinued as providing information that was too simplistic. Students' perceptions of their graphical learning and associated contexts were, in the end, obtained by semi-structured interviews.

Refining the interviews for the main study

The interviews were carried out whilst students were working on graphical tasks and conceptions of their learning approaches were elicited with the question 'what are you thinking about when you are doing [then stating the task they were currently occupied with]'. The pilot study had established that most students understood this question. Further clarification was only sought two or three times in the entire study and involved giving specific examples of tasks, such as scaling, to those who did not initially comprehend. Perspectives regarding varying classroom contexts were gathered through use of a specific question; 'is [context name] helpful to you in plotting graphs or not?' Explanations of responses were usually volunteered, but if not, students were asked 'why is this?'. Students were also asked to clarify their meaning so it became clear to the interviewer to assist interpretation (Kvale 1996). Certain question types assisted students in clarifying the meaning of their responses when necessary, such as in Table 13.2, from Sudman (2003)

Table 13.2 Question types to clarify meaning (derived from Sudman 2003)

Type of question	Example
Introducing questions	Can you tell me about…?
Follow up questions	Repeating significant words in answers to elicit further response
Probing questions	Could you say something more about that?
Specifying questions	What did you think then?
Direct questions	When you mentioned S, do you then think K?
Interpreting questions	Is it correct that you think that…?

To obtain sufficient and accurate data it quickly became apparent that usually more than one of the above questions needed to be asked. I never interviewed students until at least five minutes after they had been set lengthy tasks. These periods gave students the opportunity to consider their responses rather than replying without thought. The requirement for an honest individual response was stressed in order to obtain the students' actual opinion. Students' verbal and non-verbal communication at this stage indicated that they could relate this requirement to obtaining accurate results for science experiments. On many occasions students stated that wrong results would 'ruin your research' and that 'we won't let that happen Miss', or words to these effects. Nonverbal communication was utilised to assess statement veracity and since students were in classrooms, adjacent peers would often spontaneously corroborate their friends' statements. Consequently a high degree of confidence could be placed in students' responses indicating their actual thoughts. I had hoped to interview students singly or in pairs but classroom arrangements often made this impossible. Sometimes therefore groups of three or four students were interviewed. A wide range of responses was given in the pilot study by individuals and groups therefore it was not felt that adhering to a specific number of interview subjects was appropriate.

Classroom contexts

A further issue from the pilot study was that findings showed students to interact with many different features of the learning environment and resources than originally estimated. This aspect of the study became important in the main study as the research then focused on the patterns of LAB that were observed for different kinds of learning environment and resources. Students were observed to interact with each other, with teachers, and with physical objects such as worksheets and interactive whiteboards. To gain a more complete view of students' LAB in graphical situations it was necessary to investigate student interactions with both individuals and with objects. Classroom context refers to the physical items and individuals with which students were involved during graphical tasks. The number of these contexts in the main study was raised to 24 altogether, which included combinations regarded as single contexts. To synthesise this list required careful observation of all the recorded films. The resulting 24 contexts were: whiteboards (WB), mini-whiteboards, interactive whiteboards (IWB), listen to teacher with IWB, student talk with IWB, student-talk with IWB and DART (Directed Activities Related to Text), student-teacher talk with IWB, listen to teacher, listen to teacher with worksheet, listen to teacher with WB, worksheet, DART, student talk and worksheet, student talk and DART, student talk, student talk with WB, student-teacher talk, student-teacher talk with worksheet, student-teacher talk with DART, student-teacher talk with WB, ICT, student talk with ICT, listen to teacher with ICT, student-teacher talk with ICT. These classroom contexts were noted as such when students were plotting or interpreting scientific or mathematical line graphs. As can be seen from this list, classroom contexts had also to include one or more resource, interactive whiteboard, whiteboard, student talk, and student-teacher talk for example. This definition of contexts is specific compared with previous work on learning environments, such as that by Ramsden (1997).

Analysing data

My study eventually investigated student learning approaches from three different perspectives and set these against varying classroom contexts. Two perspectives utilised observation, in visual and audio formats. Here both descriptive accounts of student behaviours and quantitative accounts of time spent exhibiting LAB were obtained. Audio recordings of student talk allowed additional observation through sound just as film permits observation by sight. The third perspective was gained from the student interviews as they made comments regarding classroom contexts and learning approaches used in graphicacy. The interviews thus contain personal and somewhat subjective but different data which complements the visual and audio information. Therefore, the three study perspectives were quantitative observation, qualitative observation and student perceptions.

As all lessons differed in length, 30 minutes of film was analysed for each lesson. In the analysis, behaviours occurring were classified as being one of those listed in Table 13.1. There were episodes in between behaviours, but the aim here was to see the range and frequency of all these behaviours; some lasted a few minutes, others only seconds. The time for which identified learning approach behaviours were exhibited was measured for each 30 minute time slot, together with learning environment features and resources that individuals used concurrently for assistance (classroom contexts). Findings from observations were checked against those from interviews to obtain more accurate results than from a single method strategy. Data provided by conversations, interviews and observations provided alternative perspectives of graphical learning behaviours which, when combined, could give a more thorough explanation of the context than a single method approach.

Iterative film viewing and inter-rater agreement over behaviour categorisations were utilised. This process arose when viewing or listening to recordings since I could not note details of all behaviours or hear all conversation in a single session. Many repeated viewings were necessary. Notes were made on audio and camcorder transcripts as to whether statements reflected a particular learning approach. Classification in this way was repeated several times to ensure that no relevant data were omitted. Next, documents were created for each behaviour in the learning approaches (Kember *et al.* 2004). The times each learning approach was demonstrated were then calculated as well as timings for all LAB. The times each classroom context was in use were measured and the extent of each LAB per minute of context occurrence was determined. Further detail from student conversations and interviews were then used to support conclusions drawn from film observations. Eventually the analysis involved determining the range and frequency of learning approach behaviours associated with different classroom contexts.

I found overall that the LAB in mathematics and science lessons were the same. For both subjects the deep strategic learning approach (DSLA) was used most, followed by the SLA then the DLA and then a further combination, the surface strategic learning approach (SSLA). Indeed, DSLA use in science was five times that of SLA whilst in mathematics it was 11 times greater. Students' perceptions of their LA agreed with the overall findings just outlined in that they either saw themselves as using DSLA behaviours or procedural actions (SLA). There was an additional group who did not know what they thought about their learning, possibly because they did not conceive of this as an area about which to be aware. The DSLA behaviours which occurred most were sustained effort on a graphical task, attending to teachers, attending to text and note-taking. It was then fortunate that I had introduced these as novel behaviours after the pilot study as I could establish the classroom contexts in which these behaviours occurred.

Listening to the teacher alone or in association with a white-board or an IWB was conceived by students to be quite good in terms of understanding. IWB use alone was also linked to graphical comprehension by students. This was interesting as the four classroom contexts associated with the most DSLA were, from greatest to least: listening to teachers with a WB, listening to teachers, an IWB, and listening to teachers with an IWB. Here, student perceptions of classroom contexts corresponded with their actual behaviour. In both subjects there was virtually no discussion, no explaining to fellow students, no relating evidence to conclusions and no checking understanding. Students did, in some science lessons, relate what they had just learned to previous knowledge whilst talking to each other. This phenomenon did not occur in mathematics. Asking questions was a feature of mathematics lessons when students did not understand something, such as detecting anomalies. Students also eagerly volunteered their own ideas in mathematics but not in science. As previously reported, listening to teachers with an IWB was felt by students to aid their understanding. Procedural questions were also asked in all mathematics lessons. The most frequently used classroom context was the worksheet. My results are interesting in many ways; two in particular are, first, that there was so much agreement between students' opinions of classroom context, their thoughts about LA and their behaviour. Second, listening featured little in my literature reading but was strongly linked with a lot of DSLA behaviours.

Reflections on my research journey

In the initial stages of my research I managed to get a lot of work done quickly. Then I slowed down so much that it feels as if I will never finish. However, I have been involved with many research methods, even if some were not used and from this I trust that I have acquired some skills which I did not have previously. I also know a lot about learning approaches in graphical learning situations across many classrooms. Some of my findings are not only interesting but unexpected. I am pleased to say that I have plenty of results and have to give short accounts when people ask what I have found because it is not possible to summarise it all for those not involved with education. I enjoyed the analysis because much of it was a repetitive routine which I found satisfying.

References

Bain, J. (1994). 'Understanding by Learning or Learning by Understanding'. Professorial lecture, Brisbane, Griffith University, 28 September.

Beckmann, C.E. (1989). 'Interpreting Graphs'. *Mathematics Teacher* 82(5): 353–60.

Biggs, J. (1993). 'What do Inventories of Students' Learning Processes really Measure? A Theoretical Review and Clarification'. *British Journal of Educational Psychology* 63(1): 3–19.

Biggs, J. (2001). 'Enhancing Learning: A Matter of Style or Approach?' In: Sternberg, R.J. and Zhang, L. (eds), *Perspectives on Thinking, Learning and Cognitive Styles*. Mahwah, NJ: Lawrence Erlbaum Associates, pp. 73–102.

Biggs, J. (2003). *Teaching for Quality Learning at University (2nd edn)*. Maidenhead: Society for Research into Higher Education & Open University Press.

Bucher, R., Fritz, C.E. and Quarantelli, E.L. (2003). *Tape Recorded Interviews in Social Research*. London: Sage, pp. 3–11.

Byrne, M., Flood, B. and Willis, P. (2004). 'Validation of the Approaches and Study Skills Inventory for Students (ASSIST) using Accounting Students in the USA and Ireland'. *Accounting Education* 13(4): 449–59.

Chin, C. and Brown, D.E. (2000a). 'Learning Deeply in Science: An Analysis and Reintegration of Deep Approaches in Two Case Studies of Grade 8 Students'. *Research in Science Education* 30(2): 173–97.

Chin, C. and Brown, D. E. (2000b). 'Learning in Science: A Comparison of Deep and Surface Learning Approaches'. *Journal of Research in Science Teaching* 37(2): 109–38.

Entwistle, D.R. (1987). 'A Model of the Teacher Learning Process'. In: Richardson, J.T.E., Eysenck, M.W. and Warren Piper, D. (eds), *Student Learning: Research in Education and Cognitive Psychology*. Milton Keynes: Society for Research into Higher Education and Open University Press, pp. 13–28.

Entwistle, N. and Marton, F. (1984). 'Changing Conceptions of Learning and Research'. In: Marton, F., Hounsell, D. and Entwistle, D.R. (eds), *The Experience of Learning*. Edinburgh: Scottish Academic Press, pp. 211–42.

Forster, P. (2002). 'Graphing: An Area which Consistently gives Students much Difficulty'. *Australian Mathematics Teacher* 58(2): 18–20.

Glazer, N. (2011). 'Challenges with Graph Interpretation: A Review of the Literature'. *Studies in Science Education* 47(2): 183–210.

Goldsworthy, A., Watson, R., Wood-Robison, V., Sams, J. and Smith, C. (2000). *Getting to Grips with Graphs*. Hatfield: Association of Science Education.

Kember, D., Biggs, J. and Leung, D.Y.P. (2004). 'Examining the Multidimensionality of Approaches to Learning through the Development of a Revised Version of the Learning Process Questionnaire'. *British Journal of Educational Psychology* 74(2): 261–80.

Kvale, S. (1996). *Interviews: An Introduction to Qualitative Research Interviewing*. Thousand Oaks, CA: Sage.

Leinhardt, G., Zaslavsky, O. and Stein, M.K. (1990). 'Functions, Graphs, and Graphing: Task Learning and Teaching'. *Review of Educational Research* 60(1): 1–64.

Marton, F. and Booth, S. (1997). *Learning and Awareness*. Mahwah, NJ: Lawrence Erlbaum Associates.

Moschkovich, J.N. (2003). 'What Counts as Mathematical Discourse?' International Group for the Psychology of Mathematics Education held jointly with the 5th PME-NA Conference. Honolulu, HI, vol 3, pp. 325–32.

Nolen, S.B. and Haladyna, T.M. (1990). 'Motivation and Studying in High School Science. *Journal of Research in Science Teaching* 27(2): 115–26.

Norman, R.R. (2011). 'Reading the Graphics What is the Relationship between Graphical Reading Processes and Student Comprehension.' *Reading and Writing* 25(3): 739–44.

Pimm, D. (1987). *Pupils' Mathematical Talk. Speaking Mathematically: Communication in Mathematics Classrooms*. London: Routledge, pp. 22–49.

Postigo, Y. and Pozo, J.I. (2004). 'On the roAd to Graphicacy: The Learning of Graphical Representation Systems'. *Educational Psychology* 24(5): 623–44.

Preece, J. (ed.) (1983). *Graphs are not Straightforward*. London: Academic Press.

Ramsden, P. (1997). 'The Context of Learning in Academic Departments'. In: Marton, F., Hounsell, D.J. and Entwistle, N.J. (eds), *The Experience of Learning*, 2nd edn. Edinburgh: Scottish Academic Press, pp. 198–216.

Sternberg, R.J. and Zhang, L. (2001). *Perspectives on Thinking, Learning and Cognitive Styles*. Mahwah, NJ: Lawrence Erlbaum Associates Publishers.

Sudman, S. (2003). *Reducing Response Error in Surveys* 2(33). London: Sage.

Swatton, P. and Taylor, R.M. (1994). 'Pupil Performance in Graphical Tasks and its Relationship to the Ability to Handle Variables'. *British Educational Research Journal* 20(2): 227–40.

14 Insights and lessons from primary science teachers' initial professional learning and collaborative practices in questioning

Tan Ying Chin

In my doctoral thesis, my aim was to understand the processes of teacher learning and collaboration when teachers were initiated into a professional development programme focusing on questioning to promote higher-order scientific discourse. The research informed me as a science curriculum specialist on the design of school-based professional development to support schools in implementing the Singapore primary science curriculum which focuses on inquiry. The professional development of teachers is important to equip them with the knowledge and skills to facilitate students in asking questions, collecting evidence through investigations as well as explaining observations.

At the start, I had to decide on the focus of teacher learning, rationalising the choice of Chin's (2007) questioning framework among the many questioning frameworks in the literature. Besides, I also had to conceptualise how both individual and collaborative learning experiences could be introduced in the actual ecology of a primary school in Singapore. I had to find out what to focus on, based on possibilities and challenges on engaging teachers' prior knowledge and providing opportunities for enacting and reflecting on practices. My prior experiences in the professional development of teachers as well as the engagement with the literature have helped me to develop a framework for learning and collaboration in teacher questioning.

Having designed and implemented the framework for learning and collaboration in teacher questioning, I then explored various models of teacher change and growth which I could use as an analytical framework to analyse multiple evidence of teachers' learning across workshop and lesson platforms. In exploring the interconnected model of teacher professional growth (Clarke and Hollingsworth 2002), besides analysing the four interconnected domains (personal domain, domain of practice, domain of consequence and external domain) and the mediating processes of reflection and enactment, I contributed to further development of the model by uncovering new change sequences and growth networks which are unique to the Singapore context.

In this chapter, I will show how I have conceptualised teacher learning from both the literature and my practitioner experience, which then informed how I designed my study and analysed my data as follows:

- identifying professional learning of teacher questioning as focus of research
- observation of teacher questioning in practice
- conceptualising my research question
- developing a framework for learning and collaboration in teacher questioning
- analysing my research on teacher learning and collaboration in questioning
- using empirical data to inform theory and practice of teacher learning.

Identifying professional learning of teacher questioning as focus of research

In Singapore, the aim of primary science education is to provide students with experiences that build on their interest in, and stimulate their curiosity about, their environment. Through engaging in a variety of learning experiences, students construct basic scientific concepts as well as develop important skills, habits of mind, and attitudes necessary for scientific inquiry. Scientific inquiry is central to the new primary science curriculum which is designed to emphasise teaching and learning approaches that nurture students as inquirers and critical thinkers. To be effective inquirers in the twenty-first century, students should be provided with opportunities to be critical thinkers, engaging in higher order scientific discourse in various contexts of inquiry activities which incorporate essential features of inquiry such as questioning, gathering evidence, constructing explanations, making connections, and justifying explanations through communication in the teaching and learning of science (National Research Council [NRC] 2000). Teachers are encouraged to use various strategies to incorporate these essential features of inquiry: in posing and responding to questions, designing investigations using evidence to support inferences, and evaluating and communicating their learning (student-directed inquiry) compared to the degree of involvement the teacher takes (teacher-guided inquiry).

With the implementation of the new primary science curriculum in Singapore which was designed to emphasise teaching and learning approaches that nurture students as inquirers and critical thinkers, I was interested to explore how to better support teachers as a curriculum specialist-in-charge of planning and implementing the primary science curriculum. As a curriculum specialist, I oversee the design of the primary science curriculum as well as resources to support teaching and learning. I also conceptualise and conduct professional development to support teachers in implementing the curriculum.

In my study, I wanted to focus on the ways in which teachers could develop questioning practices that support students as inquirers in different topics and contexts of learning. This involved developing a programme of support to engage teachers' knowledge and beliefs on teacher questioning, develop and apply knowledge and skills by enacting questioning in practice, as well as reflect on lesson design and use of questioning in promoting higher-order scientific discourse. Hence, my aim in the research was to understand how teachers learned about effective questioning in response to the professional development programme I led.

Teacher questioning is well recognised as an important determinant of quality classroom interactions (Wellington and Osborne 2001). Science educators and researchers recognise the importance of studying teacher questioning not in isolation but using questions in scientific discourse to promote student learning and outcomes in different contexts of inquiry activities. Recently, we see research on questioning presented in terms of frameworks (Chin 2007; Mortimer and Scott 2000; van Zee *et al.* 2001). In this regard, I was particularly interested in exploring Chin's (2007) questioning framework in the primary context as it was first developed in the context of secondary science in Singapore. Her research provided insights into how individual questions were put together to influence student responses and thinking, as well as how questions could help achieve teachers' goals in science teaching and learning contexts. Besides, I found this framework useful because it not only described the features of the four questioning approaches (Socratic questioning, verbal jigsaw, semantic tapestry and framing) but included the different strategies that teachers used for each of the questioning approaches (see Table 14.1). This is a realistic reflection of actual questioning practices in everyday classrooms – different ways of using questioning approaches by different teachers.

Observation of teacher questioning in practice

Prior to conducting my thesis research, I first observed how two teachers used questioning to promote students' higher-order scientific discourse in primary science classrooms in Singapore. I found out how Chin's (2007) four questioning approaches were used with six pedagogies (whole class discussion, investigation, game, role play, concept mapping and information technology) and associated with students' higher level of cognitive responses in the topic 'Reproduction'. In this study, I looked for evidence of high cognitive level of thinking in students' responses to teachers' questioning and classified the cognitive levels of student responses within the teacher-student discourse as high or low using the Revised Bloom's Taxonomy (Anderson *et al.* 2001). Interestingly, while both teachers were observed to use a variety of questioning approaches, they were not fully aware of and did not plan questioning approaches though they planned a few specific questions. While research studies have highlighted how teacher

Table 14.1 Teacher questioning approaches derived from Chin (2007)

Questioning-based approach and strategies used	Features	When used
Socratic questioning	Use a series of questions to prompt and guide student thinking	To encourage student to generate ideas based on reasoning and prior knowledge
• Pumping	Encourage students to provide more information via explicit requests	To foster student talk
• Reflective toss	Pose a question response to a prior utterance made by the student	To throw the responsibility of thinking back to the student
• Constructive challenge	Pose a question that stimulates student thinking instead of giving direct corrective feedback	To encourage student to reflect on and reconsider his answer if he gives an inappropriate response
Verbal jigsaw	Focus on the use of scientific terminology, keywords and phrases to form integrated propositional statements	For topics with several technical terms; for students weak in language skills
• Association of key words and phrases	Guide students to form a series of propositional statements to form a coherent mental framework	To introduce factual or descriptive information and to reinforce scientific vocabulary
• Verbal close	Pause in mid-sentence to allow students to verbally 'fill-in-the-blanks' to complete the sentence	To elicit or emphasise keywords and phrases, for students who are not articulate or verbally expressive
Semantic tapestry	Help students weave disparate ideas together into a conceptual framework like constructing a tapestry of ideas	To focus on ideas and abstract concepts; for topics not associated with an abundance of technical terms
• Multi-pronged questioning	Pose questions from different angles that address multiple aspects of a problem	To help students view a problem from different angles and perspectives
• Stimulating multimodal thinking	Pose questions that involve the use of a range of thinking (e.g. verbal, visual, symbolic, logical-mathematical) using talk, diagrams, visual images, symbols, formulas and calculations	To encourage students to think in a variety of modes and understand the concept from multiple perspectives

Table 14.1 continued

Questioning-based approach and strategies used	Features	When used
• Focusing and zooming	Guide students to think at both the visible, macro level and at the micro or molecular level; or use questions that zoom 'in and out', alternating between a big, broad question and more specifically focused, subordinate questions	To help students understand a concept at both the macro, overarching level and the micro, in-depth level
Framing	Use questions to frame a problem, issue or topic and to structure the discussion that ensues	To help students see the relationship between a question and the information that it addresses
• Question-based prelude	Use question-answer propositions; questions act as an advance organiser and lead-in to information presented subsequently	For expository talk to preface declarative statements and to focus student thinking
• Question-based outline	Present a big, broad question and subordinate or related questions visually (e.g. on slides)	To visually focus students' thinking and help students see the links between the big question and subordinate questions
• Question-based summary	Give an overall summary in a question-and-answer format to consolidate the key points	At end of lesson to recapitulate key concepts succinctly

questioning can potentially stimulate students' higher order thinking (Chin 2006), questioning, like other beneficial strategies, does not guarantee student learning. This can be due to a multitude of complex and inter-related mitigating reasons that involve the teacher, learner and the social/physical surroundings such as the teacher's understanding, beliefs and practice (Spillane *et al.* 2002).

It was useful to have observed teacher questioning in practice prior to my study. As I introduced teachers to the questioning approaches that stimulate thinking (Chin 2007) to promote higher order scientific discourse, it is important to understand how teachers learn individually and learn with other teachers. Hence, in the thesis, I focused on exploring how teachers learn and collaborate to plan and use questions to promote higher order discourse in different contexts of inquiry activities. A study in this area is valuable as Darling-Hammond and Bransford (2005) highlighted that there is still a lack of research on how teacher learning affects teaching practices/student outcomes as well as how they learn successful practices. Besides, a more recent review by Capps *et al.* (2012) also revealed the lack of empirical literature on inquiry professional development.

Conceptualising my research question

Based on my observations of teachers' practice in questioning, my research question was, 'How do teachers learn and collaborate during the initiation of a professional development programme focusing on questioning to promote higher-order scientific discourse in primary science classrooms?' Teacher learning and collaborating referred to learning both individually and with others. This included involving teachers in first reflecting on the questioning typologies as well as examples of teaching and learning individually, before discussing reflections with me and the other teachers at the questioning workshop. Beyond the workshop, teachers worked with each other to develop and apply knowledge and skills of questioning in lesson design and practice for different topics and contexts of inquiry activities before customising the lessons for their individual classes. Besides lesson planning and customising, teachers also reflected on lesson design and use of questioning in promoting higher order scientific discourse individually and together with other teachers. Questioning here was confined to the four approaches from Chin's (2007) questioning framework. Scientific discourse referred to verbal interactions on science ideas or concepts between teacher-student(s) and student(s)-student(s), recognised as a means of communicating science.

Developing a framework for learning and collaboration in teacher questioning

After conceptualising my research question, I wanted to have a better theoretical understanding of learning in order to plan a learning programme for my teachers. I read more about the sociocultural theory of learning which helped me in deciding on the theoretical framework for my study on social constructivism. Central to Vygotsky's (1978) sociocultural theory of learning is how learning is mediated by other people and cultural artefacts, including physical objects (e.g. textbooks and the Internet) and social processes (e.g. various pedagogies). This theory supported my role as a curriculum specialist in designing professional development for teachers: structuring learning experiences (for teachers working individually and with others) in questioning and studying the process of teachers' learning as they initiate changes in practice in questioning to promote higher order scientific discourse. As teachers' learning is social, the roles of others including teachers and students in the learning process needed to be considered (Smidt 2009). In the learning process, teachers might build on their own prior knowledge and experiences as well as learn when interacting with other teachers during the enactment and reflection of questioning practices. As it is often said of Vygotsky's work, learning leads development and that learning appears between people on an interpsychological plane and inside the learner on an intrapsychological plane. This had implications on how learning experiences were purposefully designed for teachers to engage, enact and reflect on using questions to promote scientific discourse.

Figure 14.1 shows the framework of teacher learning and collaboration in teacher questioning, which I designed based on the principles of how people learn. The framework comprises three concentric rings. For each ring, I included considerations on how teachers learn individually and with other teachers. In the first, innermost, ring, each teacher's knowledge and beliefs on teacher questioning were engaged using questioning typologies and examples of teaching and learning as learning stimuli. Each teacher reflected individually before sharing their reflection with other teachers. In the next, middle, ring, teachers were provided with opportunities to work together to develop and apply knowledge and skills by planning lessons together before customising and enacting questioning individually for different topics and contexts of inquiry activities. In the third, outermost, ring, teachers reflected on lesson design and use of questioning in promoting higher order scientific discourse individually before sharing their reflections with other teachers. Overall, the framework was useful for my study as it provided a guide in designing learning experiences for individual and groups of teachers, from engaging their prior knowledge to enacting and reflecting on their practice in promoting higher order scientific discourse.

Using the principles of learning and the above framework of learning and collaboration (Figure 14.1), I developed a professional development model comprising three phases of 13 learning experiences (individually and with other teachers). In the first phase, teachers' knowledge and beliefs on teacher questioning were engaged through discussion and reflection using questioning typologies and videos of teaching and learning as learning stimuli. In the second phase, teachers were provided with opportunities to develop and apply knowledge and skills by enacting questioning in practice through lesson design and conduct of sixteen lessons in four topics and different contexts of inquiry activities. In the third phase, teachers reflected on lesson design and use of questioning in promoting higher-order scientific discourse. Teachers' learning experiences across the three phases were not seen as sequential but a continual process of learning, where teachers went through cycles of enactment and reflection.

The design of this model of professional development on teacher questioning was facilitated by the framework of learning and collaboration in Figure 14.1. The framework provided the focus for each phase of learning

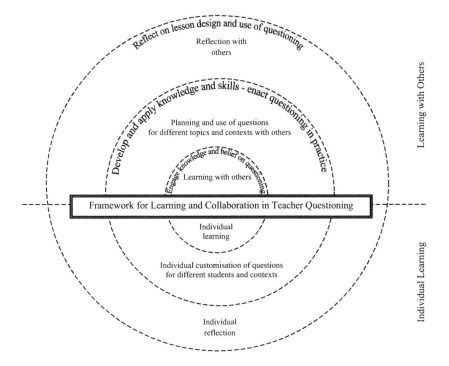

Figure 14.1 Framework for learning and collaboration in teacher questioning

(e.g. in enacting or reflecting on questioning) and guided the design of specific learning experiences (learning experiences involving individuals or with other teachers) within each phase of learning.

Analysing my research on teacher learning and collaboration in questioning

My research focus was on how teachers changed as a result of the professional development programme, what kinds of learning took place as they developed and applied what they have learned about questioning in different topics and contexts of learning. To understand how I would approach the analysis of these data, I explored the literature on teacher learning to inform my analytical approach. Fraser *et al.* (2007) perceive teacher change as a process of learning. They describe teacher change as transactions between teachers' knowledge, experience, beliefs and professional actions. Such transactions need to be considered when providing experiences that help to develop knowledge that teachers can draw on in their practice. The complexity of teacher learning is also acknowledged by Simon and

Campbell (2012), who conceptualise teacher learning as a complex combination of individual teacher's knowledge growth, the professional teacher practicing in a particular setting and the social teacher working with others in the setting. Such notions of complexity were important in my study as it is envisaged that enhancing questioning for higher order scientific discourse relies on development of new knowledge that arises from outside sources in conjunction with practice that is situated in teachers' own contexts.

To better understand the process of teacher change in the actual interplay of the school and classrooms, some researchers have identified different types (or domains) of development based on data to describe how teachers change over time. For example, Bell and Gilbert (1996) described three types of development (social, personal and professional) which occur within components of support, feedback and reflection specifically for science teacher development programmes. For each type of development, three main aspects of learning are identified. For example, for social development, teachers may initially see isolation as problematic. They may progress to valuing ways of working and reconstructing what it means to be a teacher of science and value working with other teachers. Over time, they may initiate ways of working with others. These models of teacher development reminded me that while the types of development may be defined, teachers' actual development might not follow a fixed sequence in the actual learning process and may vary from teacher to teacher too.

Other researchers tried to understand the actual process of teacher change by identifying change domains and studying the relationships between them. The common change domains which are the knowledge and practice domains, in particular the interplay between teacher knowledge and practice, now represented as a typology of 'knowledge-for-practice', 'knowledge-in-practice', and 'knowledge-of-practice' (Cochran-Smith and Lytle 1999). Goodnough (2010) used this typology to examine the relationships between teacher knowledge and practices, providing insights into the nature of teacher learning and practice. Others, such as McMeniman *et al.* (2000), tried to further understand teacher learning, by exploring teachers' roles as learners and as collaborators. This attempt to understand teachers' learning with others was also important in my study as it helped in understanding how teachers' knowledge could be socially constructed with others and in practice.

Some researchers went beyond just examining the relationship between teacher knowledge and practice to include other domains of change and mediating processes of change. The interconnected model of teacher professional growth (Clarke and Hollingsworth 2002) is one of the few models that suggests how change occurs through the mediating processes of 'reflection' and 'enactment' in four distinct domains: the personal domain (teacher knowledge, beliefs and attitudes), the domain of practice (professional experimentation), the domain of consequence (salient outcomes), and the external domain (sources of information or stimulus). The mediating processes of reflection and enaction are represented in the model as arrows linking the domains. For instance, the external stimuli can prompt teachers' enactment in practice and changes in their personal domain. Teachers' reflection on their practice can lead to changes in the domain of consequences and reconstruction of their personal knowledge, beliefs and attitudes. Hence, this cyclical model is useful in understanding the process of teachers' learning and collaboration in my study.

Clarke and Hollingsworth (2002) also provided empirical grounding of the interconnected model by reporting teachers' change of ideas or practices. They used evidence of teachers' exploration of strategies and activities and reporting of ideas. The process by which change occurs was represented as the 'change sequence', consisting of two or more domains together with reflective and enactive links connecting these domains. A change sequence associated with more lasting change is termed a 'growth network'. I was particularly interested in this model as I could understand how teachers learned and collaborated by analysing the domains of change and mediating processes. For example, based on the data collected for classroom observation and interviews, I mapped out how teachers reflected on external stimuli presented at the workshop and enacted what they learned in practice. I also included teachers' reflection on their practices and how these led to changes in the personal domain of knowledge, beliefs or attitudes and/or domain of consequences (student outcomes).

Using empirical data to inform theory and practice of teacher learning

Based on my empirical findings, I have used the interconnected model of Clarke and Hollingsworth (2002) to analyse and present change sequences and growth network in the four domains of external domain (E), knowledge (K), practice (P), salient outcomes (S). I have gained insights into the value of the model as an analytical tool to study how teachers enacted and reflected on Chin's (2007) questioning framework at the workshop sessions, lesson conduct and post-lesson discussions presented. I could study in depth how they initiated their learning with other teachers in the real-life contexts of the school and classrooms.

Firstly, I could identify the various learning stimuli within the external domain. These include Chin's (2007) questioning framework and videos of teaching and learning introduced at the workshop; stretches of scientific discourses from teachers' own lesson videos and transcripts at the post-lesson discussions; as well as teachers' discussions at both the workshop sessions and post-lesson discussions. Using the interconnected model, I could trace and understand how the stimuli led to teachers' change sequences and/or growth networks for teachers' learning and plan for learning stimuli in future professional development.

Secondly, the model could capture the multidimensional nature of teacher learning. I could use the model to analyse how the various stimuli at the workshop and post lesson discussion platforms (external domain) brought about changes in the other domains including the personal domain (knowledge and belief in questioning), domain of practice (experimentation with Chin's questioning framework) and domain of consequence (student learning and thinking in scientific discourse). Teachers' initial changes in practice included refinements/extensions rather than fundamental changes of their questioning practices. This shows the importance of considering teachers' existing knowledge, beliefs and practice in introducing new pedagogical approaches.

Thirdly, as the four domains (external domain, personal domain, domain of practice and domain of consequence) are linked by the mediating processes of enactment and reflection in the model, I could use the model to analyse teachers' change and growth across the four interconnected domains, beyond the workshop platform and across lessons. Some of the teachers' change sequences are similar but the overall growth networks for different teachers are different. This shows that the interconnected, non-linear structure of the model enabled the identification of different individual sequences and growth networks, recognising the idiosyncratic and individual nature of teacher professional growth. Hence, in designing professional development, it is important to incorporate flexibility as teachers enact and reflect differently and hence learn through different pathways. This responsive approach to professional development is aligned to the suggestion by Clarke and Hollingsworth (2002) to deliberately design programs to provide teachers with the opportunity to enact change in a variety of forms and change sequences consistent with individual inclinations.

Concluding remarks

In conceptualising my research, observations of teacher practice helped me to identify my research question which focused on understanding how teachers learn and collaborate when a professional development programme is undertaken to inform the design of school-based professional development on teacher questioning. Guided by the observations of teacher practices and the research question, I conceptualised an original framework of teacher learning and collaboration in teacher questioning designed based on the principles of how people learn. This framework was useful in guiding the design of the school-based professional development model comprising learning experiences for the individual and with other teachers. In the process, I have developed as a practitioner and contributed as a researcher to the knowledge of teacher learning. I designed my research based on the needs of teachers and what other research says about professional development of teachers.

While implementing the model of professional development, the interconnected model of teacher professional growth by Clarke and Hollingsworth (2002) was useful in analysing and understanding teachers' learning in terms of change and growth, providing insights into the complexity of and differences in teachers' learning of a new questioning framework by Chin (2007), from the workshop participation to lesson enactment to post-lesson discussions. Besides using the model to identify the interconnections of individual teacher's personal knowledge, belief, professional practice and salient outcomes, this study has contributed to the development of the model of Clarke and Hollingsworth (2002) by using it to understand how teachers enact and reflect with other teachers in the learning process.

Overall, the study has also contributed to the understanding of teacher learning as reflective and collaborative in the area of questioning. The empirical findings of how teachers learn individually and with other teachers in an authentic school setting were particularly valuable in understanding the complexity of teachers' learning and practices in questioning. These findings have made a significant contribution in informing the design of teacher professional development in questioning, an important feature of science inquiry in the twenty-first century.

References

Anderson, L., Krathwohl, R., Airasian, P., Cruikshank, K., Mayer, R., Pintrich, P., Raths, J., and Wittrock, M. (eds) (2001). *Taxonomy for Learning, Teaching and Assessing: A Revision of Bloom's Taxonomy.* New York: Longman.

Bell, B. and Gilbert, J. (1996). *Teacher Development: A Model from Science Education.* Bristol, PA: Falmer Press.

Capps, D.K., Crawford, B.A. and Constas, M.A. (2012). 'A Review of Empirical Literature on Inquiry Professional Development: Alignment with Best Practices and a Critique of the Findings'. *Journal of Science Teacher Education* 23(3): 291–318.

Chin, C. (2006). 'Using Self-questioning to Promote Pupils' Process Skills Thinking'. *School Science Review* 87(321): 113–19.

Chin, C. (2007). 'Teacher Questioning in Science Classrooms: Approaches that Stimulate Productive Thinking'. *Journal of Research in Science Teaching* 44(6): 815–43.

Clarke, D. and Hollingsworth, H. (2002). 'Elaborating a Model of Teacher Professional Growth'. *Teaching and Teacher Education* 18(8): 947–67.

Cochran-Smith, M. and Lytle, S.L. (1999). 'Relationships of Knowledge and Practice: Teacher Learning in Communities'. *Review of Research in Education* 24(1): 249–305.

Darling-Hammond, L. and Bransford, H. (2005). *Preparing Teachers for a Changing World. What Teachers should Learn and be Able to Do.* California: Jossey-Bass.

Fraser, C., Kennedy, A., Reid, L. and Mckinney, S. (2007). 'Teachers' Continuing Professional Development: Contested Concepts, Understandings and Models'. *Professional Development in Education* 33(2): 153–69.

Goodnough, K. (2010). 'Teacher Learning and Collaborative Action Research: Generating a "knowledge-of-practice" in the Context of Science Education'. *Journal of Science Teacher Education* 21(8): 917–35.

McMeniman, M., Cumming, J., Wilson, J., Stevenson, J. and Sim, C. (2000). *Teacher Knowledge in Action: The Impact of Educational Research*. Australia: Department of Education, Training and Youth Affairs.

Mortimer, E. and Scott, P. (2000). 'Analysing Discourse in the Science Classroom'. In: Millar, R., Leach, J. and Osborne, J. (eds), *Improving Science Education*. Buckingham: Open University Press, pp. 126–42.

National Research Council (NRC) (2000). *Inquiry and the National Science Education Standards*. Washington, DC: National Academy Press.

Simon, S. and Campbell, S. (2012). 'Teacher and Professional Development in Science Education'. In: Fraser, B.J., Tobin, K. and McRobbie, C., (eds). *Second International Handbook of Science Education*. Dordrecht: Springer, pp. 159–80.

Smidt, S. (2009). *Introducing Vygotsky. A Guide for Practitioners and Students in Early Years Education*. London: Routledge.

Spillane, J.P., Reiser, B.J. and Reimer, T. (2002). 'Policy Implementation and Cognition: Reframing and Refocusing Implementation Research'. *Review of Educational Research* 72(3): 387–431.

van Zee, E.H., Iwasyk, M., Kurose, A., Simpson, D. and Wild, J. (2001). 'Student and Teacher Questioning during Conversations about Science'. *Journal of Research in Science Teaching* 38(2): 159–90.

Vygotsky, L.S. (1978). *Mind in Society: The Development of Higher Psychological Processes*. Cambridge, MA: Harvard University Press.

Wellington, J. and Osborne, J. (2001). 'Talk of the Classroom: Language Interactions between Teachers and Pupils'. In: Wellington, J. and Osborne, J. (eds), *Language and Literacy in Science Education*. Buckingham, UK: Open University Press, pp. 24–40.

15 Conclusions

Shirley Simon, Christina Ottander and Ilka Parchmann

In compiling the narratives for this book we have been impressed by the depth of analysis of learning which has resulted from reflecting on the doctoral research journey. Editing the chapters involved several rounds of discussion with the PhD students, with one outcome being a clarified structure of their own thread, or red line, of research for those situated at the beginning or even in the middle of their journey. The chapters show how and when authors have made decisions regarding research focus, theory and methodology at different phases of their research. Important to this process has been the willingness to reflect, particularly on parts of the journey that have been difficult. These reflections have enlightened us as supervisors to a range of issues faced by our doctoral students at different phases of the learning journey. Authors have also identified ways in which they have been supported and found their way past difficulties.

How do our authors now continue? Once the doctorate has been achieved, there is an adjustment to be made for future direction. Most doctoral students will move back into practice, but there are issues in how they do this, and take with them the learning from the journey. Impact on practice can also be achieved by 'translating' research findings into teaching and learning materials, or by publishing the work in different outlets. Adrian has written a short account of the issues he faced in getting published that illustrates his experiences of finding a successful way of disseminating research results aimed at changing practice. Clearly, the challenge of bridging the gap between research and practice will be a continuous issue for our field of research to which this book might contribute some scaffolding ideas.

Overcoming challenges – tasks and lessons to be learnt for supervisors

One clear message from most authors in this book is that the doctoral journey has moments of uncertainty and even confusion. This correlates with the findings of Trafford and Leshem (2009) who suggest that recognising and resolving difficulties arising from intellectual confusion are 'critical points' in the journey towards achieving the doctorate. All doctoral students need to overcome these critical points in order to achieve an understanding of what 'doctorateness' means in theory and looks like in practice (Trafford and Leshem 2009). Trafford and Leshem (2009) point out the importance of understanding the research process as an integrated network of components; if intellectual difficulties get in the way of such an understanding, then the necessary conceptualisation of the research process is blocked. When such blockages occur, students need to find a way to overcome them, otherwise they can experience extreme emotions of self-doubt and low self-esteem until they are overcome.

Intellectual blockages can be identified in the narratives of our student authors, for example, in Katarina's or Karolina's and need to be recognised as a common feature in most doctoral students' learning journeys. Understanding how such blockages are overcome through a deeper under-standing of how theory can inform research design or analytical processes has been a key issue for many of our students. The students who exemplify practitioner-led design-based research have particularly long struggles if they are not guided well or find theories that they can use to interpret large data sets. Tan Ying, Katarina and Elizabeth were all guided in their research by practitioner-led design, though in different ways. Elizabeth collected data from many observations of teacher-designed graphical tasks. Katarina did design her own tasks but, like Elizabeth, had large amounts of data and no easy way to see how to get at what she really wanted until she read about interpretative repertoires. Tan Ying read widely and was able to see how a model of teacher learning could analyse the data collected from a number of sources. Finding a successful way of combining large and complex data sets with regard to authentic and therefore not reduced artefacts from practice and a clear focus with regard to theory and structured analyses can become a great challenge for those doctoral students aiming to bridge research and practice. Supervisors should keep that in mind and prepare scaffolding questions early on during the doctoral students' journeys to prevent long periods of frustration and of being lost in a 'jungle of data'.

The following account is included here as it exemplifies a further case of a practitioner who took many years to achieve the understanding needed to identify how theory could inform his research. His case shows how our conceptualisation of journeys through research can enable us to recognise these routes in other students, and hence see what their problems might be.

Birendra Singh recently passed his PhD examination after many years of periodically interrupted study that transpired from a range of problems, including changing supervisors four times due to death or retirement, changing his own practitioner role and collecting data whilst he lacked research focus. He was unable to contribute to this book, but his story is of particular interest regarding blockages as experienced by practitioners becoming researchers, and who gather large amounts of data from a prac-titioner perspective. At the time of initiating his study, Birendra was a local inspector for science teaching in London. His work took him frequently into classrooms to observe lessons. He became curious as to the reasons why formative assessment in science, so widely promoted by studies in the 1990s by Black and Wiliam (1998), was not being implemented in practice. He embarked on a long observation and interview study to explore the reasons for this, reading literature on formative assessment to inform his observations. When it came to analysing his large data set, Birendra found the task overwhelming; he entered a largely descriptive account for his 50 per cent upgrade, which failed due to lack of focus and theory. Essentially, at this time, Birendra had not managed to intellectualise his research beyond a practitioner focus (in this case of an inspector), which blocked his ability to conceptualise the research process in such a way as to achieve recognisable potential for doctorateness. In response to this failure, Birendra went to conferences, read, and found in the words and writings of Roy Bhaskar (2008) a theory (critical realism) that chimed with what, deep down, he knew to be the real issues he identified in the ways in which schools implemented formative assessment. The use of this theory enabled Birendra to analyse his data more systematically and synthesise useful messages about the implementation of formative assessments in schools. He re-submitted and passed his upgrade, and a few years later passed the final PhD successfully.

Birendra's story is very similar to Katarina's search for a theory with which to analyse her large data set of student discussions about sustainability issues. Both Birendra and Katarina needed to step back from their studies and 'breathe' around their work in order to proceed. Doctoral students should take note that there are ways to overcome such blockages in conceptualising research, yet stay true to what they believe in as practitioners. The value of both students' findings in this practitioner-led design lies in close proximity to practice that their theoretical perspectives have achieved.

Which support structures could help students to avoid getting lost for too long? One way of obtaining conceptual clarity and helping to avoid intellectual confusion has been the use of a visual model for the research; for example, Jenny's use of the iceberg model helped her conceptualise what was important in terms of motivational factors. Sofie illustrated her need to visualise interdisciplinarity through a Venn diagram. Julian found Mahaffy's tetrahedron and immediately applied this to designing his tasks and analytical foci. Supervisors can initiate this graphical reflection by asking guiding questions and by providing elements of consideration, like the 'educational triangle' of connecting the teacher's, the learner's and the content perspectives in one's own research.

A second support structure is given by the different doctoral programs and/or by larger research project groups. The doctoral programmes in the different countries show great diversity concerning their formal support structures, with Sweden being the most formalised. The reason for

Sweden's formalisation is a policy-led change in recent years to limit the time it takes to reach a PhD certificate and to limit withdrawals. Most PhD students from Sweden belong to graduate schools with a high proportion of mandatory methodological and theoretical courses within the doctoral degree. Hence in Sweden, the PhD programme includes provision of various forms of collective 'research training'. In Germany many students belong to research groups, collaborating in a common research project but focussing on their individual research questions, as described by Christine and Wilfried, for example. The examples from the UK show various types of arrangements that are possible. Even though the support structures of graduate schools or being enrolled in method and/or theory courses are not mentioned much in the students' narratives, the reflective narratives clearly show how belonging to different graduate schools and/or taking different courses have effects on research journeys and the paradigms in science education they meet (see Treagust *et al.* 2014).

Again, other sources of support mentioned in the narratives are the learning opportunities created in discussions with others during seminars, conferences and discussion of literature in meetings with supervisors and peers. These types of discussions are mentioned both by those who belong to larger project teams and those who have a more individual research milieu. Some narratives however also report about how these meetings could include very different 'voices' in the different contexts, and how they made them feel insecure and that they had almost lost confidence in their ideas, especially in the beginning. Kobayashi *et al.* (2013) report about how to transfer diverging voices into learning opportunities.

Other studies have also highlighted that it is through conversations, interactions and exchange of ideas and feedback that doctoral students grow into becoming researchers. For example, Jazvac-Martek (2009) reports about a qualitative study on doctoral student experiences in the PhD process. She uses the social-psychological notion of 'role identities' to describe doctoral experiences to highlight doctoral student agency in the PhD process and oscillations between student and academic role-identities. Some researchers of doctoral education have also asserted that the doctorate is as much about identity formation as it is about producing knowledge (Green 2005), and others use socialisation models to describe the process of acquiring attitudes, beliefs, values and skills needed in the profession (**cf.** Weidman *et al.* 2001). Our experiences from working with the doctoral students during their reflective journey are that reflection helps them to enhance a sense of ownership and academic identity.

What comes next? – Feedback into practice and personal decisions

Why do practitioners start their journey into research even though it might carry many of the difficulties reported in the different chapters of this book? The narratives of the doctoral students in this book carry a substantial and varied agenda. Some of them, like Christine, Julian or Frederike, started their graduate studies only a few years after finishing undergraduate studies; others, like Anne, Annika, Katarina and Adrian, have had substantial experience as a practitioner in school or elsewhere. Phillips and Pugh (2000) report different reasons for starting graduate studies: as a starting point in a formal academic career, as a career-enhancing strategy, or as an acknowledgement of 'cleverness' or validation of the self. The narratives in this book suggest that most of the doctoral students started with sincere questions from their own experience as practitioners. One implication of starting a research journey in this way would be to develop implications for practice that need to be transferred back into practice – either by applying findings in one's own position or by distributing them to the community of practice through training measures, publications or other distribution channels.

Three of the five PhD students from Sweden had the opportunity to start their PhD programme based on initiatives to create career paths to raise the quality of Swedish schools and teacher education. The government investment is intended to get more teachers and teacher educators with a doctoral degree to develop more practitioner-centred educational research approaches and take responsibility over more systematic research-based school developments. This initiative by the Swedish government to stimulate teachers in school and preschool to proceed with doctoral studies aiming for a licentiate or PhD degree has been very attractive, but it is too early to say how successful it has been for the possibility for more systematic research-based school development. Annika and Katarina started graduate schools aiming for a licentiate degree, but when they had completed two years of doctoral studies they realised that they wanted to continue to a doctoral degree, and found funding to enable them to continue. Now at the time of finalising this book they are both at the end of their doctoral studies planning what to do next. Katarina will start a 'three-part position' with three years funding from the university and the municipality to combine being a teacher in upper secondary school, doing research and research-based school development. Annika will temporarily continue as a part time teacher at the university and as a research assistant in an externally funded research project at the university. There can be a delay in getting more teachers with a doctoral degree or a licentiate degree into positions at schools, but during their doctoral studies they are doing practitioner-centred educational research and hopefully they will have the possibility to continue with this work in close association with schools in the future.

The UK students vary in how they are moving forward and taking their learning back into practice. For Anne, much of her learning was put into practice through the course of the actual research, through the professional development of teachers. The excitement and relevance of the research occurred while it was in progress, the doctorate then became an arduous task of writing. However Anne still values the importance of children's voices, which is highly relevant to her current role in primary teacher education. Adrian and Elizabeth see their work as transferable into classroom practice. Adrian was keen to publish his findings (see later). Elizabeth is still working to complete her PhD. Tan Ying has taken her work on teacher learning for higher order questioning back into her role as a professional developer in Singapore.

The four German students have less clear future pathways due to their different backgrounds and stages of their PhD journeys at the time of their writing. Wilfried has already gone back into his position as a high school teacher where he has been allowed to work part-time for four years to enable him to become a member of a project team at IPN. However, he aims to combine his work in school with additional activities in teacher education, if possible again by working in projects at IPN, based on his research experiences. Christine has decided to stay in research, aiming to achieve the next qualification which would be an equivalent to the former 'Habilitation' in Germany. For Julian and Frederike the future is less clear, since they have never worked as teachers. Frederike will continue to work in the large field of science communication and science outreach, for which her PhD experience has certainly enlarged her perspectives both with regard to her personal expertise and her degree of qualification. Julian is still early on in his PhD process, so his research perspectives are still developing. In the future he is planning his career in the chemical industry.

In summary, most of the PhD students who participated in this book have similar starting points as the doctoral students in the study by Shacham and Od-Cohen (2009), being experienced in a professional discourse. The learning characteristics of the PhD students' community of practice in their study show how adult learning theories and the professional discourse enhance the academic discourse through engagement in lifelong learning, and develop researchers contributing to academic culture and society. In a similar way we believe that the authors in this book will be future practitioners or researchers in a position where they can and will have influence on developing learners, learning environments, schools and teacher education.

Independently from our students' own positions, the feedback of research experiences into practice and into research is an important task for the kind of research described in this book. Gaps between research and school practice have been reported continuously in our countries over many years (e.g. Hargreaves 1996; Parchmann 2013; Utbildningsutskottet 2012). From David Hargreaves' lecture (1996) that raised the question about the value of educational research, many discussions and debates have arisen, and there is still a central demand for research in education that aims to achieve improvements in practice. Doctoral students who have started their research from experiences in practice might become a bridge between the two worlds, as they have experienced both of them and have considered both of them throughout their whole research journey. Researchers often hear from teachers that whatever they have found out was already obvious to them before. They ask for the relevance of educational research and rather wish to have the money spent on research to enhance their own school budgets. How could the stories explored in this book help to overcome this problem?

As some of the students like Karolina or Frederike have described, they had to realise the difference between thinking as a practitioner and thinking as a researcher, to become able to set up a systematic research study. One challenge was the identification of a focused problem – would this discussion not also help teachers as communities of constant learners to address challenges and to overcome problems in a more systematic way, breaking down the complexity of classroom situations into a series of criteria? A second challenge was to raise a personal observation to a meta-level and general problem of interest. What had others already done in this area, how have they solved problems and overcome challenges? Which findings could be helpful for an observation and later on research question? A summary of literature related to challenges in practice would certainly be a continuous task to which the authors of this book could add valuable information. A third challenge is to identify supporting tools that would actually help to overcome challenges in practice, like the tasks Karolina and Katarina have developed, or the instruments provided by Wilfried. Researchers that have experienced practice themselves will keep in mind that 25-page questionnaires would not be an instrument for practice; nevertheless it could be a starting point for the development of short diagnostic tools. Also analytical schemes like the ones described by Tan Ying or Christine can later on be applied by practitioners, now being grounded and validated by research and not only an individual practitioner's experience. These aspects might show ways of how to link practice and research and back into practice again; they just need to be set up more systematically.

Another related issue is that of dissemination through publications. Students who have paper-based theses will have published articles as they progressed through their study. However for those doing a monograph thesis publication is not compulsory (though final examination criteria include dissemination plans). Students working towards both types of thesis benefit from sharing their findings at seminars and/or conferences; however to get published in journals or books requires time and patience, and also a certain amount of resilience as one may face rejection, or receive negative reviewers' comments. Annika's and Karolina's difficulties in coming to terms with the limitations of their early work, yet wanting to publish it for one of their articles, highlights a further difficulty of publishing what you have 'moved on' from. Yet the exercise of trying to get published and working with supervisors as co-authors does enable students to become resilient as they learn the ropes of publication. Troman (2002) points out the value of getting published along the way for those also doing a monograph thesis. Adrian has written an account that exemplifies the task of trying to produce a book from a monograph thesis, which demonstrates the difficulties moving from an audience of supervisors and examiners to the international world of science educators. One needs a great deal of drive and belief in one's message to overcome the challenges:

> Naturally, on completing the PhD, my aim was to publish my work and so I wrote a book proposal and submitted it to a number of academic publishers; a venture which met with very little success. Of those publishers who replied, all believed that the subject would not appeal to a sufficiently large readership to justify publication. Now, on the face of it, this must be true for during the whole course of my research I rarely met anyone who shared my interest in the linguistic structures of science examination questions. Yet this is to miss an important point, for the problems that are engendered by scientific lexicology and grammar are not confined to a few examination questions. The wider problems associated with scientific language are well recognised and have been so for many years. How many children are judged to be of low ability simply because of the way in which their examinations are written? How many will children judge themselves in the same way?
>
> Yet, examination questions are not merely lexical and grammatical obstacles to the teaching and learning of science. Their study and analysis can tell us as much about the way that language is used in school science and about the difficulties that science students have with it. Anyone who is able to use Systemic Functional Analysis and who has access to a body of science examination scripts, is in a position to learn a great deal about the linguistics of science education. To my mind, any science educator or researcher would be interested in the findings of this study. Accordingly, I rewrote the proposal to show that the field of interest was greater than might appear at first sight. This second attempt did generate a little more interest and my proposal, along with a sample chapter, was taken up by one publisher for review, which was unsuccessful. On reflection I realised that, up to this point, I had been writing for a very small number of people; my supervisor, a handful of critical friends and ultimately for the members of my viva panel. Each of these had followed the progress of the research and had, either willingly or politely, discussed each stage with me. There was no reason why a new reader should be able to follow the arguments through from beginning to end. I needed to rethink the way in which I had been expressing my ideas, observations and findings. At about this time I also read *How to Publish Your PhD* and in this book Caro (2009) argues that no one really wants to read a PhD thesis. There are those who are professionally obliged to read it and those who might

read it out of kindness but no one would actually take one off the shelf in a book shop and buy it. Accordingly, she urges her readers to rework their theses in order to produce a commercially viable text. Accepting these arguments, I shifted the focus of the book away from the detection and modification of Hallidayian features and the discussions of the attendant methodologies. Instead, I took one examination question and showed how it could be broken down into its various grammatical elements and how these elements, and the relationships between them, can affect the performance of the candidates. This time, the book was accepted for publication (Day 2013). I hope that the book will help linguists, science educators and other researchers, for clearly there is a lot to learn about the language of science education and the construction of examination questions. Whether or not I have been successful in making this case, I cannot say since the book was published only two months before I began to write this chapter. Perhaps it will serve to stimulate further investigation in the same way that other writers have inspired me. I certainly hope so.

Looking back and looking forwards

What final conclusions can we draw from working on this book project? For us as supervisors, the discussions with the students as part of the editorial process gave us many different insights into difficulties and challenges of students that occur between the demands of research and practice that are hardly ever reported in articles or monographs. Each of us – and hopefully other supervisors reading this book – might plan supervision meetings differently now, setting up more guiding questions and scaffolds as bridges between these two worlds.

For the student authors who are still early on their PhD journey, writing their chapter has clearly helped them to re-structure their line of argumentation and to specify their research foci. For the older ones the exchange with the other authors, and becoming a peer-reviewer for other chapters, showed them that the difficulties they had faced were rather common for PhD students in similar situations.

Hopefully the three pathways from practice into research presented and exemplified in this book can also be useful in research training programs. Being able to talk about research projects with the notions of using a research-based design, theory-led design-based research, or practitioner-led design of the project might help future PhD students to make decisions and to have the agency to pursue their ideas and to develop their research role-identity.

As editors/supervisors we have learnt a great deal from the narratives in this book and we wish our doctoral students every success.

References

Bhaskar, R. (2008). *A Realist Theory of Science.* 4th edn. London: Routledge.

Black, P. and Wiliam, D. (1998) 'Assessment and Classroom Learning'. *Assessment in Education* 5(1): 7–71.

Caro, S. (2009). *How to Publish Your PhD.* London: Sage

Day, A. (2013). *The Structure of Scientific Examination Questions.* Dortrecht, Heidelberg, New York, London: Springer

Green, B. (2005). 'Unfinished Business: Subjectivity and Supervision'. *Higher Education Research & Development* 24(2): 151–63.

Hargreaves, D. (1996). *Teaching as a Research Based Profession: Possibilities and Prospects.* London: Teacher Training Agency.

Jazvac-Martek, M. (2009). 'Oscillating Role Identities: The Academic Experiences of Education Doctoral Students'. *Innovations in Education and Teaching International* 46(3): 253–64.

Kobayashi, S., Brian G. and Østerberg Rump, C. (2013). 'Interaction and Learning in PhD Supervision – A Qualitative Study of Supervision with Multiple Supervisors'. *Dansk Universitetspædagogisk Tidsskrift* 8(14): 13–25.

Parchmann, I. (2013). 'Wissenschaft Fachdidaktik – eine besondere Herausforderung'. *Beiträge zur Lehrerbildung* 31(1): 31–41.

Phillips, E. and Pugh, D. (2000). *How to Get a PhD.* Buckingham: Open University Press.

Shacham, M. and Od-Cohen, Y. (2009). 'Rethinking PhD Learning Incorporating Communities of Practice'. *Innovations in Education and Teaching International* 46(3): 279–92.

Trafford, V. and Leshem, S. (2009). 'Doctorateness as a Threshold Concept'. *Innovations in Education and Teaching International* 46(3): 305–16.

Treagust, D.F., Won, M. and Duit, R. (2014). 'Paradigms in Science Education Research'. In: Lederman N.G. and Abell, S.K. (eds), *Handbook of Research on Science Education* II: 697–726. New York: Taylor & Francis.

Troman, G. (2002). 'Method in the Messiness: Experiencing the Ethnographic PhD Process'. *Doing a Doctorate in Educational Ethnography* 7: 99–118.

Utbildningsutskottet (2012). 'Hur kan ny kunskap komma till bättre användning i skolan'. Rapport från riksdagen (2012/13): RFR10, Stockholm: Riksdagstryckeriet.

Weidman, J.C., Twale, D.J. and Stein, E.L. (2001). *Socialization of Graduate and Professional Students in Higher Education: A Perilous Passage?* ASHE-ERIC Higher Education Reports 28(3). San Francisco, CA: ASHE-ERIC.

Index